Enterprising Women

Enterprising Women

Ethnicity, economy, and gender relations

Edited by
Sallie Westwood and
Parminder Bhachu

Routledge
LONDON AND NEW YORK

First published in 1988 by
Routledge
11 New Fetter Lane, London EC4P 4EE

Published in the USA by
Routledge
in association with Routledge, Chapman and Hall, Inc.
29 West 35th Street, New York NY 10001

Typeset by Hope Services, Abingdon
Printed in Great Britain by Biddles Ltd, Guildford and King's Lynn
.

British Library Cataloguing in Publication Data

Enterprising women: Ethnicity, economy, and gender relations
 1. Minority women – Great Britain –
 Social conditions
 I. Westwood, Sallie   II. Bhachu, Parminder
 305.4'2'0941   HQ1593

 ISBN 0–415–00686–4
 ISBN 0–415–00687–2 Pbk

Library of Congress Cataloging in Publication Data

Enterprising women: ethnicity, economy, and gender relations
edited by Sallie Westwood and Parminder Bhachu.
 p. cm.
 Bibliography: p.
 Includes index.
 ISBN 0–415–00686–4
 ISBN 0–415–00687–2 Pbk
 1. Minority women – Employment – Great Britain.   2. Women-owned
business enterprises – Great Britain.   3. Work and family – Great
Britain.   I. Westwood, Sallie.   II. Bhachu, Parminder.
HD6057.5.G7E57 1988
305.4'8896041 – dc 19
87-32913
CIP

This book is dedicated to all minority women in Britain, especially those whose lives appear in the pages of this book.

Contents

Notes on contributors

Sue Baxter is currently completing a doctoral thesis at Aston University (Strategic Management and Policy Studies Division) in Birmingham on the Chinese community in the fast food industry. Previously she has worked on research projects relating to institutional racism in the provision of public housing in the London Borough of Camden, the availability of public services for Birmingham's Chinese community, Birmingham Inner City Partnership Programme, single parenthood and racism on public housing estates in Birmingham.

Parminder Bhachu is an urban anthropologist based at the Thomas Coram Research Unit, Institute of Education, University of London. Her doctoral research at the School of Oriental and African Studies, London University and her post-doctoral project at the Centre for Research in Ethnic Relations, University of Warwick both dealt with the Sikhs in Britain. She is currently directing a project on 'Parental Perspectives on Schooling'. She is the author of *Twice Migrants: East African Sikh Settlers in Britain* (Tavistock 1985).

Sasha Josephides is a research fellow at the Centre for Research in Ethnic Relations, University of Warwick. Her doctoral research from the London School of Economics and Political Science was on business and religion in Madang, Papua New Guinea. Since being appointed to the Centre in 1983 she has carried out research on Greek Cypriots in London and is currently researching the Indian Workers Associations.

Annie Phizacklea teaches in the Department of Sociology, University of Warwick. She has researched widely in the field of racism and female migrant labour and is currently completing work on the UK clothing industry. Her publications include, with Robert Miles, *Labour and Racism* and *White Man's Country*, and an edited collection, *One Way Ticket: Migration and Female Labour* (Routledge & Kegan Paul 1985).

Ann Phoenix is a research officer at the Thomas Coram Research Unit, Institute of Education, University of London. She is working on a longitudinal study of women who had their first child when they were aged between 16 and 19 years.

Geoff Raw works as a town planner at Surrey County Council in Kingston Upon Thames. An active shop steward, he has sustained an interest in black/ethnic minority and women workers within the historical development of the fast food catering industry, researched for a Masters degree at Oxford Polytechnic. Previously he has worked on research relating to employment patterns in the South East and Birmingham Inner City Partnership Programme.

Shrikala Warrier is a sociologist with the London Borough of Ealing's Community Education team and is mainly responsible for research and the creation of teaching materials in the field of multicultural education. Her doctoral research for the University of London focused upon family roles and sociability networks in a Gujarati community in London with special reference to changes in women's roles.

Pnina Werbner is a Research Associate in the Department of Sociology, Manchester University. She is an urban anthropologist who has done fieldwork in Botswana and Britain. Her published papers include articles on entrepreneurship, ritual, and social organization amongst Pakistanis in Manchester. She is currently directing a research project, funded by the ESRC, on immigrant entrepreneurs in the clothing industry. She is the author of *The Migration Process: Trading Networks and Ritual Bonds amongst British Pakistanis* (forthcoming).

Sallie Westwood teaches in the Department of Adult Education, University of Leicester. Her doctoral work, for Cambridge University, was on class formation in Ghana and recently her research has been in urban India and in Britain with the Gujarati populations. She is currently working on health issues. She is the author of *All Day Every Day, Factory and Family in the Making of Women's Lives* (Pluto Press 1984; University of Illinois Press 1985).

Acknowledgements

This book would not have been possible without the generous support we have received from our contributors and we offer our grateful thanks to them all. We would also like to thank Shirley Ardener and Helen Callaway· from the Centre for Cross-Cultural Research on Women, who arranged for all of us to meet at Queen Elizabeth House in Oxford early on in the course of the book. We were joined on that day by Donna Delandro who made a valuable contribution to the development of the book for which we are grateful. Elizabeth Saxby from Tavistock (now Routledge) believed in us and our book and supported us throughout. Tricia McGuane and Maureen Cottrell deserve special thanks for their technical skills and their ability to hold things together between Leicester and London. Parminder Bhachu would like to thank Jane Singh of the Centre for South and South East Asia Studies and Mark Juergensmeyer, both at the University of California Berkeley, for their keen interest and for inviting her to present some of the themes of the book at a conference in Berkeley in February 1987. Sallie Westwood would like to thank members of the Black Mental Health Group in Leicester, especially Janet Couloute, Suki Desai, Paul Matthew, and Annette Piper, for their tolerance while the book was being finished and her attention was diverted from our current research project. Between us we owe a large debt to Sartaj Kaur Bhachu, Parminder's mother, for being a source of strength, and to Harbans Kaur Bhachu for her insights. Our warmest thanks to Ali Rattansi for his incisive comments on sections of the book and for his unfailing support. Finally, thanks go to the very many minority women in Britain on whose lives and time we may have intruded and without whom this book would not have been possible.

Sallie Westwood and
Parminder Bhachu
May 1987

1 Introduction

This book introduces the reader to the lives of black and minority women in Britain; more specifically, to the working relations that characterize their lives, both inside and outside the home. In this Introduction we want to introduce the main themes of the book and the papers in the collection. The book itself has been generated out of ongoing discussions between the editors which have been exciting and energizing explorations of differences and similarities, related both to our ethnic origins and to the perspectives that we bring to the analysis of gender relations.

As a black woman of Asian descent and a white woman coming together to collaborate on this volume, we are conscious both of the polarization in the women's movement over the issue of racism, and of the way in which black women have fought for a feminist agenda which is alive to the specificities of black and minority women as it encompasses the experiences and concerns of all women (see Carby 1982; Hooks 1982, 1984; *Feminist Review* **17**, 1984; Davis 1981; Joseph 1981; Bryan, Dadzie, and Scafe 1985, for example). In raising issues we have struggled with a language which consistently reinforces stereotypes by creating sections of the population, both women and men as 'others'. To be 'other' is to be outside, to be deviant, and it allows racism to construct the categories in which understandings will be couched. Although the use of 'black' has been appropriated by black people and made powerful through its politicization, Cypriots, together with many Chinese and South Asians, do not designate themselves as black and we have not therefore used this as a general designation. Equally, the North American use of 'woman of colour' is not appropriate. It connects with contemporary politics in the USA, but it does not have that currency here. Reluctantly, we have been pushed back to the term 'minority', but we do not accept the implications of this term – that Britain is a homogenous society and minorities are outsiders. This book is about British society and British women, but many are BLACK BRITISH women of Afro-Caribbean, Asian, and Chinese descent, who struggle on a daily basis with the racism of British society. This does not mean that Jewish, Irish, or Cypriot people have not been racialized and that they do not also suffer racism – it is quite clear that they do.

In bringing this collection together we were conscious of the diversity not only of British society, but also in the forms of explanation available to us through both feminist accounts and the social sciences. During the course of this book, different perspectives have been constantly debated between ourselves and with the contributors who are themselves very diverse: Ann Phoenix is a black British woman of Afro-Caribbean descent, Sue Baxter is a black woman of Chinese descent, while Parminder Bhachu and Shrikala Warrier are of South Asian descent. Sasha Josephides is of Greek Cypriot descent, Pnina Werbner is an Israeli woman, and Annie Phizacklea, Sallie Westwood, and Geoff Raw are all white British. In this book we have not sought to gloss over differences, we regard them as part of a continuing debate which itself celebrates the lives of all women in Britain. The contributors, like us, are committed to understanding the lives of minority women as simultaneously an expression of difference and similarity. We hope, therefore, that this book will provide the materials whereby an understanding can be built of both the specificities of minority women's lives and the commonalities between them and those of white British women. The attempt to build a theoretically more adequate account of gendered lives must, therefore, take account not only of the experiences of minority women but also the explanations that they offer of their lives and of the communities in which they are situated.

Crucial to an analysis of this kind is an understanding that goes beyond an account of patriarchal relations and 'women', positing instead the articulation between racism, class relations, cultural forms, and gender in the highly dynamic situation of contemporary Britain. Thus, we see minority women as classed and white women as having a cultural background which may be regionally and class specific. This approach marks one part of the critique of culturalist accounts previously offered as a way of explaining the lives of minority people in Britain which have often cast the women of these communities in the role of victim. There are no victims in our accounts. The black and minority women in the pages that follow are seen to be active subjects calling upon diverse resources, including their ethnic and cultural contexts, for their lives in the workplace and the home, against the state and the common sense of racist stereotypes.

Before we introduce individual contributions, we wish to explore further some of the unifying themes of the book as they have developed from our initial concerns with the impact of waged work on the lives of female migrants. This is where we began, with a conception (empirically verified) that change, flux, and innovation were the contexts for migrant women's lives, and we wanted to examine the role that waged work had played in this. But it soon became clear that there was no simple and unambiguous relationship to be explored, and that the nature of women's work was itself diverse, not only because work is both paid an unpaid, but also because these categories can overlap and present contradictions for minority women. In the sections that follow we explore first the impact of migration, because many of the women in this book are migrants, we then go on to discuss the economic position occupied by migrant and settler women and their access to the labour market. Many are not part of the open labour market because they are working within the 'ethnic economy', and are therefore recruited as family labour. It is not enough, however, to position minority women as migrants or as workers *per se*; like other women workers they are subjected to the importance of domestic ideologies in constructing women as workers – labour power is gendered and this has important consequences for the conditions under which women sell their labour power. Finally, we return to the importance of culture and the critique of culturalist accounts referred to above, in this way providing the parameters within which the contributions come together and offer distinctive accounts.

Time, space, and the division of labour

Many of the women in this book are migrants who have come to Britain as part of a global division of labour which is underpinned by colonial exploitation (Mitter 1986). Some came as migrants in their own right, while others came as the daughters, wives, and mothers of migrant men. Although the experiences of migration have been within specific histories and cultures which have had a crucial influence on the way in which they operate in Britain, the women have all met the institutionalized racism of the state through its definitions and its practices and have been racialized in novel ways in Britain. Many of the women occupied very specific locations in time and space – East African Sikh women who had not known the Punjab directly and who are now part of the Sikh diaspora; Cypriot women, who in the 1960s may have come independently in search of paid work, or as family migrants as part of a familiar pattern of chain migration, may in the 1970s have come as refugees.

For some Cypriot and Asian women the notion of return remains powerful and they work alongside their menfolk to generate the resources for land and houses in Cyprus and the subcontinent. Afro-Caribbean women were recruited in the Caribbean for the developing health service and low paid employment in the postwar boom. All of these women were, and are, part of a generation that will not be repeated. It is important to be aware of this when reading the accounts in this volume.

The role of migrant labour in the generation of profits for British capital has been well documented, but it is important to underline that this labour has been both racialized and gendered. Female migrants offer capital the same benefits as migrant labour generally (they do not bear the costs of reproduction which has been borne in the countries of origin) and due to patriarchal relations female labour is subordinated to male labour, cheapened, and kept that way by exclusionary practices supported by white male management and workers (Phizacklea 1983; Bryan *et al.* 1985).

For the women who came to Britain, migration marked the beginnings of new lives because, as Sasha Josephides comments, 'coming to England meant coming to paid work'. But 'paid work' is not a simple unambiguous category in the lives of minority women and the consequences that flow from it are complex and contradictory. These complexities are explored in this book. Change is viewed in this context as multi-faceted, not as one-dimensional or unilinear; rather we are developing an understanding of minority women's lives in the context of British society and its attendant changes. Thus, migrant women coming to Britain, who had certainly worked both inside and outside the home, found that their domestic roles in reproduction (the servicing of household and family) were now articulated with roles in social production that generated wages. And we would wish to underline the enormous impact that this has had on changes in the lives of minority women and their position in the domestic sphere, emphasized, for example, by Shrikala Warrier (this volume) who writes, 'the opportunity to work and earn a regular wage has been one of the most significant aspects of the migration to Britain'. But it is also quite clear that the divisions of labour between paid work and domestic work were, and are, for many minority women not clear-cut divisions, but are interwoven through their participation in what has been designated the 'ethnic economy'.

Economy, class, and the labour market

The ethnic economy is not an enclave outside the overall economy but a sector of entrepreneurial activity characterized by family firms operating at the margins in terms of profitability. Far less is written about the opposite end of the scale where profits are large and companies are now engaging in takeovers.[1] It is the corner shop, the Cypriot café, and the Chinese takeaway that are the public face of this sector and which form the basis of discussions in this collection.

The fact that many minority women came as 'family women' or on vouchers acquired through the promise of a job in a relative's business has had a major impact on the way in which they have been integrated into the capitalist economy. They have not been 'free labourers' in the conventional sense and, therefore, part of an open labour market (which is an ideal that is often cross-cut by familial and social relations in all sectors). Family businesses have been able to access minority women's labour power through the mediations of kinship and an appeal to ideologies which emphasize the role of women in the home as wives and mothers and as keepers of family honour. Annie Phizacklea's important critique, in this volume, provides a corrective to our understanding of the ethnic economy, emphasizing that it is a gendered economy where women's labour power is the mainstay of cheap labour costs and low wages. The 'ethnic economy' underlines the way in which migrants call up the resources available to them in a hostile environment where economic decline and racism combine to oppress them. Using ethnicity and family as resources generates a network which produces workers committed to common goals held within the family. This situation means that the worlds of production and reproduction are enmeshed in relations that it is possible to separate analytically, but which may not appear to be separable in the lives of minority women. Cypriot women, Chinese women, and Indian women do not necessarily view themselves as exploited by their husbands because they are committed to a joint stake in the family business. But women are conscious of the constraints of these types of employment and the next generation of women do not want to work within the ethnic economy, although some are committed to entrepreneurial activities. They want to move out and up through the social structure as evidenced in Sasha Josephides's account of Cypriot women and Sue Baxter's and Geoff Raw's paper where they describe Chinese women who hope to protect their daughters from manual, menial, low paid work.

Women working with their husbands in small businesses, where they do not receive wages, are in a position which reproduces dependency very similar to that of domestic labour. Again, subjective understandings of these processes may be very different and individual situations highly variable, but as Parminder Bhachu (this volume) suggests, if women withdraw from the labour market in order to participate in a family business where they do not receive wages, they are drawn back into the reproductive sphere and patriarchal relations are reinforced. Women in this situation bring together production, reproduction, and the ideologies of domesticity in particular ways which are often repeated in relation to home-workers. Women homeworkers produce goods by the piece for tiny wages without any of the benefits of being workers. But we would argue that it is important not to adopt a simple view of homeworkers as victims, because this type of work is part of a strategy to secure paid work, and as Martha Roldan comments, 'industrial outworking is better for working class women than having no paid work at all' (Roldan 1985: 279). The impact and importance of women's earnings in this sector is no less than in other sectors and is highlighted by Swasti Mitter, writing about the Bangladeshi community in East London: 'Women's increased earnings shifted, even if only slightly, the balance of power between men and women' (Mitter 1986).

Minority women who have a different work history involving paid work outside the home prior to their inclusion within the family firm come with very different notions about wages and effort, trade union rights and their effectiveness within business, as evidenced by Parminder Bhachu's paper. Far from the drudgery of family labour, the Sikh women of her study are empowered by their involvement in family firms in which they have specific roles and responsibilities, with both access to and control over the products of their labour. Changes in familial ideologies and the structures of kinship also provide an important context for Sikh women who find themselves in situations where the ethos of common economic goals within the extended family is tempered by a shift towards nuclear units with their own economic agendas.

The current government emphasis upon enterprise culture and self-employment is part of the restructuring of the British economy. Hundreds of thousands of workers have been ejected from the workforce, and some have used redundancy pay to start a small business or a basement factory using machinery sold off in the closures. Migrant workers, black workers, and those in the old industries have been hardest hit, and racism and economic decline combine to keep a new generation of black people out of the labour force. Instead, there is a rise in part-time, insecure work, much of it female. It is this type of work that has been contrasted with secure employment; the periphery workers versus the core workers. This language is interesting because it is borrowed from the earlier analysis of post-colonial economies with the metropolitan core exploiting the periphery or drawing the periphery to the core, where those who came as migrants in search of economic opportunities find themselves once again at the margins of the good life, servicing an economy designed for the metropolitan centre, in this case the south-east of England. Clearly, many black and minority women workers find themselves at the periphery. But part-time work has never been favoured by them; instead, we find that black women and minority women have clung tenaciously to their positions in the labour market and have fought to defend their jobs.

Contrary to popular myths about the labour market participation of minority women it is clear from the statistics that the rates are high. Afro-Caribbean and non-Muslim Asian women are more likely to be in the labour market than their white counterparts in full-time employment. Among women aged 25–44, 66 per cent of indigenous white women are economically active compared with 77 per cent of those of West Indian origin and 62 per cent of those of Indian origin. Only 17 per cent of women of Bangladeshi and Pakistani origin are economically active, but this does not take account of homeworking. Among Asian women those of East African origin have a higher rate at 67 per cent (Labour Force Survey 1984, reported in the *Employment Gazette*, December 1985). These figures reproduce those found within the PSI study (Brown 1984: 150–1). The ratio of full-time to part-time workers is highly variable with ethnic groups: 44 per cent of white women employees are part-time compared with 29 per cent of West Indian women and 16 per cent of Asian women. These figures demonstrate the very high level of economic activity among black women in Britain and that, overall, they are more likely to be in full-time work than their white counterparts. The exceptions are Muslim women, but the lack of data on paid homeworking does not allow us to present an accurate picture. For many of the women in these statistics, coming to Britain meant their first encounter with paid work outside the home, but the level of their involvement speaks for the importance of women's work as a resource within the household and family, an importance that has grown with the deepening recession and the ever-rising levels of male and youth unemployment.

The jobs migrant women came into were mainly low paid manual work in manufacturing or the state sector. Black nurses are an integral part of the health service in Britain, but because many were shunted into SEN training, their earnings and promotion prospects were very limited and they found that they were working overtime or doing two jobs to make up their income. Asian women in factories found they were part of a gender division of labour which gave to women the low paid, unskilled work with few bonuses and no overtime – routine monotonous work, injurious to mind and body.

But, as Sallie Westwood's contribution shows, many black women found that working lives in factories were not just about technical processes. As workers they were inducted into working-class culture and the forms of resistance developed in response to the capitalist labour process. It is important to insert these issues into the debate on the articulation between racism, gender, and class because it too easily falls into an analysis of inert categories, rather than the material processes whereby subjects become classed, 'raced', gendered. Asian women on the shopfloor have shown themselves to be a militant and fighting group conscious of their rights as black workers and of the division between the interests of capital and labour. In this sense they have become proletarianized, not just as wage labourers, but also as part of a working class that is currently being restructured by the ways in which Thatcherism handles the current crisis in the economy and the processes of deindustrialization. Minority women are part of a fractionalized class in which ethnicity, racism, gender and skill, alongside regional cultures and the development of new forms of paid work, crosscut and stratify the class as a whole. Nevertheless, the Asian women in the papers by Parminder Bhachu and Sallie Westwood show a keen awareness of their class position in social production and its implication for them as black women. The importance of the small business sector has been explored, but it is in the relations between this petty bourgeois sector and the manual working class that many minority women are positioned and where they work out viable strategies as workers and women.

Gendered labour power

There is ample evidence (Pollert 1981; West 1982; Phizacklea 1983; Westwood 1984; Knights and Wilmott 1986) to suggest that

> women do not enter the labour market on the same terms as men. They are bearers, not simply of labour power, but also of gender characteristics rooted in a prior division of labour which finds its

empirical expression in specific family-based household forms. The terms upon which women may compete in the labour market are thus dictated by the social relations within which they operate – as daughters, wives, mothers, widows etc. – and which impose both ideological sanctions upon their identifications as 'free labour'.

(Hilary Standing in collaboration with Bela Bandyopadhyaya 1985: 23)

For the women who are represented in this book these social relations are articulated with the racism of the social formation of which minority women are a part, the ethnic context to which they belong, and the dynamic between this context and the British economy. Consequently, the issues surrounding honour and shame, discussed most especially in Sasha Josephides's paper, come to have a new meaning in the context of the capitalist economy and the role that daughters, wives, and mothers will play in relation to social production and work outside the home. Family firms can invoke familial ideologies, and with this offer a 'safe' environment, which is not constructed as part of the public sphere, to minority women as a way of overcoming the contradiction between the need to use women's labour power to generate material resources in the household and the need to reproduce the honour of the family. In the same way that, in the past, some firms in a local area were designated as 'good' companies by white working class people and as being appropriate places for women as daughters, wives, and mothers to work without damage to their reputations, and thereby the reputations of male family members.

Mothers are the most crucially distinguished category of female labour power, both economically and legally within work relations. The position of 'mothers' in the labour market demonstrates clearly the way in which economic relations are both gendered and ideologically constructed. For black mothers ideologies of racism also intervene to construct very specific positions within the labour market for black worker-mothers. The labour market statistics demonstrate the very high level of participation by black women, of both Afro-Caribbean and Asian descent, many of whom are mothers (these statistics do not include homeworkers or some family labourers who are more likely to be mothers). For economically active mothers the crucial issue is childcare. 'Childcare is a critical issue to working mothers regardless of race, income or occupation' (Maveaux 1986: 70) although the outcomes differ with class. In Britain, professional women solve the problem by employing women, whereas working-class women, black and white, look to family help, childminders, the twilight shift, or weekend work. Women who have children are made vulnerable to low pay and insecure work by the necessity to take on part-time work which is offered by employers as a means of maintaining a pool of available and easily retrenched workers. But, as we have noted, black and minority women have shown themselves very resistant to this form of exploitation, trying instead to use childminders and relatives to help with childcare. Shrikala Warrier's paper explores the contradictions posed by the importance of motherhood and the necessity and the desire for employment in the lives of South Asian women in London. Contrary to popular myths that suggest Asian women have a ready supply of older female kin to help with childcare we find Asian women sharing the problems of many other women. There is a very real sense in which childcare issues are a unifying force for black, white, and minority women, especially currently, where women's rights to maternity benefits, security of employment, and adequate child care provision are under attack and diminishing as we write.[2]

The ideology of motherhood and domesticity affects the working lives of *all* women and impinges on the schooling of daughters and their access to paid work, training, YTS, etc. However, the postwar recruitment of migrant women into full-time, low paid manual work suggests that the ideology is more complex and that it has racist overtones which stop migrant women workers, especially those of Afro-Caribbean descent, from being seen as mothers. As Bryan, Dadzie, and Scafe (1985: 29) comment: 'In the early 1960s, the State was still busy trying to encourage (white) women to stay home and embrace domestication and consumerism. It wasn't prepared to offer any childcare support to black women who had to work.' Instead, black women were separated from their domestic lives and their children were fostered or sent back to the Caribbean for care, thus simultaneously denying the gendered nature of their labour power and underlining it in the jobs offered to women of Afro-Caribbean descent.

However, it is also clear from Westwood's account of shopfloor life that black and white women workers reappropriate motherhood and idealize it as a counter to the routine of factory labour. For the women of the shopfloor, motherhood and mothering constitute real and important work, and are worthy of celebration, offering all women status and pleasure as well as responsibilities.

Culture, ethnicity, and ethnography

One of the central premises of this collection is that culture is a dynamic and multi-textured entity, requiring 'thick description', not a set of fixed characteristics which are used to distinguish the normal from the abnormal. We reject the way in which 'culture' has been used in the ethnic relations literature to mark out specific populations and practices as aberrant. In this book culture is understood as a material and collective expression of social life. Our understanding, therefore, connects with the work of the Centre for Contemporary Cultural Studies (Hall, Johnson, *et al.*) where the importance of cultural forms in generating strategies, defences, and forms of resistance have been emphasized. On this model cultural change becomes a complex interaction between contradictory elements which generate change in uneven ways and simultaneously reproduce patterns and innovate. All the papers in the book are concerned with the processes of change in the articulation between minority peoples and the contemporary socioeconomic structure, but the case against naive culturalist accounts is most cogently argued in the paper by Ann Phoenix who, using material from a study of young women both black and white, demonstrates the inadequacy of an explanation of early motherhood for young black women in terms of cultural traits seen to be located in the island cultures of the Caribbean. In contrast, Ann Phoenix argues for the importance of contemporary British society as the context for young black mothers and young white mothers and the relevance of racism, class, and gender in explanations of behaviour.

To start with the lived experience of black and minority women in British society and generate explanations within the structure of that society is itself a critique of common-sense accounts in which ethnic and cultural elements were abstracted from the whole structure of relations of which they were a part. Cultures were dissected and pieces of them offered as a means of understanding minority peoples and their lives. Now, it seems extraordinary as a basis for understanding, but it was born out of the empiricist account of social and cultural life. Once we dispense with this and present a material and dynamic account of cultures and ethnicities we can see the ways in which cultures and ideologies, and cultures and economics, are embedded one within another. It is also possible to move beyond simple unitary views of cultures and to see differences and complexities that, like ethnicities, are called up as resources socially and economically, in addition to offering a sense of self and identity to minority peoples. Family and household are essential elements in the analysis. But, like cultures and ethnicities these are not viewed as static, timeless entities which bind women to men in conditions they do not make. Clearly, the social construction of familial ideologies is very important throughout the papers of this book – Phizacklea's account of ethnic business alerts us to its importance in generating workers and in a very different way Warrier's paper shows the importance of familial ideologies in the lives of Gujarati women, while Westwood and Bhachu present further examples of its impact. However, familial ideologies are articulated with the practices that make up family life in all its variety. On the ground it is quite clear that families are very diverse and that they have been throughout history, given context and difference by region and class, cultures and ethnicities. The consensus, however, has constructed the family by reifying the white, middle-class nuclear family in law and through state practices. Consequently, ideologies are embedded in state structures and the materiality of power relations. This has been powerfully demonstrated in the ways that minority and black families, of both Afro-Caribbean and Asian origins, have been denied their integrity by the British state through the implementation of the immigration laws and nationality acts. The problems attendant upon the reification of the family and the household have been the subject of critiques elsewhere (Harris 1981) which have developed our understanding of the shifting and dynamic nature of the household. Clearly, in considering the impact of economic relations upon the domestic sphere we are interested in both generalities and specificities and our attempt has been to hold these together in relation to an account which is gendered. Households are viewed as operating at the economic level in three areas – production, reproduction, and consumption (Goody 1972; Rapp 1982). Consequently, households are most essentially about work – and this may include paid work as part of a family business or paid work as outworking where production relations are centrally placed within the household. It is clear from the papers in this volume that women do the bulk of the work within households and that they have specific roles in relation to consumption and reproduction whereby their wages are often used for immediate consumption, and turned into food and nurture for other household members. In Pnina Werbner's paper we are shown a larger world in which British Pakistani women have a crucial role in maintaining intra-ethnic networks within the community. The networks of social relations decribed are gendered and support specific ideologies held within the communities of which the women are a part. Equally, networks are about resources and the circulation of resources – 'what goes round comes round' (Stack 1974) – while at the same time they play a major role in maintaining the status of certain families and the importance of male heads of these families. This is work of status reproduction which falls to women and which has a crucial role in class reproduction through its articulation with the world of wages and the economy. Pnina's paper echoes the world of women presented in other literature on Muslim women (Beck and Keddie 1979; Saifullah Khan 1976). Women's work in these accounts is as much about social reproduction as it is about domestic labour, reproducing solidarities and distance between families outside the group, maintaining cohesion and cultural identities through social relations.

Networks in this sense may be seen as a form of cultural capital, both extending and using the cultural competences that minority women possess. For those who have entered the world of paid work outside the home, networks may be further extended through inter-ethnic and inter-caste relations which increase the range of social contacts beyond the family and kinship group, as well as the flow of knowledge and information, especially in relation to the world of paid work, evidenced in the papers by Bhachu, Josephides, and Westwood, for example. These relations and the networks that construct them become part of the cross-cutting patterns of class, gender, and ethnic identities and solidarities currently being forged in British society, which have a direct bearing upon the domestic domain and the lives of minority women and men within the home.

In an attempt to unravel the complexities of social change many of the papers in this volume (including those that address the issues of changing networks) have emphasized the way in which ethnography is crucial to our understanding of the lives of all women in Britain today. Anthropology has long striven for theoretical complexity, but it has remained committed to a methodology and an account of social forms which is grounded in the substantive lives of people. We believe that it is important for feminism to take note of ethnographic materials and to integrate these within current discourses so as to move the debates forward. Ethnography is, therefore, a positive tool in our struggle against the racism of British society and a means whereby insiders' accounts can construct both the detail and the parameters in which minority cultures and lives will be understood, academically and more generally.

Our broad aim in bringing together the papers in this collection is to offer some insight into the lives of minority British women who, while they are culturally diverse and ethnically distinctive, share the lived reality of racism through the institutional and discursive practices in the social formation. The Introduction has concentrated upon the ways in which economic relations are embedded within gendered and culturally specific relations which offer minority women, as daughters, wives, and mothers, particular economic roles in the processes of production and reproduction. It is not surprising, therefore, that the volume begins with a paper by Annie Phizacklea which reconstructs our understanding of the ethnic economy, providing a corrective to much of the extant literature which emphasizes the role of family labour in generating workers and the success of family firms. Her paper argues strongly for 'gender transparency' in our accounts of economic relations and an understanding of the way in which ethnically variable patriarchal relations intervene in production relations to provide not family labour but *female* labour in the case of the ethnic economy. This labour power is accessed through the family and kinship relations and underpinned by familial ideologies. Using a case study of home workers Phizacklea demonstrates the way in which this form of labour exploits the position of minority women (a situation reproduced for all homeworkers) by ensuring that they carry all the burdens of waged work without any of the benefits.

Having asserted at the outset the importance of a gendered account of economic relations the papers that follow, by Sasha Josephides, Sue Baxter and Geoff Raw, Parminder Bhachu and Sallie Westwood demonstrate the complexities of this, showing that patriarchal relations are neither monolithic nor static but contexted by cultural elements with which they interact, including the means available to minority women to contest and negotiate patriarchal relations. Thus, while analytically labour power is exploited, minority women do not necessarily conceive of themselves as exploited. On the contrary, many of the minority women in this book take pride in their contributions to family firms and their abilities to generate income.

The paper by Sasha Josephides introduces us to a world of enterprise beyond the familiar Cypriot café, demonstrating the tenacity with which Cypriots pursue entrepreneurial activities and the way in which enterprise strategies are articulated with ideologies surrounding honour and shame in the family. Josephides's paper provides us with an account of change over time, too often lacking in ethnographical work, between the migrants' world and the second generation of British-born Cypriots who, as young women, are forging a novel sense of self. The paper suggests that there is no simple relationship between wages and greater power for Cypriot women in the household because the division of labour in that sphere has a major impact on the lives of Cypriot women still. The position is a contradictory one and Josephides's perceptive account helps us to tease out some of the complexities and to generate an analysis rooted in the experiences and understandings that minority women themselves have had of their lives.

The contradictions in the lives of Cypriot women are reproduced in the lives of the Chinese women of Sue Baxter's and Geoff Raw's paper which concentrates on one sector of the fast food industry, Chinese takeaways. This paper makes visible a very important sector of the ethnic economy and situates this in relation to the history of the Chinese communities in Britain, showing how laundry work gave way to food outlets and the manner in which Chinese women were integrated into this, initially as subordinated labourers but latterly as joint participants in family ventures. The early migrant women suffered the loss of their children who were sent back to Hong Kong to be cared for because childcare was not available to them. This situation replicates that of many black women from the Caribbean. Again, the account here demonstrates the arduous nature of this kind of work and the way in which Chinese women have struggled to overcome privations, expressing their pride in their contribution to the family income, in a situation which offers them very little opportunity to come together.

Parminder Bhachu's fascinating account of the lives of Sikh women in Britain shows none of the ambivalence discussed in the cases of Cypriot or Chinese women. Countering earlier discussions of Indian women which present them as lacking autonomy in their lives (Sharma 1980, 1984; Brown *et al.* 1981; Standing 1985), Bhachu's paper argues strongly for the way in which waged work empowers Sikh women in Britain and has had definite effects within the domestic sphere giving Sikh women more resources with which to negotiate changes in the division of labour within the home and also in the patterns of expenditure which they control at a much earlier stage in the developmental cycle of the household than in the past. All this has had an impact on kinship structures, which as a result of women's wages are becoming more bilateral and tending towards nuclear forms. The Sikh women in her study have had experience of paid work outside the home before they have become involved in the family businesses and through their work experiences have learnt the essentials of workers' rights and the power relations of industry. They come into family firms, therefore, as workers with a definite sense of their own contribution and their worth to the ventures. It is a powerful combination explored through a series of case studies in the paper. The world of business was until recently a novel area for most Sikhs but in response to racism, the economic climate, and the ideological calls to enterprise the communities have placed themselves much more centrally within the world of business with plans to expand, not to remain as small businesses. Sikh women are clearly going to have a major role to play in the development of this business sector, not simply as manual labourers but as managers exercizing power and control. Parminder Bhachu's paper is an important corrective to any conceptions of Asian women as powerless in relation to the accumulation and management of resources, or the creation of cultural patterns specific to women. Sallie Westwood's powerful paper continues this account, concentrating on the life of the factory in which Gujarati women, like other black and white working-class women, generate and sustain a powerful resistance to management and the capitalist labour process through a highly ritualized and complex shopfloor culture which celebrates the life-cycle events of women's lives as brides and mothers. The paper develops previous work in the area (Westwood 1984, 1985) by considering the ways in which the wages generated at the factory are used as a resource in developing business projects by family members. Like many other women in this book, Gujarati women express great pride in the businesses of which they are a part, although they exercise less control over these projects and the world of business and enterprise is conceived as a masculine world offering status and power to men. It is unclear how long this will remain so, given the militancy of Gujarati women in the workplace and the aspirations of a new generation of British-born Gujaratis. The paper analyses the class contradictions expressed in the importance of petty bourgeois ideologies and the commitment to enterprise among Gujaratis while the women have become proletarianized in the factories.

The importance of paid work and the way in which women are socially constructed through familial ideologies as wives and mothers is given prominence in Shrikala Warrier's paper, which provides new data on the forces impinging upon the opportunities available to Gujarati women in London who wish, or need, to be 'working mothers'. The difficulties experienced by Gujarati women in solving the problems of adequate childcare are difficulties reproduced for most mothers and the data in this paper makes real the notion of 'gendered labour' and its consequences for individual women. Shrikala Warrier's perceptive discussion introduces the notion that Gujarati women, who have previously been resource managers, have, since migration to Britain, taken on the task of resource procurement, and that this latter role is increasingly important and crucial to family survival, allowing few Gujarati women the opportunity to be full-time mothers. The statistics on labour market participation reinforce this conclusion. But of greater interest is the way in which Gujarati women in the study now have a conception of themselves as workers outside the home, although, as Shrikala Warrier comments, 'few women in the sample . . . regarded paid work as a liberating experience' (p. 141).

Motherhood, we have argued, is a social and cultural construction which may be celebrated or denied depending upon the context and the women involved. The complexities of this are interwoven in the discussion by Ann Phoenix who, using data from a study of young black women of Afro-Caribbean descent and young white women in the process of motherhood, argues against simple cultural relativism and its use, for example, as an explanation of the behaviour of young black women. Instead, following an incisive critique of narrow definitions of culture, Ann Phoenix turns her attention to the underlying structures of economic, social, and ideological relations which frame the lives of young black and white women in Britain. This emphasis concentrates attention upon the articulations between racism, class relations, and gender as a means of explaining and describing the processes whereby young black and white women become mothers. It allows us to see what they share as class subjects and as women and what experiences are specific to black women and to white women. There is a great need for more analysis of this kind and Ann Phoenix's work marks a breakthrough in our understanding of the way in which the lives of young black British women are contexted by racism in Britain, rather than a fixed notion of cultural traits from specific regions of the Caribbean, and by the same class forces that impress upon the lives of young white women.

Finally, Pnina Werbner's paper explores the articulation between gender, cultures, and British society through the life of the British Pakistani community in Manchester, most especially the lives of Pakistani women. Here, in the rich descriptions and careful analysis of the intra-ethnic networks that are serviced and maintained by Pakistani women, it is possible to unravel the ways in which life in Britain both reproduces previous ways of life and inevitably changes them, widening the field of contacts and presenting Pakistani women with new challenges. This paper explores more fully areas that are touched upon in many of the other papers and gives substance to the understanding that in Britain maintaining networks is an essential part of reproductive work. The processes of reproduction are linked to status and class both within and without the communities linking families and individuals into the wider socioeconomic structure, pushing the limits of women's lives further out. It is quite clear from this account that while networks may reproduce status for Pakistani men and women, they also offer Pakistani women solidarity and strength in the British environment.

It is this vision and the reality of the strength and power of minority British women as 'enterprising women' that impresses upon us and, we hope, those who read this book.

Notes

1 See, for example, the Patel takeover of Finlay's newsagents.
2 The Maternity Alliance is one response to this.

References

Beck, L. and Keddie, N. (eds) (1979) *Women in the Muslim World*, Cambridge, Mass.: Harvard University Press.
Brown, P., Macintyre, M., Morpeth, R., and Prendergast, S. (1981) 'A daughter – a thing to be given away', in Cambridge Women's Studies Group, *Women in Society: Interdisciplinary Essays*, London: Virago.
Brown, C. (1984) *Black and White Britain: The Third PSI Survey*, London: Heinemann.
Bryan, B., Dadzie, S., and Scafe, S. (1985) *The Heart of the Race: Black Women's Lives in Britain*, London: Virago.
Carby, H. (1982) 'White Woman Listen! Black feminism and the boundaries of sisterhood', in Centre for Contemporary Cultural Studies (eds) *The Empire Strikes Back: Race and Racism in 70's Britain*, London: Hutchinson.
Department of Employment (1984) *Labour Force Survey*, London: HMSO.
Davis, A. (1981) *Women, Race and Class* London: The Women's Press.
Feminist Review **17** (1984) *Many Voices, One Chant: Black Feminist Perspectives*.
Goody, J. (1972) 'The evolution of the family', in P. Laslett and R. Wall (eds) *Household and Family in Past Time*, Cambridge: Cambridge University Press.
Hooks, B. (1982) *Ain't I a Woman: Black Women and Feminism*, London: Pluto Press.
—— (1984) *Feminist Theory: From Margin to Center*, New York: Southend Press.
Harris, O. (1981) 'Households as natural units', in Kate Young *et al.* (eds) *Of Marriage and the Market: Women's Subordination in an International Perspective*, London: CSE Books.
Joseph, G. (1981) 'The incompatible menage à trois: marxism, feminism

and racism', in L. Argent (ed.) *Women and Revolution: The Unhappy Marriage of Marxism and Feminism.* London: Pluto Press.

Knights, D. and Wilmott, H. (1986) (eds) *Gender and the Labour Process*, London: Gower.

Maveaux, J. (1987) 'The political economy of black women', in M. Davis *et al.* (eds) *The Year Left 2: Towards a Rainbow Socialism, Essays on Race, Ethnicity, Class and Gender*, London: Verso.

Mitter, S. (1986) *Common Fate, Common Bond: Women in the Global Economy.* London: Pluto Press.

Phizacklea, A. (ed.) (1983) *One Way Ticket: Migration and Female Labour*, London: Routledge & Kegan Paul.

Pollert, A. (1981) *Girls, Wives, factory Lives*, London: Macmillan.

Rapp, R. (1982) 'Family and class in contemporary America: notes towards an understanding of ideology', in B. Thorne and M. Yalom (eds) *Rethinking the Family: Some Feminist Questions*, New York: Longman.

Roldan, M. (1985) 'Industrial outworking, struggles for the reproduction of working-class families and gender subordination', in N. Redclift and Minglone (eds) *Beyond Employment: Household, Gender and Subsistence*, Oxford: Blackwell.

Saifullah Khan, V. (1976) 'Purdah in the British situation', in D. Leonard Barker and S. Allen (eds) *Dependence and Exploitation in Work and Marriage*, London: Longman.

Sharma, U. (1980) *Women, Work, and Property in North-West India*, London: Tavistock.

—— (1984) 'Dowry in North India: its consequences for women', in R. Hirschon (ed.) *Women and Property – Women as Property*, London: Croom Helm.

Stack, C. B. (1974) *All Our Kin: Strategies for Survival in a Black Community*, New York: Harper.

Standing, H. with the collaboration of B. Bandyopadhyaya (1985) 'Women's employment and the household: some findings from Calcutta', in *Economic and Political Weekly* **XX**, April 27. (Review of Women's Studies, pp. 23–38.)

—— (1985) 'Resources, wages and power: the impact of women's employment on the urban Bengali household', in H. Afshar (ed.) *Women, Work, and Ideology in the Third World*, London: Tavistock.

West, J. (ed.) (1982) *Work, Women, and the Labour Market*, London: Routledge & Kegan Paul.

Westwood, S. (1985) *All Day Every Day: Factory and Family in the Making of Women's Lives*, London: Pluto Press; Chicago: University of Illinois Press.

2 Entrepreneurship, ethnicity, and gender

Annie Phizacklea

Introduction

For nearly twenty years, migration studies in advanced Western European societies have concentrated on contemporary labour migration flows largely as a source of low wage labour (see for instance Castles and Kosack 1973; Castells 1975; Carchedi 1979). More recently, some research has focused on the female component of these migrations and how minority women have played an important and gender specific role within this low-wage labour force (see the different contributions to Phizacklea (ed.) 1983). It is argued elsewhere that this 'political economy of labour migration' perspective constitutes a reasonably distinct literature, in so far as those who advocate such a perspective work within a largely Marxist or Marxist-feminist tradition (Phizacklea 1984).

Alongside, but in comparative isolation from this literature has emerged another perspective which for want of a better label we might call the 'ethnic business' school. Much of this literature in the UK is theoretically rooted in what has been termed the 'sociology of ethnic relations' (Phizacklea 1984: 205). Such studies have been keen to move away from an emphasis on the migrant/immigrant as object of racism, discrimination, and exploitation to analysis of the way in which ethnic ties can be used as a resource, for example, in creating alternative employment opportunities. A good example of the growing literature on ethnic entrepreneurship in the UK is the volume edited by Robin Ward and Richard Jenkins, *Ethnic Communities in Business*. In focusing on entrepreneurship in settled minority communities, implicitly, therefore, on the process of class formation therein, this literature provides a necessary corrective to the overemphasis on black and ethnic minority communities as passive victims of racism and discrimination.

Nevertheless it is suggested here that the gender blindness of most of the ethnic business literature and its failure to treat seriously the implications of ethnically variable patriarchal social relations within the family, and how these relate to the viability of a particular economic form (labour-intensive business), results in inadequate theorizing.

This argument will be elaborated through a case study of the clothing industry, particularly in the West Midlands of the UK. Testing hypotheses on a single industry is obviously problematic, raising questions about the extent to which findings can be generalized to other labour-intensive industries, for instance. Attempts will be made wherever possible to draw on evidence from other industries.

But ultimately this chapter has limited aims: to provide a feminist critique of extant theorizing and to raise some questions that might inform further research.

Lumpenproletariat to lumpenbourgeoisie

The stereotypical representative of ethnic entrepreneurship is the 'rags to Mercedes' immigrant who through hard work and risk taking 'makes it' into the ranks of the comfortably off. A small proportion of Britain's postwar black and ethnic minority immigrants have built up over time large sums of capital through international trading and multiple shop ownership (see for example articles in the *Director*, June 1983 and *The Sunday Times*, 2 October 1983). Nevertheless this does not by itself constitute a barrier to racism and discrimination and does not in any case represent reality for the vast majority of ethnic entrepreneurs in the UK.

Entrepreneurship constitutes an escape route for many minority men from the drudgery of the dead-end manual jobs to which they are confined by racism and racial discrimination. During the 1980s, entrepreneurship has become a necessity for many shaken out of the labour-intensive manufacturing industries in which they were located, whose residential concentration in the decaying inner cities has further reduced the alternatives for those made redundant.

In this respect, entrepreneurship can be seen as a form of disguised unemployment, a shift from the lumpenproletariat to the lumpenbourgeoisie with subsequent earnings often much lower than those that prevailed during wage labouring days (Aldrich, Jones, and McEvoy 1984).

But minority women have not escaped the experience of dead-end, low paid manual work and redundancy either. In this context, work in the so-called 'ethnic economy' is viewed as creating alternative employment structures for women shaken out of manufacturing or those who perceive obstacles to working outside a 'safe' environment for language or cultural/religious reasons (Shah 1975).

With meagre start-up capital, minority entrepreneurial projects include small-scale manufacturing enterprises (clothing being the most important), service, and retail outlets. Such projects have low entry barriers and are highly labour intensive, with continuing access to a cheap and flexible labour force crucial to their economic viability.

But ethnic business is predominantly male controlled and labour intensive; men are bosses and women are either workers or can expect to control or give orders only to other women. This is not unique to 'ethnic' business, in so far as fewer women than men are entrepreneurs in the population as a whole. But it is argued here that those ethnic groups deemed to be more 'successful' in the business world than others are characterized by social structures which give easier access to female labour subordinated to patriarchal control mechanisms.

Patriarchy is used here in a materialist sense and in accordance with Cockburn's and Hartmann's definition; both view patriarchy as:

A set of social relations which has a material base and in which there are hierarchical relations between men and solidarity among them, which enables them in turn to dominate women. The material base of patriarchy is men's control over women's labour power. That control is maintained by excluding women from access to necessary economically productive resources and by restricting women's sexuality.

(Cockburn 1985: 84, following Hartmann 1979)

The encouragement of small business has of course been a much publicized plank of Thatcher government policy (though apart from the appointment of the infamous Abdul Shamji as head of the party's Small Business Bureau it is difficult to see how government policy has in any way supported the cause of small business). Backed up by Lord Scarman arguing, in the wake of the Brixton disturbances in 1981, that black people had to secure a real 'stake in their community' through business enterprises (Scarman 1981) it was clear that the Conservative Government was keen to get the front line victims of deepening recession and deindustrialization picking themselves up by 'their ethnic boot-straps'.

The publication in 1984 of the Third PSI study, *Black and White Britain*, testified to the rise in self-employment among Asians in Britain compared to the 1974 Survey. Ten years on, Asian men and women were more likely to be self-employed than white men and women, while Caribbean men and women remained under-represented within the ranks of the self-employed (see Table 2.1). Labour Force and other surveys also indicate over-representation of Turkish and Greek Cypriot men (22 per cent) and Chinese amongst the ranks of the self-employed.

Much of the ethnic business literature has of course been preoccupied with theorizing about why some ethnic groups are over-represented within the ranks of the self-employed and in business and why others are under-represented. Before evaluating some of those theories we need critically to examine the concept of self-employment itself.

Table 2.1 *Self-employed by ethnic group*

	Self-employed as a percentage of all in work		
	White	*West Indian*	*Asian*
men	*14*	*7*	*18*
women	*7*	*1*	*14*

Source: Table 104 in Brown (1984) *Black and White Britain: The Third PSI Survey* (p. 210).

Self-employment: being your own boss?

First, self-employment is not necessarily synonymous with entrepreneurship. Many of the clothing workers I interviewed during the course of my research were technically self-employed because their boss was not interested in shouldering the costs or responsibilities of being an employer. In reality they receive work from only one company, many are actually working on its premises, and they are supervised. Thus they are expected to behave as employees without any of the benefits of employee status. Second, what does it mean in class terms for a woman to be self-employed in a family firm? In the clothing industry many wives and daughters of Asian, Turkish, and Greek Cypriot entrepreneurs supply unpaid labour as machinists and finishers, but also as supervisors, mediating between the 'boss' and other machinsts (Hoel 1982; Anthias 1983; Morokvasic, Phizacklea, and Rudolf 1986). Sometimes they are the 'middle-woman' in the organization of production based on the labour of homeworkers. How are these women rewarded for their labour? The evidence that exists suggests that such women do not receive any 'independent' reward but view any surplus that might accrue from their labour as an essential contribution to the family income. As far as Southern Asian cultures are concerned, a departure from this norm would strike at the heart of a clearly demarcated sexual division of labour. In generalizing about such cultures Saifullah Khan argues that:

> throughout the Indian sub-continent the mother has responsibility for the domestic sphere of activity. This includes childcare, housework and the domestic comforts of her husband. The husband is responsible for gaining the livelihood of the household.
> . . . Employment [of mothers] beyond the home can be condoned only if it does not jeopardize the affection and care of young children, nor threaten the husband's position as main wage-earner and his exemption from housework.
>
> (1979: 120–1)

Do members of a family firm share an identical class situation or not? I think the answer is no. All female members and young male members of the family are working under patriarchal relations of production, they remain dependent for their maintenance on the 'boss' who is usually also the head of the household, in return for their efforts.

But women and men working in this context may have differing expectations of their jobs. In the London clothing industry it is quite common to find men as well as women working as machinists. But for women the most one might expect of a machining job was faster speeds and higher pay or at very best a supervisory role. For men the confinement to low-wage 'women's' work was a necessary part of the apprenticeship for entrepreneurship (Anthias 1983; Morokvasic, Phizacklea, and Rudolf 1986). These gender differences are commonly ignored or viewed as tangential to explanations of both the form and differential rate of entrepreneurship between ethnic groups. When they are noted there is often slippage on the gender front. For instance, Mars and Ward argue that in the case of Turkish Cypriot clothing firms and restaurants,

> The 'captive' labour supply provided by immigrant wives, whose way of life keeps them largely separate from the wider society, is vital to the success of the enterprise, as is the interest of potential entrepreneurs in accepting low wages for their work in return for gaining the experience which will equip them to set up on their own in due course.
>
> (1984: 4)

What they fail to distinguish is the fact that the 'fringe benefit' of entrepreneurial training is reserved for men. It is with such considerations in mind that we turn to a critical evaluation of existing theory in the field.

Why the differences?

A wide range of theory claims to explain why some ethnic groups are more widely represented than others among entrepreneurs.

'Middleman minority' theories aim to analyse the position of groups distinguished by their concentration in independent trading and commercial activities, occupying a petit bourgeois class position. A range of theories fall within this category. Some commentators see such groups as creations of the dominant class in a society, acting as a go-between for the ruling élite in their dealings with subordinate classes. This in turn generates a hostile reaction towards the 'middleman' group (Blalock 1967; Hamilton 1978).

A variant of this approach is adopted by Pierre van den Berghe, who argues that any similarities which do exist among middleman minorities must be sought 'principally in the social structure of the plural society as a whole, and only secondarily in the characteristics of the immigrant groups' (1975: 198).

Edna Bonacich and John Modell argue that such contextual theories are unsatisfactory if they assume that the minorities are the creation of the society in which they reside. They suggest that there is plenty of evidence to show that some groups become concentrated in the middleman category regardless of context; they list these as Jews, Chinese, and Indians (Bonacich and Modell 1980: 31 and Appendix B).

In her earlier work, Edna Bonancich suggested that the initial orientation of the group towards its territory will have a significant impact on the group's future economic role. Her view is that groups who see themselves as temporary migrants or 'sojourners' encourages their concentration in trade and similar middleman activities. It promotes hard work, risk-taking, and concentration in areas where assets can be quickly liquidated. Indirectly it encourages the retention of ethnic solidarity which aids ethnic business (1973). Her later work with John Modell concentrates on whether or not the ethnic ties dissolve once the viability and/or necessity of the economic form declines (1980).

Some of the most widely propagated theories are cultural in form.

Rather than viewing 'middleman' groups as creatures of the society they come to sojourn or settle in, such theories concentrate on the characteristics they bring to this environment. For instance Ivan Light argues that strong ascriptive ties enable some ethnic groups to succeed in entrepreneurial activity where the contractual relationships characteristic of industrialized societies may be less successful (1972). Other theories are based on the belief that certain ethnic groups have an elective affinity with business. Such theories draw heavily on Weber's *The Protestant Ethic and the Spirit of Capitalism* (1958). Culturally valued attributes, such as hard work and risk taking, are seen to be particularly well suited to entrepreneurial success. One can take issue with cultural explanations on a number of grounds. First, if it is suggested that these 'cultural traits' are inherent then such theories verge on racist explanations. Second, if groups possess such characteristics why is it that over generations, sometimes just one, they move from over-representation as entrepreneurs to an employment profile identical to the population as a whole?

Third, such theories take no account of the impact that racial discrimination, harassment, and violence may have on the retention, even development, of so-called ethnic ties, solidarity, and social structure, including the retention of a clearly defined sexual division of labour and the confinement of women to 'safe' environments. If the mainstream avenues to lucrative employment are cut off by racism and discrimination then the adaptation of available skills and resources within a particular group to alternative income-generating mechanisms is a reasonably predictable outcome.

Fourth, of vital importance to that strategy is the use of women's so-called 'natural' skills and their labour as a resource. All the theories stress the importance of the 'family' (real or fictive) based economy, yet they ignore the gender-specific mechanisms of subordination therein which generate a supply of low-wage or unpaid labour, ensuring the viability of the labour-intensive enterprise. When authors refer to 'the family' they are nearly always referring to women, for example:

> Labour costs can be kept down, where the time of family members is available to assist with the business and where, either through racism, economic factors or cultural prescriptions, there is little alternative to working, in a firm run by a community member. A community where immigration is largely by males, or at least not in complete family units, as with the Irish, is therefore at a disadvantage in this respect. Since most ethnic business is labour

intensive, access to family or community members as employees at low rates is a key advantage for many entrepreneurs.'

(Mars and Ward 1984: 18)

Finally, cultural explanations can become self-fulfilling prophecies. The 'ethnic economy' provides employment for minority women confronted by continuing high levels of racism and racial discrimination and a reduction in traditional job opportunities in manufacturing industry (Phizacklea 1985). But it is also argued that work in this sector is dictated by certain 'disadvantages' that they carry around with them, such as 'language deficiencies', 'cultural preferences', and 'lack of recognized skills', facets of what Morokvasic describes as a conventional stereotype of minority women (1983). That stereotype can provide a useful justification for exploitation, as the following quote from one Asian entrepreneur in Coventry illustrates:

I see the majority of women working for me as benefitting from my job offer. They are illiterate and have no skills, hence no British factory will make use of them. . . . Their £20 a week will help towards the family income, and we are like a big family here

(Hoel 1982: 86)

Following Mars and Ward (1984) and Waldinger (1986) I want to suggest two conditions for the creation of the ethnic business. One is access to resources that native entrepreneurs cannot lay their hands on. A low-wage, flexible labour force is crucial in this respect. The other is to find an economic niche in which the small firm can viably function. The next section outlines why the cheap, high-fashion sector of the clothing industry in the UK has become a favoured niche for 'seed-bed' ethnic business.

Getting it all sewn up

The clothing industry has provided an economic niche for successive waves of immigrants to the UK. Between 1881 and 1886 Russian and Polish Jewish refugees entered out of necessity what were referred to as the 'sweated' trades in London. Previously, women workers had borne the brunt of 'sweating'; now they were joined by male immigrants. Very often the production unit and the family unit were the same and Birnbaum argues that the sexual division of labour in the production of clothing and the relegation of women to 'unskilled' tasks allowed Jewish male refugees to reassert themselves as the 'head of household' (Birnbaum n.d). Hall argues that clothing as a sweated trade was bound to go into decline in London as employment options for women expanded, as 'alien' immigration was restricted in 1911, as factory production expanded and legislation tightened (Hall 1962). Between the First and Second World Wars factory production developed rapidly in London but never replaced production based in sweatshops and on the labour of homeworkers. This 'secondary' sector remained intact, awaiting a postwar revival.

In the postwar period a number of 'new' immigrations led to a resurgence of the clothing industry in London and other inner cities, such as Manchester. Cypriots, both Turkish and Greek, and Asian migrants (excluding Bangladeshis) entered the industry as entrepreneurs from the early 1960s onwards (Birnbaum *et al.* 1982). While the majority of Turkish and Greek Cypriots migrated as family units, there was a brief time-lag in family reunion for Indians, (Brown 1984). This was not the case for Bangladeshis, whose migration throughout the 1960s was almost entirely male. It is perhaps no coincidence, therefore, that Bangladeshis entered the clothing industry not as entrepreneurs but as unskilled machinists who 'learnt the ropes' the hard way (Perry 1983). Bangladeshis have now moved into a dominant position as entrepreneurs in leather manufacture in London and have emerged in other parts of the industry as well (Birnbaum *et al.*). The pattern of family reunion is probably quite closely connected, therefore, with the rate of business start-ups in labour intensive industries such as clothing. In the Federal Republic of Germany, family reunion and self-employment has never been encouraged and there is no evidence of any involvement of migrants as entrepreneurs in the clothing industry there (though there is a small Greek involvement in the fur trade) (Morokvasic, Phizacklea, and Rudolf 1986). The same was true of the Netherlands until 1975 when the regulations on family reunion were liberalized. Boissevain reports that this coincides with the re-emergence of a 'secondary' sector of clothing production in Amsterdam.[1]

But why have ethnic minority firms moved into this sector, and what makes them viable? It costs very little to enter the clothing industry, as we shall see below. If production is based on a pool of homeworkers it totals the purchase price of a cutter, a van, and some materials. There is a continuing need for a sector of the industry producing unstandardized garments to meet increasingly unpredictable demand. Ethnic entrepreneurs are prepared to take the risks on such production. The advantages of 'sourcing' close to the point of sale is not lost on retailers and manufacturers without their own production facilities. If the latter send their designs abroad to be made up in low-wage developing countries they must expect long lead times, must anticipate demand well in advance and must be prepared to have a build-up in stocks at certain periods of the year. At a time when demand has become more and more unpredictable, retailers and manufacturers have sought to minimize their risks by sourcing very close to 'home' and in line with demand. Under these circumstances they have turned to sub-contractors who can accommodate stringent demands of flexibility in production and speed of delivery (Phizacklea 1986). It is exactly this role that the small inner city workshop with its retinue of homeworkers has come to play.

The viability of the sector rests on the payment of very low wages for long hours and in many cases the evasion of statutory employment practices such as the payment of National Insurance contributions (Anthias 1983).

In the English West Midlands a whole 'new' clothing industry has 'taken off' on this basis largely since 1978. Asian male workers were recruited throughout the 1960s to work in West Midlands metal manufacturing and engineering industries. Yet between 1975 and 1982, 74 per cent of all industrial job losses in the area were in those industries and in areas of Asian residential concentration; unemployment rates had risen to between 40 and 47 per cent (Gaffikin and Nickson, n.d.).

A small redundancy payment is enough to set oneself up as a clothing producer if there is also access to skilled, cheap, and flexible labour. Asian women have become the predominant suppliers of that labour in what has become the only manufacturing growth sector in the West Midlands economy. It is estimated that at least 20,000 new jobs have been created in small clothing firms in the area since 1979 (West Midlands Low Pay Unit 1984). The West Midlands Low Pay Unit's survey of such firms indicated that average pay was well below the minimum. And if a garment is assembled in the home the worker may receive as little as fifteen pence a garment for simple work. Within the trade it is estimated that imported goods must be at least 20 per cent cheaper than domestically produced goods if retailers and manufacturers are to buy or subcontract production abroad. Thus we have in these very low labour costs one simple factor in explaining any expansion of domestic subcontracting to this sector of the clothing industry. If we add to this the speed with which deliveries can and are made to the high street retailers then there is a real competitive advantage over Third World producers.

But competition between the small, inner-city sub-contractors is fierce and unregulated. If a firm does not complete an order in the time and at the price agreed it will lose any future orders from that manufacturer. Competitive pressures such as these can only be passed one way, to the already under-rewarded workforce through intensified work and further casualized working practices (Phizacklea 1986).

Yet with staggeringly high levels of unemployment for Asian men and women in the West Midlands, racism and exclusionary practices in other sectors of the labour market and the claims of 'ethnic loyality', workers are in a very weak position to resist such exploitation. The threat of unemployment and the knowledge that there are other minority women who can be substituted for the same job, acts as a powerful deterrent to resistance amongst an already vulnerable workforce. Nevertheless, such pressures have not deterred Asian women from struggling for union recognition in their workplaces in a number of notable disputes in the region (for example the Kewal Bros dispute in 1984). In most cases employers have won by using the tactic of closing down the firm and reopening under a new name and with a completely new workforce (Bishton 1982). In other circumstances, employers have used husbands and other male kin to discipline their 'women' (Hoel 1982). As Mitter has argued, 'the servility, subservience and passivity that the communities expect of wives towards their husbands, daughters-in-law towards fathers-in-law in the home, were reproduced to an important extent in the factories' (1986).

Yet the West Midlands clothing industry has been built on the skills of women. There is no evidence to show that the entrepreneurs in question have any previous experience in the industry; unlike many of their counterparts in London, they have built their businesses out of meagre redundancy payments and savings and the skills and labour of Asian women. I will illustrate this with reference to an entrepreneur I interviewed in November 1984.

Mr X had been made redundant from a plastics factory six months prior to the interview. Redundancy money was used to buy an Eastman cutter, textiles, wood for making tables, and to pay rent for very small premises. Through a relative he made contact with an agent exporting dresses to Saudi Arabia and they made a deal for a small test contract at a very competitive price. He and his brother marked up and cut out the cloth for women's and girl's dresses. These were put in his van and delivered to twelve homeworkers, all Asian women, known personally to himself and his wife. The sewn garments were picked up, brought back, and trimmed and finished by his wife. If there was no work, he had no employees to be retained.

Homeworkers are therefore in a very precarious position and all those interviewed in Birmingham reported that the uncertainty attached to their work was the greatest drawback. The vast majority of homeworkers are women confined to the home because of domestic responsibilities, particularly the care of pre-school children. Most fail to recognize the hidden costs involved in homeworking, which include the purchase or hire of their own machine and running costs. Most homeworking is 'off the books' and therefore completely precarious.

Conclusion

The main argument in this paper has been that access to 'family' or community members as low-wage workers is a key competitive advantage for many ethnic businessmen. This point is well supported in the literature. What is usually glossed over in the literature is the extent to which this 'family' and 'community' labour is female and subordinated to very similar patriarchal control mechanisms in the workplace as in the home. Ethnic groups which have very different social structures, for instance Afro-Caribbeans in the UK (Phizacklea 1982) will therefore be at a competitive disadvantage as far as labour-intensive 'start-up' business is concerned. In fact, Caribbean businesses in the UK are not characteristically labour-intensive (Ward and Reeves 1984).

On both the analysis and policy front this paper constitutes a plea for gender transparency. On the policy front supporting the 'ethnic economy' appears to make good sense to local authorities frantically searching for ways of regenerating economic activity in decaying inner city areas and for alternative employment opportunities for ethnic minority men and women in the face of deindustrialization and continuing high levels of racism. But does the 'ethnic economy' open up the possibility of breaking out of gender specific and ethnically segregated low pay labour markets for minority women? If it simply means more of the same then support for the ethnic economy needs to be treated with some scepticism.

Note

1 This point was made by Jeremy Boissevain at the 'Clothing Industry'

Workshop held during the Ethnic Business Conference, Aston University Management Centre, Birmingham, May 1985.

References

Aldrich, H. Jones, T., and McEvoy, D. (1984) 'Ethnic advantage and minority business development', in R. Ward and R. Jenkins (eds) *Ethnic Communities in Business*, Cambridge: Cambridge University Press.

Anthias, F. (1983). 'Sexual divisions and ethnic adaptation: the case of the Greek-Cypriot women', in A. Phizacklea (ed.) *One Way Ticket: Migration and Female Labour*. London: Routledge & Kegan Paul.

Birnbaum, B. (n.d.) 'Women, skill and automation: a study of women's employment in the clothing industry, 1946–1972', unpublished paper.

Birnbaum, B., Evesley, J., Clouting, T., Allard, D., Hall, J., Morgan, S., Woods, K., Allan, R., and Tulley, R. (1981) *The Clothing Industry in Tower Hamlets: An Investigation into its Structure and Problems*, Tower Hamlets Council.

Bishton, D. (1984) *The Sweat Shop Report*, Birmingham: All Faiths for One Race (AFFOR).

Blalock, H. (1967) *Toward A Theory of Minority Group Relations*, New York: John Wiley.

Bonacich, E. (1973) 'A theory of middleman minorities', *American Sociological Review* **38**: 583–94.

Bonacich, E. and Modell, J. (1980) *The Economic Basis of Ethnic Solidarity: Small Business in the Japanese American Community*, Los Angeles and Berkeley: University of California Press.

Brown, C. (1984) *Black and White Britain: The Third PSI Survey*, London: Heinemann.

Carchedi, G. (1979) 'Authority and foreign labour: some notes on a late capitalist form of capital accumulation and state intervention', *Studies in Political Economy* **2**: 37–74.

Castells, M. (1975) 'Immigrant workers and class struggles in advanced capitalism: the Western European experience', *Politics and Society* **5**, (1): 33–66.

Castles, S. and Kosack, G. (1973) *Immigrant Workers and Class Structure in Western Europe*, London: Oxford University Press.

Cockburn, C. (1986) 'The Relations of Technology', in R. Crompton and M. Mann (eds) *Gender and Stratification*, Oxford: Polity Press.

Crompton, R. and Mann, M. (1986) in R. Crompton and M. Mann (eds) *Gender and Stratification*. Oxford: Polity Press.

Gaffikin, F. and Nickson, A. (n.d.) *Jobs Crisis and the Multi-Nationals: the Case of the West Midlands*, Birmingham Trade Union Resource Centre.

Hall, P.G. (1962) *The Industries of London since 1861*, London: Heinemann.

Hamilton, G. (1978) 'Pariah capitalism: a paradox of power and dependence', *Ethnic Groups* **2**: 1–15.

Hartmann, H. (1979) 'Capitalism, patriarchy and job segregation by sex', in Z. Eisenstein (ed.) *Capitalist Patriarchy and the case for Socialist Feminism*, New York and London: Monthly Review Press.

Hoel, B. (1982) 'Contemporary clothing sweatshops: Asian female labour and collective organisation', in J. West (ed.) *Work, Women and the Labour Market*, London: Routledge & Kegan Paul.

Light, I. (1972) *Ethnic Enterprises in America*, University of California Press.

Mars, S. and Ward, R. (1984) in R. Ward and R. Jenkins (eds) *Ethnic Communities in Business*, Cambridge: Cambridge University Press.

Mitter, S. (1986) 'Industrial restructuring and manufacturing homework: immigrant women in the UK clothing industry', *Capital and Class* **27**, Winter: 37–80.

Morokvasic, M., Phizacklea, A., and Rudolf, H. (1986) 'Small firms and minority groups: contradictory trends in the French, German and British clothing industries', *International Sociology* **1** (4): 397–420.

Perry, N. (1983) *The Leather Garment Industry in Tower Hamlets*, Tower Hamlets Council.

Phizacklea, A. (1982) 'Migrant women and wage labour: the case of West Indian women in Britain', in J. West (ed.) *Work, Women and the Labour Market*. London: Routledge & Kegan Paul.

—— (ed.) (1983) *One Way Ticket: Migration and Female Labour*, London: Routledge & Kegan Paul.

—— (1984) 'A sociology of migration or 'race relations'?: a view from Britain', *Current Sociology* **32** (3) Winter: 199–218.

—— (1985) 'Minority women and economic restructuring: the case of Britain, France and West Germany', paper given at the Racial Minorities and Economic Restructuring Conference, September 1985, ESRC Research Unit on Ethnic Relations at the University of Warwick.

—— (1986) *Fashion Clothing Production in Britain, France and Federal Republic of Germany*, Final Report, ESRC, London.

Saifullah Khan, V. (1979) 'Work and network: South Asian women in South London', in S. Wallman (ed.) *Ethnicity at Work*. London: Macmillan.

Shah, S. (1975) *Immigrants and Employment in the Clothing Industry: The Rag Trade in London's East End*, London: Runnymede Trust.

van den Berghe, P. (1975) 'Asian Africans before and after independence', *Kroniek van Afrika* **6**: 197–205.

Waldinger, R. (1986) *Through the Eye of the Needle: Immigrants and Enterprise in New York's Garment Trades*, New York: New York University Press.

Ward, R. and Jenkins, R. (eds) (1984) *Ethnic Communities in Business*, Cambridge: Cambridge University Press.

Ward, R. and Reeves, F. (1984) 'West Indian business in Britain' in R. Ward and R. Jenkins (eds) *Ethnic Communities in Business*, Cambridge: Cambridge University Press.

Weber, M. (1958) *The Protestant Ethic and the Spirit of Capitalism*, New York: Scribner.

West Midlands Low Pay Unit (1984) *Below the Minimum*, Birmingham: Low Pay Unit.

3 Honour, family, and work: Greek Cypriot women before and after migration

Sasha Josephides

Introduction

Mediterranean cultures, including that of Cyprus, have been typified as ones where the concepts of honour and shame underly every aspect of social and economic life, and where women's actions are controlled through rigid norms and practices (Davis 1977; Campbell 1964; Peristiany (ed.) 1965; Gilmore 1982). In such societies the honour of men, women, and entire families is apparently more easily maintained if women do not go out to work.[1] Where a woman does go out to work it means first, an open admission that the man cannot support the household himself, and second that the woman is mixing with outsiders. Neither of these is helpful in promoting family honour. However, in London we see thousands of Cypriot women serving behind the counters of small shops and cafés or working as machinists in the Cypriot clothing factories that abound in north London. These are the various branches of the Cypriot 'ethnic economy' and indeed, as Anthias has shown (1983), women have been the building blocks of this economy. Younger Cypriot women are also 'out there' working, but they have rejected the ethnic economy and are to be found in clerical jobs of all kinds, particularly in banking, insurance, and travel agencies; in hairdressing and beauty therapy; in the rag trade as designers; and in retail as buyers and trainee buyers. There are also increasing numbers of women in teaching and the social services, often employed in reference to their ethnic group. The fact that these younger women are working outside the ethnic economy entails a significant departure from the position of older women, since not only are they working outside the home, but they are also working for complete outsiders.

What have these developments meant in terms of family honour and gender relations within the household? In order to explore these questions we must start by looking at the situation in Cyprus prior to migration. Although much of what is contained in this paper applies to both Greek and Turkish Cypriots there are also differences between the two groups, so what follows can only be properly taken to refer to Greek Cypriots.[2]

Women, work and the household in Cyprus

Cyprus is an island in the Mediterranean which was under constant occupation until 1960 when it gained formal independence. Britain was its most recent colonizer (1878–1960) and Cyprus is, therefore, part of the New Commonwealth. The population of Cyprus consists of a majority of Greek Cypriots, substantial numbers of Turkish Cypriots, and pockets of Armenians and Maronites. Its economic base has been agricultural and the island has been characterized as consisting of peasant farmers. Agriculture in Cyprus has changed over the years due to increasing mechanization, the introduction of irrigation systems, and a shift from mixed farming to the growing of cash crops, such as citrus fruits. Since 1974, due to the war on the island and the subsequent occupation of a large area by Turkey, there have been still more changes. However, even before the occupation it was not possible for the land to support everyone in the rural areas, particularly because of indebtedness which sometimes caused people to sell their land to richer men, and the inheritance rule which results in land fragmentation, many people had no holdings at all or holdings that were too small to support them. So not all the people living in the rural areas were necessarily peasant farmers; some worked as wage labourers on other people's land, others performed a number of skilled and unskilled jobs within the village, and there has always existed a cottage industry, consisting of processing foodstuffs, weaving, and lacemaking. These goods were produced both for use at home and for trading and their production was almost exclusively the work of women. Furthermore the present century has seen a definite shift of population to the towns, which have seen the development of some light industry.

In both town and village the Cypriot household is a self-sufficient unit consisting of a married couple and their unmarried children. With the passage of time it is common for a widowed parent to form part of the household. What is less common is for newlyweds to live with their parents, as the ideal is for a couple to be able to set up in their own house as soon as they are married and for this house to be the girl's dowry. In cases where parents cannot provide a house for their daughter it can be difficult to 'marry her off' properly; a tragic situation for a Cypriot woman since there are very few roles available to her other than that of wife and mother. In common with many societies adult status for women is related to marriage and motherhood. Through the dowry system marriage also has implications for the economic base of the household.

The issues of marriage and the family bring into focus all those values in Mediterranean culture that come under the label 'honour and shame'. Honour is carried by both families and individuals and involves the notions of respectability, reputation, and integrity as well as the idea that each person should act correctly according to their role and position in society. There is thus a difference between the way honour applies to men and women. Furthermore it appears that honour is only applied to women in a negative sense, in the form of 'shame', the counterpart of honour. Women display appropriate shame by being generally modest and obedient but the essential ingredient of shame is sexual modesty. Peristiany writes: 'women's foremost duty to self and family is to safeguard herself against all critical allusions to her sexual modesty' (1965: 182). What is at issue here is not just that unmarried girls should be virgins and married women faithful (which they should) but that they should have a reputation for being so, since gossip regarding a woman's sexual modesty is almost as harmful as evidence of sexual activity. Because of this, contact with unrelated men is discouraged. Even if the relationship is innocent tongues can wag. If there is gossip it is not just the woman who is harmed but the whole family, as everyone related to the woman, particularly her close kinsmen if she is unmarried or her husband if she is married, lose honour. The importance of the honour/shame syndrome is therefore totally related to the public sphere and to how the actions of individuals and families are interpreted by their neighbours and the 'world'. Unlike women, men are not required to be sexually modest – if anything they are expected to prove their sexual prowess through premarital sex. It is also socially acceptable for men to have other liaisons once they are married. The only way in which sex can dishonour men is if the women they are connected with behave inappropriately, so in order to retain their honour men have to control women's sexuality.

Because of issues of social standing and honour and the fact that these attach to whole families, making appropriate marriages is important to Cypriots and they operate a form of arranged marriage known as *proxenia*. Prior to any formal discussions a discreet investigation takes place to ensure that the person in question is suitable: i.e. that they come from a respectable family, that they are economically acceptable, and that, in the case of girls, there are no adverse reports regarding their sexual purity. *Proxenia* can take a number of forms, from inviting the boy and his family to the girl's house and then sending the girl into the room to hand coffee round so that she can be seen (and see), to slightly more casual and discreet ways of giving the young people an opportunity to see one another (although arranging a meeting might be a relatively recent phenomenon). The young people normally have the power of veto, though this too may be a recent phenomenon. *Proxenia* is normally put into motion by the parents, who may employ a trusted go-between at the initial stages. The negotiations after the initial meeting take place between the two sets of parents and usually include discussions of the dowry and any property transfers. When everything is agreed the young couple get engaged, a relatively binding contract involving a church ceremony, and it is usually a few years later, when a house is available and all the other arrangements are made, that the couple get married.

Within a marriage the roles of the two partners are very rigidly defined: Loizos applies Davis's dictum to Cypriot families that: 'a man's rights are sexual and his duties economic while a woman's rights are economic and her duties sexual'. He goes on to elaborate, 'Men must support their families economically; women must nurture their families by housework; women must submit to the sexual demands of their husbands; and women must never by their actions give the community the slightest cause to doubt their sexual shame' (Loizos 1975: 54–5). Women also have total responsibility for childcare. Daughters as well as wives are expected to be constantly attentive to the father's wishes and to help with household chores. In the case of sons, although they are not expected to help in the house or to service the father in the same way as his womenfolk, they are expected to show him respect in every way (see Peristiany 1965: 181).

In spite of the idea that the economic domain is totally the responsibility of the man, because of the nature of household arrangements based on a tradition of peasant farming, women have always worked in the fields and have always been involved in the kinds of cottage industries listed above. However, as this can be considered to be an extension of women's work within the household and does not provide a wage it is still possible to see this kind of work as part of the woman's lot and to claim that men are fulfilling their economic duty. Also, this is the kind of work in which women are least likely to come into contact with dangerous unrelated men thereby running the risk of public gossip and loss of family honour.

However something more surprising and less easy to reconcile with the idea that women had no economic responsibilities is the fact that as well as working in the contexts described above, Cypriot women also worked for a wage in both rural and urban settings. Writing in 1930 Surridge had already observed women in Cyprus working as agricultural labourers on the road in cases where the family holding was insufficient (1930: 26). In 1954 there was a substantial female workforce in Cyprus as can be seen from the official statistics. Tables 1 and 2 only refer to specific industries or specific locations so they do not indicate the overall female workforce but they do show the ratio of male to female workers.

Table 3.1 *Number of persons working in mining and quarrying and manufacturing industries, by sex (1954)*

	total	male	female
number of persons	49,527	39,400	10,127
percentage	100	79.5	20.5

Source: Cyprus Government Statistical Abstract 1955
The detailed tables in the Statistical Abstract show the majority of women appearing in the present *Table 1* (5,389) to be employed in the 'manufacture of footwear, other wearing apparel and made up textile goods'.

Table 3.2 *Number of persons employed in the six district towns, August 1953 (excluding domestic service)*

	total	male	female
number of persons	44,528	38,293	6,232
percentage	100	86	14

Source: Cyprus Government Statistical Abstract 1955
The detailed tables in the Statistical Abstract show the majority of women appearing on Table II (3.058) to be employed in 'Commerce and Services'.

Tables 3.1 and 3.2 are not compatible. However, we can make the overall assessment from them that a significant percentage of the workforce in the mid-1950s was made up of women; if we knew the figures for domestic servants and agricultural workers the percentage would probably be even greater. From ethnographic sources we also find evidence of women working for a wage. Loizos, during research carried out in a Cypriot village in the late 1960s, found that out of eighty-two households thirty-four had wives or daughters who sometimes took paid work outside the home (1975: 55). In more recent years women have made up over a third of the working population in Cyprus. Table 3.3 includes agricultural workers.

Table 3.3 *Women as a proportion of the employed population in Cyprus*

	total	female
1976	159,286	58,831
1980	197,311	73,727
1981	205,244	79,232
1982	205,776	80,098
1983	209,328	82,034

Source: Cyprus Government Statistical Abstracts 1984.

The ideology is that women should not be economically active but the reality is that they are. Davis summarizes the situation for the Mediterranean in general and comments on what this means in terms of prestige: 'The ideal may be that women should do no work at all in the fields or that they should only work at harvest, or that they should never work for other men; but whatever the ideal, some fail to attain it and they and their men consequently lose prestige' (1977: 43). He then reviews the evidence and cites examples from all around the Mediterranean of societies where women are not supposed to work outside the home but where some do.

On the question of prestige Loizos also says that in the thirty-four households mentioned above where women worked for outsiders the status of the man was slightly diminished. However he goes on to add, 'It does not mean that his honour is affected, unless that is, one of his women misbehaves sexually' (1975: 55).

Another point to emerge from Loizos's work is that women can progress from working outside the home to *not* working outside the home and that change does not necessarily take place the other way round. Loizos writes that whereas in the past all village women did both housework and agricultural work on their own land, no matter how rich they were, in the last twenty years women who have married teachers or civil servants have not had to do much agricultural work: 'to assert family status, husbands with regular salaries sometimes prefer to pay other women to weed around the trees and pick the ripe fruit. This leaves nothing for their wives to do' (1975: 55–6). This suggests that an emerging class structure is as important to whether or not women work as more traditional concepts of honour, and pinpoints the intersection of ideologies and economics.

Data from other parts of the Mediterranean support this perspective and also imply that the question of the acceptability of women's economic activity is related to the urban/rural divide, to whether husbands are salaried employees or peasant farmers, and on the form of the family. Davis, referring to these points, mentions 'reports from Islamic communities of poor men who leave the land and become wealthy, [and who then] seclude their women and veil them'. He also cites Silverman writing on Colleverde in Italy who 'contrasts the farmstead dwelling women of extended families whose capacity for work is highly valued, and town-dwelling women of nuclear families whose chastity is highly prized' (Davis 1977: 44–5).

A further point which needs to be raised is the question of how women's prestigious jobs are viewed in these kinds of societies. Unfortunately this question does not receive much attention in the literature, since the issue of honour and women's economic activity is mostly discussed in terms of how women's work affects men's honour and prestige. Nevertheless one interesting example is given by Loizos in an examination of sibling sets in a village in Cyprus: two of the sisters of the set leave the village to study and come back as teachers. The status of one of the sisters, a gym teacher, contributed to the prestige of the whole sibling set (which included men). The other sister married without difficulty. She had many suitors and her husband accepted that she would continue working to pay off the debt for her dowry house. This example implies that when it is a matter of receiving an education and coming back to a professional job, even leaving the village and spending time in a big city is acceptable and can add to the prestige of both the family and the woman herself rather than detracting from it. No mention of honour is made by Loizos (1975) in this account.

Looking at honour more generally, Davis (1977) argues that it is a mechanism for ranking and affects only the middle ranges. The wealthy are at the top of the hierarchy and their status cannot easily be shaken, so they can do as they please. The poor cannot afford honour and certainly cannot afford for women not to work. It is only the people in between who can potentially be ranked on the honour scale and who vie for position. Although many anthropologists would disagree with Davis's analysis, since it goes against some of the more romantic notions of honour (e.g. Campbell 1964), clearly wealth and class are central to the issue of honour, while urbanization and family structure influence the form it takes and the importance attached to it.

As must be evident from this brief review, the relationship between honour and women's work outside the home is highly complex and changes with the situation. The relationship between honour and prestige/status is not clear from the literature and when wealth is brought into the equation there is a certain amount of disagreement among writers on the subject. For the purposes of the present paper the main point to emphasize is that women going out to work, and the adjustments and renegotiations that can result, were issues that were relevant in Cyprus and did not arise in London as a consequence of migration.

Cypriots in London: the first generation

MIGRATION AND SETTLEMENT IN LONDON

The first wave of Cypriot migration to Britain was between the wars and consisted mainly of Greek-Cypriot men who found work as waiters in London's West End and seasonal work in southern seaside towns. The smaller numbers of women who came at this period worked as machinists in Jewish factories in Soho. In the 1950s and 1960s, the main period of migration, substantial numbers of Cypriots, men and women, Turkish and Greek, came to Britain and found work in the same industries as their predecessors. The last influx of Cypriots were the displaced persons and refugees who had to leave Cyprus after the upheavals of 1974. Those who were not deported by the British Government have by now been absorbed by the Cypriot community.

Cypriots migrated for economic reasons, choosing Britain because of work opportunities and their colonial connection. Despite this connection, migration to Britain was subject to controls. From 1937 the Colonial Government in Cyprus imposed a system of affidavits, preventing would-be migrants from coming to Britain unless they had sponsors, already settled in this country, who could guarantee their support. This contributed to the form that the migration took, which was a chain migration along kinship and patronage lines (Oakley 1979). After 1962, with the implementation of the Commonwealth Immigration Act, Cypriot entry into Britain, like that of all other new Commonwealth citizens, was controlled by the British Government through the voucher system. Only in the years between 1959 and 1962 were there no controls and those were the years when the largest number of Cypriots came to Britain. The status of most Cypriots once in Britain is that of British Subjects, and as New Commonwealth immigrants they have the same priviliges and the same restrictions as migrants from the Indian subcontinent and the Caribbean. However, as white immigrants they do not suffer the same kind of racism as other New Commonwealth immigrants[3] and it is possible for them to become ethnically 'invisible' in Britain, although in fact few of them have done so.

At the present time, the mid-1980s, there are some 180,000 Cypriots living in Britain with the great majority settled in London. London's Cypriot population displays almost the same Greek to Turkish ratio as in Cyprus, has an even sex ratio, and consists of people of all age groups (including the elderly): the Cypriot settlement in London is no longer young. Greek Cypriots in London are spatially concentrated in certain areas and they have tended to work, socialize, and marry within the group. Greek Cypriots operate as a community in many ways, including the maintenance of a vast number of ethnic organizations which aim to keep the group together (Constantinides 1977: Josephides 1987; Oakley 1987a).

Cypriot women migrated to London in a number of ways. Married women either came with their husbands or joined them later (not usually more than a year or two). Young women sometimes came with their families but there are also many cases of young women coming on their own and joining married siblings or other relatives. In some cases they came and lived with their employers. There were also divorced or widowed women who brought their children with them. For the majority of Cypriot women, coming to England meant coming to paid work, whether they were married or not. And for the majority of them the jobs they came to, at least initially, were as machinists in the clothing industry. Whether it was because they knew that that was what they were destined for (and in many cases employers would have had to sponsor their migration) or whether it was because that was the work they were doing anyway (see Table 3.1), of the women who gave an occupation on emigrating from Cyprus a vast majority appear in the statistics under the category 'tailors, dressmakers, and related garment makers'.

Although Table 3.4 is for all emigrants from Cyprus the majority of the women in this Table came to London.

WOMEN AND 'ETHNIC BUSINESS'

One of the most distinctive aspects of the Cypriot settlement in

Table 3.4 *Female emigration from Cyprus*

	1956	1957	1958	1960	1962
all female emigrants	3,493	2,682	2,320	6,425	2,956
female emigrants aged 15 to 59	2,346	1,945	1,668	4,606	2,036
numbers classified by occupation	804	692	759	1,969	789
'tailors, dressmakers and related garment makers'	663	657	630	1,568	702

Source: Government of Cyprus Migration and Vital Statistics.

London is the degree to which Cypriots have developed their own businesses, particularly in the clothing and catering industries. Data from the 1971 census indicates that 22.2 per cent of male migrants from European countries in the New Commonwealth (principally Cyprus and Malta) are self-employed. This is more than twice the national average, with more than one in five males in this group being recorded as self-employed. Furthermore, a greater percentage of men in this group have employees (11.3 per cent) than work on their own (10.9 per cent) (Reeves and Ward 1984).

We do not have parallel statistics for women's employment, but we know that large numbers of Cypriot women are the employees of self-employed Cypriot men (cf. Phizacklea, this volume). In the clothing industry women work for men as machinists in factories, or as homeworkers, while in catering women work alongside their husbands running small cafés. Women who work in cafés perceive themselves as building up a family business with their husbands rather than working for them. However, officially it is the man who is registered as managing the business and in some cases the woman might be registered as his employee.

Cypriots have gone into business in such large numbers because they came to the UK in order to work and improve their economic position. For many of them, going into business was seen as the only way to make money and fulfil their dream of going back to Cyprus with the potential of buying property and having some capital besides, or of getting an education either for themselves or their children. In fact, for most Cypriots going into business has not meant making big money but making enough to live on, and they do this by working long hours and putting up with the worries and uncertainties of being in business. In other words, they are very much at the margins of the economy. People in the clothing industry are the most insecure, and for every entrepreneur who makes it big, dozens of others close down every day.[4] A current joke is that the only way to make money at the present time is by becoming a liquidator.

In most cases, Cypriot men's and women's business aspirations are different: whereas for men the aim is to work for themselves, for women it is more a question of contributing to a family business. For this reason, even if analytically we can see that women's labour is used in the same way by their husbands as by other Cypriot entrepreneurs (e.g. Anthias 1983), there are important distinctions to be made because the women experience these situations differently and relate differently to the wealth which is produced through their labour power in each case. This point is elaborated below.

Except for the very small numbers of professional women, female students, and women who went to areas of Britain without a strong Cypriot community, first generation Cypriot women have nearly all worked in Cypriot businesses one way or another. Many of the women whose family/husband's businesses were a success and are now wealthy no longer work on a regular basis and along with the wives of Cypriot professional men are involved in the various Cypriot parents' associations and the 'Ladies Branches' of other associations. Parallels can be drawn between this situation and the situation in Cyprus since families which have become economically secure can afford the luxury and the status implied when the woman does not have to work outside the home. However most Cypriot women continue to work outside the home and the majority of women working as employees work within the clothing industry while the majority of those working with their husbands work in catering. Before looking at women's role in these two industries in greater detail a few examples of the kinds of work that women have done in this country will indicate the range and combinations of enterprises with which women become involved. In addition the women have all raised families.

Georgia came to London in 1960, aged eighteen, to live with her married sister, to work, and to find a husband. She worked in a relative's grocery shop for a while then found a job at a Cypriot record shop. She eventually married the owner of the shop and then, mainly through her efforts, they started a clothing factory. This was not successful and was eventually abandoned after all the capital they had saved from the shop and invested in the factory had been used. Now, after a series of jobs, including homeworking and running a dry cleaning shop, Georgia manages an hotel of which she is part-owner. Her husband is involved in another business in his own right but will eventually pull out of that and join Georgia in the hotel.

Ellou has done everything! Her husband was the initiator of all the projects but she was an equal partner, albeit behind the scenes. They began by running an accommodation agency from their front room, then they 'did Greek weddings', which involved providing drink on a consume or return basis and seeing to various other details of the reception. Many projects later they are now raising quails for London clubs and restaurants. This is apparently such a smelly and unpleasant job that they cannot find anyone to go into the business with them so there are only the two of them working together.

Maria came to London in the late 1950s with her husband and three children. Shortly after they arrived in London she and her husband split up and Maria raised her family on her own. She has worked as a machinist both in factories and at home; she ran a café, a post office, a launderette, and a guest house; she has been involved in an interpreting and translating service; and she has tried to get into property conversions. When Maria first came to this country she worked in order to raise the capital to start a business and has since been working in order to raise enough money to enable her to get out of business. In common with many small business people she has neither a pension to look forward to, other than the state pension, nor investments which would help provide a comfortable retirement. She still has financial commitments. Maria therefore feels she has to make more money before she can retire. This is proving difficult. Maria is tired and suffering some ill health due to continuous overwork. However she has no choice but to continue working.

Frosso came over in 1960. She was a dressmaker in Cyprus, and except for a brief period helping in her sister's fish and chip shop she has worked almost exclusively in the clothing industry. She has worked for different firms, both Cypriot and Jewish, and is now a homeworker. However she has now become very slow and has a back problem so she cannot spend as long at the machine as she used to. Her husband works as a presser but does not make enough to support the whole family.

Helen and her husband worked for other people to raise the capital to start their own fish and chip shop. They have been working it together for years and made enough money to buy a house so they no longer have to live above the shop. Helen prefers not to go to the shop every day now so they have taken on a part-time worker (an Englishwoman) and Helen only works there herself two or three days a week. The rest of the time she stays at home where she works as a homeworker to bring in some extra money.

These examples are not given because they are typical – in fact the cases of Maria and Georgia who entered business in their own right are fairly unusual – but to show the range of work that Cypriot women become involved with and to indicate that they can be involved in more than one type of work at any one time. The cases outlined here also suggest that Cypriot women (like Cypriot men) are tenacious entrepreneurs constantly looking for openings in the market and that, in part, they are like this because they have no option. The more typical situations will be discussed in the next two sections. Although some women in the clothing industry are employers and some in catering are straightforward employees, the following section looks at the role of the majority of women in each of these two industries.

1 The clothing industry
The form the Cypriot niche of the clothing industry has taken has been well documented (Anthias 1983; Ladbury 1984). The main points which need reiterating here are:

(a) Cypriot entrepreneurs established themselves in the clothing industry through using other Cypriots as employees.[5] These employees were often not registered and although this was considered to be an advantage to the employees themselves, as they received 'clear money', it certainly meant that they provided a source of cheap labour for the employers and it is doubtful that Cypriot entrepreneurs would have been successful if it had not been for these practices.
(b) There is a division of labour in Cypriot firms, with the women working as machinists, overlockers, and finishers and the men working as pressers and cutters. Pressers and cutters are paid much more than machinists.
(c) Large numbers of women homeworkers are employed. Home-working is a flexible form of employment enabling the women to work in their own time and the employers to take less responsibility for their workforce. This kind of employment can lead to the worst forms of exploitation.
(d) Employers and employees are linked by many ties. They are often kin or fictive kin, they socialize with one another and

attend one another's ceremonies and celebrations. This means that the relationship is not seen in simple economic terms.

Consequently, women workers in this industry have been a source of cheap labour and have been severely exploited, in terms both of the wage they receive and the conditions under which they work (see Anthias 1983).

Although many women went into dressmaking because of the skills they brought with them from Cyprus, in some cases their skills were almost a disadvantage because ability to machine fast is the main requirement in these jobs (see Westwood 1984). Two women told me that because they learnt dressmaking in Cyprus they were too slow and still had to be put with another woman to 'train' when they started work here. The implication is that the more skill-oriented women from Cyprus have to relearn their trade to satisfy the new conditions. But besides their skills there are other reasons for women working in this industry which have to do with exclusion from other openings and easy, almost inevitable inclusion into this one. The exclusions at the time were due to the fact that most Cypriot women did not speak English or have qualifications and generally lacked 'know how' regarding how to operate in this country. In terms of the inclusion, working in the clothing industry, particularly for Cypriots or for firms employing Cypriots, was in some cases part of the migration package and in others, through informal recruitment, an almost inevitable consequence of it. This kind of work also had the advantage that it could be done at home; a necessity for women with small children.

Another encouragement to this type of work is to be found in the importance of honour and the idea that it is 'safer' for women to work with people known to the family (Anthias 1983: 79; Ladbury 1984: 111). ·

But despite there being so many reasons why women find themselves working in Cypriot clothing factories and so many reasons why they stay, their main reason for working is to make money and even if there are dimensions to their relationship with their employer which are not simply economic this does not necessarily blind women to their own interests or prevent them from changing their situation if the right time comes. For example, Marro worked as a dressmaker in Cyprus for a woman with a small workshop. Her boss then migrated to London and sent for Marro to come and work for Mr and Mrs Stavrides who had a prosperous dress factory. The Stavrides sponsored Marro to come to London and when she arrived in 1960 she both worked and lived with them. When she married in 1965, the firm provided her with a wedding dress and her employer's brother became a best man. Shortly after her marriage she left the firm because the pay was too low (£8 per week) and started working for a Jewish firm in Harley Street. The salary there was £13. This firm closed down and she obtained work as a homeworker through her neighbour's contacts. Then she started a family so she remained a homeworker. Marro related differently to the ethnic economy at different stages of her life in Britain. When she needed patronage as a newly arrived unmarried woman she worked for Cypriots but later as a better established married woman she tried to get a better deal for herself and when she had small children, she found it necessary to work at home.

Possibly, once Marro married 'honour' was satisfied and it was possible for her to take work outside the Cypriot context.

2 Catering

Unlike women working for someone else whose concern is with how much is in their wage packets, women working with their husbands want the business to prosper.

The majority of Cypriot cafés are fish and chip shops; they tend to have a few tables, but most of their trade is takeaway. Cypriots also run day cafés which cater for working people. Greek restaurants, although some may be run as family businesses, generally rely on the employment of outside staff and are on a different scale and of a different type from the cafés I am describing here.

In most Cypriot cafés the man is seen as having the main responsibility for running the café while the woman 'helps' and is also responsible for running the home. This involves the normal routines of housework, looking after the children, etc., and also, in most cases, preparing an evening meal.

How this is organized depends on the opening hours of the café, whether the family live on the premises, and whether there are small children. A woman without small children living above the café will spend all the busy times with her husband in the café and the lulls upstairs doing her housework, cooking, and so on. Where the café is a fish and chip shop, because many of them close after lunch, the women spend afternoons doing household jobs and preparing the evening meal. Some women cook the family meal in the café kitchen so that they can keep an eye on that and serve the customers at the same time. Women are usually responsible for keeping the shop clean. When a woman cannot be at the café during all the busy times, either because she has very small children or because they live off the premises and she has to spend some of her time at home, an older child or a part-time employee helps the man.

Although it is generally acknowledged that the man could not run such a business without his wife's hard work it is nevertheless the man who is seen as the essential ingredient in the business due to his organizational ability. One woman said that she and other women can work hard but they do not know how to deal with things like VAT forms and could not keep the business going without their husbands. Where the women cannot read or write this is felt even more strongly. The women I know who work in such businesses and who also run the home and cook special Greek food for their husbands every night, do not feel resentful in any way or suggest that their husbands should help in the home. They complain about having too much to do but they are proud that they are able to keep everything ticking over. They even manage to make Cypriot delicacies to take to friends they are visiting at the weekend or for community events, and if they are sitting in front of the television in the evening it is with some work in their hands. Nor do they consider it a problem that the man is in charge of the business and, in most cases, the money. The money they make in the business goes towards their common aspirations which are to buy a house and move away from the business, and eventually to buy a house plot in Cyprus. On a day-to-day basis their money is used to maintain the household and for their children. But the women I talked to felt that their husbands were 'fair'. They said if they were with the kind of man who spends jointly earned money on other women or on gambling then they would feel very differently, and as for cooking for such a man, one woman summed up their attitude by saying: 'let him eat poison!'

Following this discussion of women's roles in ethnic business, we can draw together some of the issues which emerge. First, when women work for outside employers, they are exploited in the same way as all workers and perhaps more severely because of the particularly bad conditions in the clothing industry. Women are well aware of this though often they can do little about it. Where women work with their husbands, on the other hand, they cannot be said to be exploited in the same way when their joint income is jointly controlled, nor do they perceive themselves as being exploited. The situation is different when a man spends this income on himself. Secondly, when a couple run a shop jointly a women's actual economic contribution remains hidden and is therefore not quantifiable. But when she works for an outside employer her earnings are quantifiable and each spouse's contribution to the household budget is clearly visible. This means that a woman working for an outside employer is in a stronger position vis-a-vis her husband as her labour cannot be incorporated into his. It would therefore be easier for a woman receiving a wage to assert her independence from her husband than for a woman who is working with him. Finally, whether women work for outside employers or together with their husbands in their shop, they still have to be housewives at home. Men do not see their wives' economic contribution as placing them under any obligation to contribute in the home nor do women expect such a contribution. Women who work for an outside employer (particularly those who go out to work each day) can clearly be seen to have two jobs. When women work with their husbands in the shop, this can sometimes be seen as an extension of a woman's domestic duties.

In conclusion, it is clear that women employees are exploited by their employers but might, in the long run, be in a stronger position vis à vis their husbands. Women working with their husbands, on the other hand, are not exploited in that way because they share jointly in the product of their labour. However, they have no way of asserting their economic independence. This raises the question of whether women working for outside employers have a greater potential for being independent of their husbands in a more general sense. Part of the answer to this question is that women's independence is also related to whether the society in which they live can accept them as independent beings and on whether there are any roles available to them other than as daughters, wives, and mothers. There was no such acceptance or alternative roles in Cyprus and nor is there within Cypriot community life in London, although attitudes are changing. But in London women theoretically are able to opt out of Cypriot community life, though this is unlikely to be an attractive proposition for most first-generation women.

One final question is whether Cypriot women are *forced* to work only in the ethnic context because of Cypriot ideologies of honour and shame. A curious characteristic of ideologies is that they always seem to be there when they are needed to justify a particular practice, but they can just as easily be absent or change. Cypriots, both men and women, can cite the 'dangers' of working with unrelated men in order to show the desirability of women working in a Cypriot factory or, better still, of not working at all, but in the next sentence they can talk about a woman getting a 'good' job with better pay in a non-Cypriot factory and only comment on this in respect of whether the woman gets lonely not having other Cypriots around her. Also, when Cypriot women first came to London none of them worked for Cypriots because there were no Cypriot factories in those days and although through informal recruitment practices they usually found themselves working with other Cypriots there is nothing to suggest that those women who worked entirely with outsiders were in any way considered to be without shame. Honour and shame ideologies can be used to control women's activities when appropriate but they do not shape women's working lives in a universal or uniform way.

The second generation

In 1986 in both Cyprus and among London's Cypriots it is expected, accepted (and hoped!) that every girl leaving school will either go into higher education or get a job. For the daughters of rich families this may only be an interim period until they marry but there is no question of keeping them at home until a suitable bridegroom is found. However girls in London would not dream of doing the kinds of jobs their mothers did and nor would their mothers wish it.[6] Yet although Cypriots in London are not faced with the kind of racism suffered by black minorities, unemployment among them as a group is comparable to the unemployment levels among other immigrant groups (Anthias 1982: 211 ff). Also, young Cypriots suffer from the same kind of educational disadvantage as their New Commonwealth immigrant peers (Swann 1985: 686). Within these constraints young Cypriots are making certain choices. The second generation go for what they perceive to be glamour jobs. Beauty therapy, hairdressing, and fashion are high on the agenda but because they fear getting stuck in the same kinds of jobs as their mothers it can be difficult for them to get started in certain industries. According to a careers officer who has young Cypriot women clients, when it is suggested that in order to work in fashion design they have to learn things like pattern cutting they shy away, as this is too reminiscent of seedier aspects of the clothing industry. In fashion retail, although they like the idea of being buyers (and several of those I interviewed at youth clubs were trainee buyers) they are frightened of anything that looks like a straight selling job. Cypriot girls are also going into clerical jobs, anything to do with travel or banking being popular. Although they want to get away from the Cypriot economy the spirit of self employment is not altogether gone. For example, Helen is working in an insurance firm and is engaged to a Cypriot man who runs his father's off-licence. They hope that once they are married they will be able to go into business together and are looking around for possibilities. Many women who are going into beauty therapy and hairdressing hope eventually to be able to set up on their own. Some have already done this, mostly by going to clients' homes, which is easier to do and requires less capital than setting up a clinic or salon.

Most young women would rather not work for Cypriots at all. For example, there are openings for Cypriots in the branches of the various banks of Cyprus which have opened in London, in Cypriot tourist agencies, and other Cypriot offices. Young Cypriot women stand a better chance of getting into these offices than any others because they require Greek language skills which means that they would only be competing against other Cypriots. However in my interviews, except for one girl who was taking extra Greek lessons because she desperately wanted to work for a Cypriot bank, most young people felt that it was better to work for non-Cypriots if possible and there was more prestige attached to finding work in the open market. One respondent told me that she would not work for Cypriots because they are stingy and they take advantage of you by making you make the tea all the time. She also said they were two-faced and that most youngsters would agree with this and do not want to work for Cypriots. Many others were concerned about having to make the tea and felt that Cypriots were bad employers. So not only do young Cypriot women choose not to work within the traditional spheres of the ethnic economy, but they also choose not to work for Cypriots if they can help it.

Paradoxically, one of the few groups which is working increasingly within the ethnic context is young professional women. Because of Section II funding and the blossoming of race relations units and ethnic specialists many Cypriot women are being channelled into this area and are working as social workers, community development officers, multicultural advisers, and so on with reference to the Greek-Cypriot community. In different circumstances many professional young women may not choose to work in an 'ethnic' capacity.

New jobs do not mean that young women have broken away from Cypriot values. To begin with, most live at home with their parents until they marry. If they move from home to go to university they move back when they finish their studies. Of all the young women I spoke to when conducting interviews at youth clubs and community centres only one, an actress, lives away from home. When they live at home, although most of them are critical of many of their parents' attitudes and some of them are considered to be rebels, they nevertheless follow the dictates of their parents. In theory, since they are in work they live an independent life and do not have to submit to their parents' control. However there are a number of reasons why they do. One is that they are economically better off living at home as they do not have to contribute to the household economy and all their money can go on clothes or be saved up for the time they marry. Also parents often try to provide cars for their daughters and a generally comfortable home, something they are unlikely to get if they move out. A second reason is that young Cypriot women do accept many of their parents' values and appreciate the safety and security of feeling that they are part of the Cypriot community and of having parents who care about their welfare and their future. This they would have to give up if they were to be really rebellious and leave home or behave in a way which is unacceptable. Finally, although young Cypriot women complain about their lack of freedom they do not admire the kinds of freedoms that they perceive young English women as having and they are horrified by what they see as the lack of caring in English families.

Most of the other central Cypriot practices and values are still there although there have been shifts. *Proxenia* is mocked by most young people and many older Cypriots feel it is an outmoded method of finding a marriage partner. On the other hand older Cypriots (and some young people) believe that a marriage which has been properly looked into by the young person's family, by people who are likely to care for that young person and be able to anticipate potential problems, has more chance of success than a pure love match. Many parents feel that they want to give their daughter a dowry, and if they cannot manage to provide a house, they do try to give help towards getting one. The dowry is often approached from the point of view that young people need help to set up on their own as it is too difficult otherwise, though there is prestige involved in doing the right thing by a daughter and settling her down properly. In the case of parents whose families were too poor to provide the daughter with a dowry house on their own marriage, being able to do it for their own daughter sometimes means a great deal to them and justifies the expectations that migration would reverse their economic position. There is no longer the feeling that the bridegroom's people can demand a dowry but there are often stories of dowry expectations, particularly when they have not been fulfilled. There can also be the feeling that a man has been taken advantage of when a marriage has not involved a dowry. For example, a young male solicitor who became engaged to a woman without having asked for any dowry was told by his people that it was a waste for someone with his prospects and education to make no demands and that the woman's family must take him for a fool. His family then started negotiating for both the bride's family's house and business. However, in general dowry is less of an issue in London than it is in Cyprus. In some ways dowry could never have retained its old stranglehold in London because young Cypriot women outside Cyprus at least have the possibility of marrying non-Cypriots (although few do) so the bargaining power of Cypriot men is lessened.

Reputation and sexual modesty, on the other hand, are almost as important to London's Cypriots as they were in Cyprus. In fact many Cypriots claim that values have loosened up in Cyprus and it is only in London, where people are maintaining the attitudes they brought with them in the 1950s that it is so rigid. Most issues around reputation centre on the question of 'being allowed out'. Most Cypriot daughters are allowed out with family members, particularly brothers, and with other young Cypriot women who are known to the parents and whose family is considered respectable. The controversies arise out of allowing young women out without constraints and more specifically, allowing them out with young men. At present there is a lot of variation in how much freedom parents allow their daughters. At one extreme there are horror stories such as that of a young woman whose father took her to Cyprus, locked her up at her grandmother's house, and took her passport with him so that if she escaped she could not come back to London and mix with 'undesirables' (this account was given to me by her friend in London), at the other, there are those who are allowed out as freely as their English counterparts but are expected to 'behave' and not do anything to embarrass their families. Some are allowed out more freely than others and the precise restrictions imposed vary. The time they have to be back, whether or not they must be escorted, who they can go out with, and the places they are allowed to go to are the relevant elements in these restrictions, and whatever their individual situation the vast majority of young women I spoke to felt that parents in general did not allow them enough freedom. This is a very lively issue at the moment and is being discussed within the Cypriot community both in the pages of the newspapers and at meetings of ethnic organizations. The youth and social services also take an interest in this issue, perceiving it as a 'problem' for young Cypriot women.

So for the second generation the issue of honour has been divorced from that of women's work and has become exclusively attached to girls going out socially.

Conclusion

Because of honour and shame ideologies Cypriots may say that they do not like women to work outside the home, but in fact women always have worked outside the home. In the context of London, Cypriots may also say that it is 'better' for women to work for other Cypriots because this is 'safer'. However, Cypriot women in London have always worked for outsiders; the first migrant women came over at a time when there were no Cypriot firms in any case and they worked for Jewish firms. Other women have shopped around and found the best jobs open to them. The second generation, backed by their parents, are choosing, if they can, not to work for Cypriots. Honour and shame, as regards women's employment, is a useful ideal which can be picked up when needed and allowed to lapse when the circumstances demand it.

In the majority of households women have sole responsibility for looking after the home and the family. The fact that they are also economically active has not made Cypriot women question the division of labour within the household. This was so in Cyprus, and particularly among the first generation of migrant women, continues to be so in London.

Women in London who are working with their husbands are in any case not in a position where their economic power is seen independently from that of their husbands. Women working for a wage are in a slightly different position but the fact that they can be economically independent does not necessarily give them extra bargaining power. To have this they also need to live within a society which can accept them as independent beings (which is not the case within the Cypriot community in London). What might bring about changes is the coupling of wage labour with living in a wider society, that is, the ability to exit from the Cypriot community if necessary. This may happen with the second generation. What I mean by this is not that they will take on English values, which they do not necessarily see as preferable to Cypriot ones, or English lifestyles, but that there are other options in a cosmopolitan society and therefore the kinds of constraints that are all-powerful when there is no choice other than to accept them are likely to be weakened. In other words I am not suggesting that Cypriot girls will 'exit' from Cypriot community life but that because the option is there they can have greater bargaining powers within the community.

Notes

This paper is based on data collected during an ESRC funded research project on second generation Greek Cypriots in London (1983–85) and on my own knowledge of Greek Cypriots.

1 Work/working is used here to denote economically active, but this is not meant to imply that women at home 'involved' in domestic labour do not work.

2 Unless it is necessary to specify for reasons of clarity I am using the term 'Cypriot' to refer mostly to Greek-Cypriots. Official statistics from Britain are calculated from a category which includes all Cypriots and Maltese while statistics from Cyprus are based on all Cypriots prior to 1974 and to Cypriots living in the South (mostly Greek) after 1974.

3 This has not always been the case. In the 1930s Cypriots appear to have been a racialized group (see Oakley 1987b).

4 This has always been the case and is not just due to the present crisis in the industry.

5 Though significantly fewer Cypriots are now employed by these firms. The secretary of DACA (the Cypriot dressmakers association) at a public meeting in 1984 remarked that whereas ten years earlier a Cypriot firm employing fifty people was likely to employ forty Cypriots and ten outsiders, the ratio is now reversed. This has been explained to me in terms of Cypriot women no longer being willing to be either cheap or unregistered labour, and certainly younger women are not going into these jobs. However it may also be that more homeworkers are now employed as this is one way of cutting costs and increasing profit margins.

6 Ladbury makes the point that young Turkish-Cypriots are sometimes forced into the ethnic business sphere as a last resort when they fail to find work in the open market (1984: 122).

References

Anthias, F. (1982) 'Ethnicity and Class among Greek-Cypriot Migrants', unpublished PhD thesis, Bedford College.

—— (1983) 'Sexual divisions and ethnic adaptation: The case of Greek-Cypriot women', in Annie Phizacklea (ed.) *One Way Ticket*, London: Routledge & Kegan Paul.

Constantinides, P. (1977) 'Factors in the maintenance of ethnic identity', in J.L. Watson (ed.) *Between Two Cultures*, London: Oxford University Press.

Campbell, J.K. (1964) *Honour, Family and Patronage* London: Oxford University Press.

Cyprus Government Statistics
  Statistical Abstract 1955–1959. Published by Financial Secretary's Office, Cyprus.
  Statistical Abstract 1984, Department of Statistics and Research, Ministry of Finance.
  Migration and Vital Statistics 1955–1959. Published by Statistics Section, Financial Secretary's Office.
  Migration and Vital Statistics, 1960–1962. Published by the Statistics

and Research Department, Ministry of Finance.

Davis, J. (1977) *People of the Mediterranean*, London: Routledge & Kegan Paul.

Gilmore, D. (1982) 'The anthropology of the Mediterranean area', *Annual Review of Anthropology*: 175–205.

Josephides, S. (1987) 'Associations amongst the Greek-Cypriot Population in Britain', in J. Rex *et al.* (eds) *Immigrant Associations in Europe*, Aldershot: Gower.

Ladbury, S. (1984) 'Choice, chance or no alternative? Turkish Cypriots in business in London', in R. Ward and R. Jenkins (eds) *Ethnic Communities in Business*, Cambridge: Cambridge University Press..

Loizos P. (1975) *The Greek Gift*, New York: St Martin's Press.

Miles, R. (1982) *Racism and Migrant Labour*, London: Routledge & Kegan Paul.

Oakley, R. (1979) 'Family, kinship and patronage: The Cypriot migration to Britain', in V.S. Khan (ed.) *Minority Families in Britain*, London: Macmillan.

—— (1987a) Patterns of spatial distribution, *Research Paper No. 5*, Centre for Research in Ethnic Relations.

—— (1987b) 'The control of Cypriot migration to Britain between the wars', *Immigrants and Minorities*, Vol. 6, 1: 30–43.

Peristiany, J.G. (1965) (ed.) *Honour and Shame*, London: Weidenfeld & Nicolson.

—— (1965) 'Honour and shame in a Cypriot highland village', in J.G. Peristiany (ed.) *Honour and Shame*, London: Weidenfeld & Nicolson.

Phizacklea, A. (1985) 'Jobs for girls: production of women's wear in the UK'. Seminar presented at the Centre for Research in Ethnic Relations.

Reeves F. and Ward, R. (1984) 'West Indian business in Britain', in R. Ward and R. Jenkins (eds) *Ethnic Communities in Business*, Cambridge: Cambridge University Press.

Surridge, B.J. (1930) *A Survey of Rural Life in Cyprus*. Nicosia: Cyprus.

The Swann Report (1985) *Education For All: The Report of the Committee of Inquiry into the Education of Children from Ethnic Minority Groups*, London: HMSO.

Westwood, S. (1984) *All Day Every Day: Factory and Family in the Making of Women's Lives*, London: Pluto Press.

4 Fast food, fettered work: Chinese women in the ethnic catering industry

Sue Baxter and Geoff Raw

For a quarter of a century, Chinese restaurants, chip shops, and 'takeaways' have been a common feature of towns and cities throughout the country. Yet although they are the third largest ethnic community in Britain, the Chinese have received relatively little attention from politicians and researchers. Partly a result of their demographic dispersal, the low profile of Britain's Chinese has been due more to their isolation from the mainstream economy. For not only is the Chinese community concentrated in the fast food catering industry,[1] in which workplaces are atomized and workers' organization difficult, but also ownership as well as the staffing of firms tends to lie in Chinese hands. This was confirmed by a Home Affairs Committee report in 1985 which estimated that about 90 per cent of Britain's Chinese were employed in the catering industry and that of these, perhaps 60 per cent were employed in small, family shops (Home Affairs Committee 1985: xi). However, so little is known about the lives of those who work in this insular trade that there has developed a popular misconception that Chinese people are culturally inclined towards economic and social detachment (see, for example, Jones, 1979; Watson 1974; Swann Report). Less still is known about Chinese women in the ethnic economy, yet it is their experiences in particular that can provide the most penetrating insight into the Chinese catering niche.

Whilst scarcely any serious literature exists on the Chinese community in general (let alone on Chinese women), what little there is tends to focus exclusively on its cultural features (e.g. Ng 1986; Watson 1977; Baker 1977). This is not to say that such contributions are unimportant. However, because so little is known about the structural factors that to a large extent dictate the lives of Chinese people in the fast food industry, it is necessary to establish a wider explanatory framework within which to understand their specific experiences. In relation to Chinese women, this means first apprehending the way in which gender roles have been and continue to be transformed as a consequence of the erratic development of capitalism in southeast China. Imposed with the expansion of

British and other imperial powers, rapid capitalist industrialization entailed the destruction of the local agricultural economy and prompted massive demographic movements which stretched far beyond the borders of China to the developing colonies and to Britain. Second, the lives of Chinese women must be seen not only within the context of racist and sexist immigration laws affecting female workers and dependants but also with a critical appreciation of employment conditions within the fast food industry. From this perspective it is evident that the concentration of Chinese women in an ethnic sub-economy is a direct result of the postwar economic demand for cheap, colonial labour to provide inexpensive, ready-cooked meals. In this sense, Chinese women in the catering trade share a common historical oppression with other women from New Commonwealth countries, despite appearing often to enjoy a petit bourgeois class position. Such findings challenge the conclusions of a growing body of research on exclusively ethnic economic 'enclaves' which maintain that migrants employed in these sectors fare considerably better than those who are not, and that the underlying impetus for such differences is rooted in cultural practice (e.g. Waldinger 1984; Wilson and Portes 1980; Model 1986; Light 1972; and see Phizacklea, this volume).

The changing role of Chinese women

According to traditional Chinese cosmology, the world was composed of two complementary elements – the *yin*, the female, symbolizing all things dark, weak, and passive, and the *yang*, the male, symbolizing the bright, strong, and active. Codified in Confucian epigrams, this dichotomy reflected the centuries-old status of women and men in dynastic China. Property transmitted along agnatic lines meant that women were economically, socially, and politically subordinate. Subject first to their fathers, then to their husbands, finally to their sons, Chinese women could never be independent. This was enshrined in the lineage and clan institutions that regulated village life. If women held any power at all, it was only in their ability to manipulate their kinsmen.

In peasant China, the role of the female was rooted in domestic production for the household while men generally farmed the land. Women's main task was to spin and weave cotton but they also made pottery, shoes, and other textiles. This function, along with the low technology, 'cottage industry' mode of production, remained static for centuries. During peak demand for agricultural labour, such as planting and harvest, women worked with men in the fields, but their contributions were never sufficiently sustained to constitute a threat to the established patriarchal structures. In the nineteenth century, however, the onslaught of Western imperialism effectively obliterated the traditional economy of southeast China, displacing and rendering even more precarious the position of local women.

Tea and silk were the main commodities sought by the colonialists in China, while in return they illegally sold vast quantities of opium, their largest and most lucrative source of local profit. The British trade monopoly was ended in 1834 and 'free trade' concessions were subsequently wrested from the Chinese government in two 'Opium Wars' declared on China by Britain during the latter part of the nineteenth century. This resulted in the devastation of the economic stability which had become established around controlled trading through China's southeastern sea ports. The disruption of inland trade routes, the spread of foreign owned industries in the coastal cities, and massive imports of Manchester cotton yarn, kerosene, cereals, and sugar (Riskin 1978: 362) amongst other items, systematically undermined and eliminated the traditional roles of both men and women.

Hundreds of thousands of economically displaced women migrated to the rapidly developing urban centres in search of work (many dying in the process), providing the new industrialists with a vast reservoir of cheap, female labour. In many areas, this migration had involved *all* those who were economically active (Siu 1982: 84). Even into the twentieth century, working conditions for urban women were so severe (particularly in foreign-owned factories) that they were sometimes forced:

> to urinate at their workpoint or to give birth to babies in the hallways of the factories. In fact, due to the 'complications' attached to married women, factory employers were usually reluctant to hire them, with the result that most women workers were between 10 and 18 years old.
>
> (Siu 1982: 89)

From the rapid destruction of the peasant economy of southeastern China emerged mass movements of resistance and rebellion directed against both the colonialists and the impotent Qing dynasty. Women played an active role in these forces for change and not least in the Taiping Rebellion, the largest and most influential of revolts, which swept the southeast between 1853 and 1860. Often hailed as the precursor to revolution in China, the Taiping Rebellion was very much predicated upon women's rights; namely an end to polygamy, female slavery, exclusive male adultery, and footbinding. It was also during this period of economic and political turbulence, and as a consequence of it, that a Chinese community became established on British shores.

A history of self-employment in Britain

The first Chinese settlers in Britain during the eighteenth century were virtually all men who had come as merchant seamen, recruited for British trade ships to fill the gap left by indigenous seamen who had been impressed into the Navy for the Napoleonic Wars. Growing trade links between Britain and China prompted by the end of the East India Company's trade monopoly in 1834, the acquisition of Hong Kong by Britain following the Opium Wars, and the opening of the Suez Canal in 1869 entailed increasing recruitment of cheaper Chinese workers by British trading companies. The need to service off-duty seamen passing between ports around Britain eventually led to the development of small 'Chinatowns' in many coastal cities, which catered specifically for the needs of the sailors. Thus, running boarding houses, social clubs, and laundry shops soon emerged as the means by which former Chinese seafarers were able to carve out a meagre living for themselves on British shores in the face of growing labour hostility towards the employment of cheaper, non-unionized Chinese workers, whose low wages undermined the strength of indigenous labour unions. In response to continued strike breaking by unorganized Chinese seamen during the 1911 Seamen's Union strike, for example, anti-Chinese riots in Cardiff left every single one of the city's thirty Chinese laundries in ruins.

The early Chinese settlers also suffered under increasingly restrictive racist legislature, which nurtured and consolidated the trend towards self-employment amongst the ethnic community. The 1905 Aliens Act not only consigned 'aliens' at the point of entry to a marginal economic status dependant upon the position of organized indigenous workers; it also limited their activities once they were admitted. Further legislation in 1914 and subsequent amendments extended the discretionary powers of immigration officers and restricted both the geographical movement of 'aliens' and the extent of their industrial militancy. Legally bound to be self-supporting, many Chinese who failed to prove Hong Kong birth faced deportation. With unemployment running high after the First World War, agitation by domestic seamen grew and increasingly they refused to sail with Chinese crews when there were 'thousands of Britishers wanting berths'. By 1931 over 500 Chinese laundries had become established throughout Britain, the vast majority owned and run by Chinese men. In due course, however, automation throughout the laundry industry forecast the imminent demise of labour-intensive Chinese hand-laundry shops, so that by the 1960s hardly any were still to be seen.

The drastic economic reordering wrought by the Second World War may have heralded the end of Chinese hand-laundry shops but it also opened up a new avenue for survival into which many of the precariously placed laundrymen could channel their efforts. It was also the sector into which a new generation of postwar migrants from Hong Kong and China would be drawn, building upon the niche already carved out by their dwindling predecessors.

Fast food

During the Second World War both migrants and women were drawn into industrial catering on a massive scale, a response to the sudden need for publically provided, ready-cooked meals caused by the new demands of a society at war. As women were drafted into waged work, families separated through the evacuation of children, and men conscripted into the armed forces, new methods of satisfying the basic needs of housing, clothing, and eating had to be found. One measure taken towards meeting those needs which was introduced by the Government was the setting up of British Restaurants and Factory Canteens. Factory Canteens (instituted under the Factory Canteens Order of 1940 No. 1993) catered for employees in factories where the workforce exceeded 250, whereas British Restaurants provided subsidized and unrationed hot meals to the community as a whole. For it was observed that 'If women are to enter industry . . . they must be freed from the necessity of providing meals for husbands and children. The extension of canteens in schools and factories accomplishes this purpose' (Labour Research Department 1943: 4). Similarly, it was noted, 'Hotels, restaurants and pubs have had to fall back on refugee and Irish labour to a great extent' (Labour Research Department 1943: 24). Doubtless, Chinese in Britain during this period entered the burgeoning catering trade along with other European migrants. By 1942 over 108 million meals per week were being consumed outside the home, over half of these being provided through private rather than state catering outlets (Labour Research Department 1943: 10).

During the same period, the economy of Hong Kong (formerly China's best trade port) was also undergoing considerable change. Its transition from an *entrepôt* and trading foothold for Britain in southeast Asia into a lucrative industrial and financial centre accelerated after the Japanese retreat and the rise to power of Mao in 1949. The latter propelled the majority of remaining capitalist interests from China to the colony, where they met with a ready supply of refugee labour. (By 1972 one American source calculated that Hong Kong was providing as much as half all the backing for the pound' Hong Kong Research Project 1974: 30.)

Rapid industrialization in Hong Kong soon outstripped the food supplies produced by its rural hinterlands, the New Territories. Agriculture was transformed into cash cropping of specialized rice grains and vegetables, whilst the main bulk of the colony's rice was imported cheaply from Thailand. This led to the swift demise of previous forms of rice production as a viable source of income throughout the New Territories and the hastened disintegration of the local economy, as pressure for industrial, commercial, and housing land encroached into rural areas. This was at a time when Britain was beckoning cheap, colonial workers to staff new jobs in the postwar 'boom'.

Postwar economic restructuring and expansion in Britain gave rise to the rapid growth of public and private 'service' industries. Subsequently the need for ready-cooked meals was kept alive. Founded upon labour-intensive production techniques, the new service jobs necessitated the employment of a flexible 'reserve army of workers' (whose labour power could be utilized and shed according to the rate of labour-saving technological development) in order to secure the fastest rate of capital accumulation.[2] As cheapness and docility of labour was a prime consideration in this process, women and migrant workers – who lacked a strong organizational power base and thus were most vulnerable – were a preferred source for the development of the service sector.[3] The evidence for this is well documented. Women, who in 1951 constituted less than one-third of the labour force (Breugel 1979: 16) now account for roughly half of all employed workers (1981 Census: Economic Activity, Table 1). Moreover, their patterns of employment reveal a substantial shift towards service work (see Foord 1984). Hence, the expansion of the fast food market was not merely a source of profit in itself; it also potentially released women from time-consuming home cookery (i.e. simply producing use values) in order to sell their labour power (i.e. to produce surplus values). In Hong Kong, the response to Britain's brief period of active encouragement of New Commonwealth immigration resulted in many Chinese men departing for the colonial metropolis (most of them from the New Territories). Following in the tradition of their forefathers who had arrived as seamen, they used established contacts – by now mostly concentrated in the restaurant industry – to find work.

Chinese fast food

By the time the majority of men began to leave Hong Kong, relying upon Chinese sponsors already established in Britain had become a statutorily codified condition of emigration, as those arriving during the 1960s were subject to the work voucher system imposed by the 1962 Commonwealth Immigrants Act. The legislation, designed to tailor immigration more specifically to the demands of the British economy, served to channel incoming Chinese migrants into the ethnic fast food industry. As highlighted by Rees, by the latter part of the 1960s and early 1970s, 'the majority of permits were issued to workers in the hotel and catering industry and in hospital employment' (Rees 1982: 85). Lacking industrial skills and speaking little or no English, most of those who came from the New Territories were therefore forced to rely on Chinese sponsors who would guarantee them specific jobs in Britain. Moreover, under the terms of the Act, men were allowed to bring their wives and dependants under the age of eighteen to join them, whereas women were not. Migration under these conditions was thus inevitably male-led, whilst other members of the family remained in Hong Kong and lived off the money sent home from abroad. In this way, it was not uncommon for entire villages to be dependant upon remittances sent from kinsmen in Britain (see Watson 1975): returns from farming and industrial work performed by women left behind in the New Territories during this period were so scarce that they could but supplement the frail and declining village economies.

'When my daughter was born in 1974, her father went to England after she was six months old. So it was me and my mother-in-law who brought her up. He used to send money to us for our living expenses – about £50 a month – and we could earn about £25 from farming. He had some land, you see, about one or two acres, and I worked on that. Everyone was the same then, not just my family.'

Confined to a system of economic patronage based on kinship networks, and due to their linguistic and technical differences in the context of a racist society, the migrants were obliged to take restaurant jobs. However, the proliferation of Chinese restaurants during the 1960s and 1970s to a large extent masked the conditions upon which their success was founded. Total reliance on Chinese employment channels put workers completely at the mercy of their employers. Long hours of split shift work, flexible duties, and lack of statutory entitlements (such as sick pay, holiday pay, overtime pay, payslips, and National Insurance payments) all too frequently accompanied tied housing and arbitrary management. Nevertheless, despite being below average British rates, remuneration levels were very much higher than any of the workers could have expected to receive back home.

'1968 I came to England because you couldn't get a job in Hong Kong to put food in your mouth. My uncle worked in a restaurant, you see – The White Lotus in Richmond, just outside London. He signed the form for me to come. In those days, someone I knew would be coming over every week. My uncle came first and I came later. He got me a job working in the restaurant. No wages – just food and somewhere to live – no money. It wasn't supposed to be a real job, you see. But once I found a job with pay, it was so much better than Hong Kong. I got £17 for the week. In Hong Kong I got £15 for the month!'

The universality of such conditions of service mitigated their perpetuation, as did the 'sojourner' orientation[4] of workers who remained separated from their families.

Whatever rights the Chinese restaurant workers had been accorded under the 1962 Act were subsequently eroded with the Immigration Act of 1971. Despite the introduction of concessionary Rules to administer the 1971 Act, it officially removed the automatic right of entry to wives and children of men already established in Britain. This prompted a 'beat the ban' wave of dependants' immigration, such that between 1971 and 1973 (when the Act came into force) dependants accounted for upwards of 90 per cent of total immigration from Hong Kong (Baxter 1986: 14). Dependants, however, were obliged to demonstrate that they could be supported by their sponsors, which rendered them in a far more subordinate position than women who had emigrated independently from urban Hong Kong and Singapore and who, on the whole, filled jobs in other areas of the service sector.

Chinese women in Britain

'When I came in 1968 I went to live with my husband above his uncle's takeaway shop for a year. We both worked there in the evenings and he gave us free food and never asked for any rent. . . Oh no, we didn't get paid. Then we rented a fish and chip shop for a couple of years but it didn't do too well, so we moved to Chinese Street. I had two kids by then. In those days, all the Chinese used to live there in the big houses. There were five families in ours – well, one was only a single man. But the rent was only £3 a week, which was all we could afford. Only three families used to cook there – the others ate at work. So things weren't too bad.

Housing was the immediate problem confronting women and children upon joining their male relatives in Britain. The dormitory work system suited families even less than it had done single men, and delapidated, overcrowded staff houses became standard accommodation for the Chinese community.

'I came here in 1972 but I just couldn't get used to it. My nephew was here already with his wife but I brought their three children with me so we could all live together again. My nephew and his wife slept in one room and I slept with the children in another room. The youngest one was so young, she had to use a potty all the time. We had to cook and eat in the same room. It was really horrible. There were mice everywhere. There was only two good things about it: the rent was only about £6 or £7 a week for all of us and it was easy to make friends. Everyone was Chinese so we could all look after each other.'

For some wives, reunification with their husbands in itself was a bewildering experience.

'My husband has been here twenty years now. His father before him was here for many, many years. I never met him because he died over ten years ago. He had an English wife as well, you know, and had two kids but they lost contact. I know when he sent for his son, it was a lot of hard work. I hadn't seen him for about six years before he came to England because he had already gone to Hong Kong to work in a clothing factory. But the wages here were good, I think. I stayed on our farm in China and grew vegetables and my husband would send us quite a lot of money. The only time I went to Hong Kong was to catch the aeroplane to England. It was very different, so modern and so busy. When I came to

London Airport, I didn't even recognize him! I waited and waited for about two hours and still nobody came for me. In the end I talked to someone in Chinese and they announced me on the loud speaker. Then it turned out he had been there all the time in the same place as me!'

Many women (and children) were absorbed into Chinese restaurants as kitchen hands and cleaners, often for no wages at all since it was assumed by employers that their labours were spent in part payment for their accommodation.

'My sister can't speak English so she just washes dishes in a restaurant. I was the same when I first came to this country. My husband got me the job in the same place as he was learning to be a cook but it's hard work and I didn't get much money.'

'I remember when I first came to this country we lived above a Chinese restaurant in Wales. I had to work there on Thursday and Friday nights and every weekend because my parents had to work so hard on those days, they couldn't keep up with the business. Sometimes the boss would give me 50p pocket money for the week but that's nothing, is it?'

From the mid-1970s onwards, Chinese restaurants increasingly met with competition from fast food 'chains' such as Kentucky Fried Chicken (introduced to Britain during the 1960s) and McDonalds (first established on this side of the Atlantic as early as 1974) (Jones 1985: 56). The advantage of the fast food chains lay in their heavy investment in cost-cutting technology which obviated the need for labour-intensive production, a saving passed on to customers. Since, by this period, rapidly diminishing new work permits kept wages reasonably stable for Chinese restaurant workers, the relative profitability of restaurants began to decline as economic competition began to bite. Together with the availability of family workers upon which to draw and the total unsuitability of dormitory, tied accommodation to family life, the falling profitability of restaurants transformed the Chinese catering economy into one composed of smaller capital units operating on lower running costs but with a similar rate of profitability to restaurants. In short, the mid- to late 1970s witnessed the simultaneous decline of Chinese restaurants and the rapid spread of Chinese 'takeaway' and fish and chip shops, the majority run as family businesses.

'running a restaurant involves a lot of money. But to open up a takeaway only costs about a third of what it costs to open up a restaurant. The profit margin is about the same – in fact it's more without the heavy outgoings. All you need is one chef in the kitchen and one waiter at the counter.'

'Twenty years ago there wasn't any takeaways. It was all restaurants. Me and my husband used to work in one of the big ones in the city centre. He was just learning then, like me. It was no good, though. Then we got a job in this place here for two years. He worked in the kitchen and I worked at the counter. There was another cook as well but he got the sack soon after because business wasn't very good then – not enough customers. After two years, we bought the business. That was ten years ago. The old owner, he's only got one business now. That's where he works with his family. I work seven days a week – but only in the evening, not in the daytime. We don't open for lunch. Some of our friends do, though. We both have to work at night but we can have a rest during the day, although we've still got to prepare the food for 5 o'clock, when we open. Thursday, Friday, and Saturday we work quite hard in the day – cutting the meat, getting it ready, chips, vegetables – things like that. Some of the stuff we get delivered but other stuff we've got to get from the wholesale market. You have to get up early for that. It's very difficult sometimes because we can't go to bed until about 2 o'clock (a.m.) and the market closes at 11 (a.m.). Weekends, it must be 2 or 3 (a.m.) before we're even finished in the kitchen. You have to clean everything after you've closed at night, you know. There's a lot of cleaning.'

Whilst it is true that the lives of both Chinese women and men are dictated by the opening hours of the takeaway shops, it is nevertheless women who generally bear the brunt of the social and economic marginality such a living imposes. Time and again the sentiment, 'It's his business, he makes the decisions' is reiterated and this is noticeably reflected in community life.

John is a waiter with a dependent wife and three children. A description of how he spends his spare time reveals that he and his wife have little in common socially.

'This is my second job. The first is in the casino or down the bookies. I go out with all the others in the restaurant all the time. In this business, there's nothing – nothing. Last weekend I played Mah Jeung for seventy-two hours – seventy-two hours and no sleep but I couldn't stop. We finished at 5 o'clock in the morning and I got in the car and drove straight back to work. Last night, quarter to four (a.m.) I'd lost £90. By four o'clock I won £230. That's about £300 in fifteen minutes. The other night, we all put money in the kitty – about £50. In four spins we'd made £500. But what happened? We lost it again. Easy come, easy go. If I was in Hong Kong, I would save all my money for my children's future and buy my son and his family a house but it's not the same here. When they grow up, they say, "bye bye Daddy, I'm off". So what's the point? I might as well enjoy myself – as long as they've got enough to eat.'

John's social life contrasts sharply with that of many Chinese women, not least his wife:

'There's nothing for me here. That's the truth. Everybody's too busy in England to make real friends. If you want to be friends with the English, you have to make an appointment to see them. Back East you can go and see people any time you like and do anything you like. My husband doesn't feel the same as me. He likes it here. But he's got more friends and he can go out more than me. I've got to look after the kids.'

Social isolation is a far more acute problem for Chinese women than for men. John's wife is not alone in her frustration. Whether as dependent wives of workers or themselves working in the family takeaway, the monotony and alienation of life in the Chinese fast food industry for all women is striking.

'My husband gives me pocket money whenever we can afford it. Most of the time I'm too busy or too tired to spend it, though. Sometimes I go to play Mah Jeung at my friend's house. A lot of Chinese like to do that – or go to the casino. That's where my husband goes. That's all there is to do at 1 o'clock in the morning when we finish work. Catering makes you very cut off from other people. The only time you have off is when most people are in bed and when most other people are off, that's when you're working hardest. Some of my friends just go to the casino to watch the Chinese films. They're not even interested in the gambling. It's a very boring life really, but what else can I do?'

'I used to cry a lot – not really for any particular reason. There was just no-one I could really talk to. I've been trying to learn English ever since I came but it's very difficult when you've got nobody to talk to'.

A second generation of fast food workers

The demanding hours of Chinese restaurant and 'takeaway' work has meant that for many women, rearing young children has been a virtual impossibility. As a consequence, a new generation of British-born Chinese children has not been automatically brought up with their parents in their country of birth. Instead, many were sent back to Hong Kong to be looked after by relatives and friends, paid and unpaid. Thus, even before 1973, whilst Chinese people already established in Britain enjoyed the same *de jure* legal and political rights as the indigenous population, their concentration in the ethnic fast food industry meant that they were *de facto* relegated to a position similar to migrant workers admitted after 1973 under the much less secure work permit system with regard to their families.[5] The situation has arisen, therefore, whereby many Chinese children born in this country have nevertheless entered it as much strangers as their parents did before them.

'I was actually born here, you know. But you wouldn't think so ten years ago because I didn't actually come here till I was eight. I lived with my auntie in Hong Kong until then, from when I was a baby. I really wanted to come here, though. I remember it very clearly. All I knew was my parents were over here and I'd always expected to come some time or other. So when the day came for me and my sister, I didn't think nothing of it. It was almost automatic. But my parents, they were like strangers. I thought I knew my mother, but I hadn't seen her for four years and she was really different to how I remembered.'

'My brother – he grew up here; he spoke English – he ganged up on me with his classmates when I came to England from Hong Kong. He never could identify with me.'

'By the time me and my sister arrived they'd settled down in their own shop. It was good business then. We helped sometimes, chopping potatoes for chips and things like that. We helped quite a lot really, especially at weekends. I didn't get any homework, so it didn't disturb my schooling. I didn't like school anyway. When I came, I only knew simple English like "pen" and "pencil", so I didn't learn a lot. I just sat round and watched what was going on. I was in a class where everyone was slow, you see, so how could I learn much? There were only three girls including me and the other two didn't like me, so that was that. My parents were too busy to teach me anything – my Dad speaks English you see – so I never learned to speak it, not having any friends or anything. All my friends now are from my village in Hong Kong. It's still good business. There's five of us working. We also get paid now because me and my husband, we do most of the cooking. Actually we get over £100 a week. That works out about £10 a day each and we get every Monday off. I'd like to go to Hong Kong for a holiday. It's just so boring here. All we do is watch a video and go to bed. In Hong Kong you could just step outside the front door and all your family and friends would be around to talk to. In the future I'd like us to get our own shop. My parents will probably give this one to my brothers, you see, even though me and my sister are older. No, I don't resent it. It's not really unfair because it's always been like that, right from my great grandfather. Everyone does it; not just my parents – so I know what to expect.'

New horizons

For Chinese women the isolation of the family workplace mitigates against conscious, collective struggle. However, it would be incorrect to conclude that Chinese women are merely the passive recipients of the adversities imposed upon them through migration. Working in a family business where profitability depends as much upon the efforts of the wife as upon those of the husband, actually means that there is a material basis for Chinese women to assert a certain degree of control, albeit on an individualized level. Indeed, an increasing minority of women are becoming joint partners in their husbands' businesses and others are running businesses themselves. This is tempered however, by a growing awareness of the economic and social trap that running an ethnic takeaway shop or restaurant holds in store for future generations of Chinese women. Consequently, it is accompanied often by a desire to see children leave the fast food trade through educational attainment:

'I'll tell you one thing, I don't want this life for my daughter. I want better for her. I want her to speak English and get a good job.'

This attitude finds resonance with a younger generation of Chinese women and girls:

'A few years ago my Dad kept asking us if we would help him run a takeaway and we all said "no way". I don't want to work like a

slave. I know what it's like because I've got friends who work in
their parents' takeaway shops and they have to work like dogs.
My Mum saw it from our point of view. She said it would be
better for us to carry on at school so we could choose what we
wanted to do when we finished.'

'I quite resented it when I was younger, about fourteen or fifteen.
I couldn't go out most nights because I was working. All my
friends would go to discos and parties and I could never go
because I was working. I just used to look at my friends and how
they lived with their families and I'd get so envious. I just wished
and wished I was like them. Plus all that, I had my homework as
well. That was very important to me, not just because my Mum
and Dad wanted me to do well, but because for me it was a way
out. We had a little table in the corner and I'd spread my
homework out and do it when there were no customers about.'

Conclusion

The problems presented by precarious employment, and long and
unsociable working hours for relatively few material rewards
compounded by a lack of organizational support, exist as much for
Chinese people in the ethnic fast food industry as for other catering
workers. However, the Chinese are at the sharp end of this postwar
development in that they have been pushed by immigration laws
and by a historical legacy of indigenous racism towards a form of
self-exploitation which has forged new ground for the development
of the fast food market. Increasingly, they are forced to pitch the
cheapness of their labour against the unabated, 'high tech'
competition of multinational firms. For Chinese women, the
situation is doubly oppressive. Whereas a formally paid female
kitchen hand might earn a weekly £82.70, many Chinese women
working in family takeaway shops or restaurants receive no wage at
all, except for that which they might personally negotiate from
husbands, fathers, or sons on a weekly basis. This confounding of
economic and domestic roles has rendered them even more
vulnerable to marginalization and isolation. When these experiences
are placed within a broad historical context, it becomes apparent
how the contemporary predicament of many Chinese women falls
within the mould cast over a century ago with the imperialist
penetration of southeast China. However, whilst the self-exploitation
and oppression within the family remain at a high level, Chinese

women are no longer content to accept the narrow horizons of the 'take-away'.

Notes

1 The term 'fast food' denotes a technological and organizational trend within food catering whereby standardized meals are produced at a rapid rate for immediate consumption, either on or off the premises where they are purchased. Production characteristically comprises extensive use of highly developed, labour saving cooking equipment combined with simplified cooking techniques making for quick, 'component assembly' of meals from standardized ingredients. Whilst the major hamburger, fried chicken, and pizza outlets have taken this trend to its most advanced form by capital investment on a massive scale in labour-saving technology, 'fast food' is a term which also describes the trade of 'fish and chip shops', cafés, snack bars, 'takeaways', and many restaurants. The term is least applicable to haute cuisine restaurants, where labour-intensive meals are produced on an individual basis by specialists.

2 'Marx (1867) saw the expansion of a reserve army of labour as an inevitable outcome of the process of capital accumulation (*Capital* Vol. 1). As capital accumulated, it threw certain workers out of employment into a reserve army; conversely, in order to accumulate, capital needed a reserve army of labour. Without such a reserve, capital accumulation would cause wages to rise, and the process of accumulation would itself be threatened as surplus value was squeezed' (Bruegel 1979: 12).

3 For example, see Baudouin *et al.* (1978), 'Women and immigrants: marginal workers', in C. Crouch, and A. Pizzorno. *The Resurgence of Class Conflict*, Vol. 2. London: Macmillan.

4 This concept is discussed at length in relation to Chinese migrants in Siu 1952–3.

5 The removal of reproduction and all its attendant costs to the country of origin facilitates optimum use of migrant labour power in the accumulation of capital in the receiving society.

All excerpts are taken from interviews conducted with Chinese respondents in Birmingham during 1985/6 as part of fieldwork for a forthcoming PhD thesis entitled 'A Political Economy of the Ethnic Chinese Catering Industry', to be submitted by Susan Baxter to Aston University, Strategic Management and Policy Studies Division, 1988. The research was supported by the Economic and Social Research Council.

References

Baker, H. (1977) '*The Cultural Background*'. Report of a conference entitled 'Chinese Children in Britain', April 1977, Commonwealth Institute, London.

Baxter, S. (1986) *The Chinese and Vietnamese in Birmingham*, Race Relations and Equal Opportunities Unit, Birmingham City Council.

Bruegel, I. (1979) 'Women as a reserve army of labour: a note on recent British experience', *Feminist Review* **3**: 12–23.

Foord, J. (1984) 'New technology and gender relations', Discussion Paper No. 58, Centre for Urban Regional Studies (CURS): University of Newcastle Upon Tyne.

Home Affairs Committee (1985) *Second Report and Proceedings on the Chinese Community in Britain*, Vol. 1., London: HMSO.

Hong Kong Research Project (1974) *Hong Kong: A Case to Answer*, London and Nottingham: Hong Kong Research Project & Spokesman Books.

Jones, D. (1979) 'The Chinese in Britain: origins and development of a community', *New Community* **7**: 397–402.

Jones, P. (1985) 'Fast food operations in Britain', *Service Industries Journal* **5** (1): 55–63.

Labour Research Department (1943) *Works Canteens and the Catering Trade*, London: Labour Research Dept.

Light, I. (1972) *Ethnic Enterprise in America*, Berkeley and Los Angeles: University of California Press.

Model, S. (1986) 'A comparative perspective on the ethnic enclave', *International Migration Review* **XIX** (1): 64–81.

Ng, R. (1986) 'My people: the Chinese community in the North East', in *Multicultural Teaching* **4** (3): 30–33.

Rees, T. (1982) 'Immigration policies in the United Kingdom', in C. Husband (ed.) '*Race' in Britain*. London: Hutchinson.

Riskin, C. (1978) 'The symposium papers: discussion and comments', *Modern China* **4** (3): 359–76.

Siu, B. (1982) *Women of China: Imperialism and Women's Resistance 1900–1949*, London: Zed Press.

Siu, P. (1952–3) 'The sojourner', *American Journal of Sociology* **58**: 34–44.

Waldinger, R. (1984) 'Immigrant enterprise and the structure of the labour market', in R. Finnegan and D. Gallie (eds) *New Approaches to Economic Life*. Manchester: Manchester University Press.

Watson, J. (1974) 'Restaurants and remittances: Chinese emigrant workers in London', in G. Foster and R. Kemper (eds) *Anthropologists in Cities*. Boston: Little, Brown & Co.

J. Watson (1975) *Emigration and the Chinese Lineage*, Berkeley and Los Angeles: University of California Press.

—— (1977) 'The Chinese: Hong Kong Villagers in the British catering trade', in J. Watson (ed.) *Between Two Cultures*. Oxford: Basil Blackwell.

Wilson, K. and Portes, A. (1980) 'Immigrant enclaves: an analysis of the labor market experiences of Cubans in Miami', *American Journal of Sociology* **86**: 295–319.

5 *Apni Marzi Kardhi** Home and work: Sikh women in Britain[1]

Parminder Bhachu

Introduction

The work patterns and the labour market positions of migrant/settler women have already been the subject of discussion. This paper addresses, more specifically, the impact of wages on the domestic domain.[2] While I am not arguing the simple thesis that wage labour equals liberation, because it is clear that the patriarchal relations of the household and the wider socioeconomic structures remain powerful, I am arguing in the discussion that follows that women's increased ability to develop more self-defined roles has been aided by their increased access to cash, which has allowed them to invest and consume in their own interests and for their own benefit. This is contrary to the emphasis in the existing literature on the lack of women's control over productive resources (Sharma 1980, 1984; Brown *et al.* 1981), even when they themselves have generated them (Standing 1985). The reasons cited for this include the power of the patriarchy and the all-dominant men who are portrayed as definers of the very parameters of women's existence (Brown *et al.* 1981) and as controllers of their property and the conditions of their lives. In such a picture, Asian women appear as passive victims unable to make any significant dents in these features of their societies, which are presented as static, oppressive, non-negotiable entities free of women's input.

In this paper I attempt to show that not only do women have an active relationship with the labour market since migration,[3] a situation that differs from the one prior to migration, which was characterized by the absence of resources acquired from their own relationship to the cash economy, but that they are also neither inert nor impotent in controlling and in generating resources, and in making a significant impact on the household and on culturally defined masculine and feminine roles, i.e. on the very kinship that appear from the outside to be oppressive and static.

* 'I

The argument is many faceted and in the pages that follow I present data from my research with Punjabi Sikh women, especially those of East African origin, settled in London and the Midlands. I want to consider initially some of the parameters that mark out Sikh culture and religion and then to relate these to the ethnographic material presented as a series of cases which demonstrate the impact of wage-earning women on the households of which they are a part. The discussion then moves to salient points raised by the case studies and how these relate to the move from wage work into commerce and entrepreneurship, an area of discussion common to many of the papers in this book. Finally, I consider the conclusions that can be drawn in relation to the impact of cash and women wage earners not only in relation to the gender division of labour and power relations in the domestic domain, but also in relation to the women who are the subjects of this discussion.

Sikhism: women's position

Why is it that Punjabi Sikh women in Britain are able to exercise control over the wages they earn? What is it about Sikh social structure and religious ideology that enables them to do so despite the descriptions to the contrary in the literature on women, property, and the household (Sharma 1980, 1984; Vatuk 1972; Wilson 1978; De Souza 1980), even when the women are themselves educated professionals (Kapur 1970: 152)?

The independence of Sikh women, and their ability to exercise control over their own wages, is linked not only to the predominance of nuclear households with no authoritarian elders and gatekeepers of expenditure, but also to the Sikh religion, which accords equal status to men and women. They are not in *purdah* and they occupy a different position from that of Muslim women (Saifullah Khan 1976a, 1979) who are much more secluded, and of whom only 18 per cent are in the labour force, as compared with 62 per cent of women of Indian origin and 67 per cent of East African Asian women (Labour force survey 1984, reported in the *Employment Gazette*, December 1985), and from that of Gujarati women amongst whom the group ethos is stronger and extended families with common economic bases and goals are more predominant (Westwood, this volume).

Sikhism emphasizes egalitarianism and   'us for all (Mcleod 1968: 86, 1976: 5; Khushwant Singh 1.   ?). There are cases of Sikh women who have shown gr   nce and courage in the face of adversity, and are us   nodels to illustrate the elevated position accorded to women by the founding Gurus, who attempted to upgrade the lowly status of women. For example, Sardarni Sada Kaur (1762–1832) in the eighteenth century 'planned a surprise attack on Lahore and conquered it for Ranjit Singh (The Maharaja) in 1799' (Sidhu 1977: 23) and Mai Bhago in the seventeenth century went into battle by organizing a band of women including wives of deserters who had left Guru Gobind Singh's troops to fight the armies of Wazir Khan, the local Moghul chief.

My purpose in referring to the above cases is to illustrate that the active role of Sikh women within the community and the labour market in Britain has historical roots, Sikh religious ideals allow women to 'lead religious congregations, to take part in the continuous recitation of the holy scriptures, to work as priests, or preachers, and to participate freely in all religious, cultural, social, political and secular activities'. They even fought in wars by organizing themselves into *jathas* (armed bands) (Sidhu 1977: 7). They have always been active participants alongside Sikh men in protest marches (*morchas*) in the past and present both in India and the UK. This was especially obvious from their vociferous presence in the Sikh demonstrations in Central London against Indira Gandhi's Congress Government, immediately after the army action at the Golden Temple in Amritsar in 1984.

In Britain this is reflected in the key positions that women have taken in public institutions. For example, in the past five years in a South London temple, women have twice been elected president. These women are also in full-time employment and participate in what are frequently referred to as masculine spheres of public services as decision makers.

This is not to suggest that women have equality within the community, because they do not: men remain dominant. However, Sikh religious ideology and community ethos has a considerable impact on perceptions of gender roles and helps to modify the male dominance. It is precisely this kind of cultural and religious background that spurs women on to manage their own earnings and to negotiate their position within the domestic unit.

Home and work

In previous publications (Bhachu 1985, 1986), I have demonstrated the ways in which traditional practices related to marriage and dowry have been reinforced and elaborated through the entry of women into the labour market, albeit at the unskilled level and doing mostly the lowest paid jobs (Harris 1972; Phizacklea 1982, 1983; Parmar 1982). Despite the confinement of women to 'low skill therefore low paid work' (Phizacklea 1983: 6), women's command over economic resources through a direct relationship with the productive process had lead not only to the 'traditionalization' of particular female-related cultural values despite changing economic conditions, but also to the renegotiation of the sexual division of labour and to an increase in their territory within the reproductive unit. This has lead to actual changes in the structure of the household, in the expenditure and authority patterns within it, which have favoured them – or, rather, have strengthened their power base within the domestic domain. Exposure to the external world of waged employment has lead to internal changes within the household which are reflected in structural changes within the organization of the Sikh community. For example, this is reflected in the kinship system which is much more loosely organized and much less patriarchal than in the past. The seniority of the elders and their authority which accrued from their command over productive resources has been severely dented by the increasing nuclearization of households which are 'couple-focused' and not 'extended kin group focused', as in the past. The establishment of nuclear households has been *catalyzed* by the increase in women's earnings in Britain, even though, this trend represents a continuous process being linked to urbanization in India (Vatuk 1972) and to migration in urban Britain.

Among younger couples especially, gender roles have been redefined in nuclear households and are more conducive to egalitarian relationships and joint decision making. For example, men are much more involved in domestic tasks and childcare than ever in the past. This is not to say that there is a radical shift in perceptions of what is 'feminine' and 'masculine' or that there is a reversal of roles, but that there is a revision of male and female roles, which have resulted in the men being more involved in the household because of women's move into the labour market. All this has modified both gender role models within the household and sex-segregated spheres.[4]

In my West London sample of older women, more than half (i.e. 17 out of 31 women) were wage-earning, and had been since their arrival in Britain, although, generally they had not worked in Africa. The majority were employed in factory work ranging from sausage, ice-cream, sweet, and biscuit making to airline food packing, canteen work, and electric circuits and coils production. None of these women did cleaning jobs, which according to them are restricted to '*churi-chamaris*' belonging to the lower caste groups of *churas* and *chamars*, which constitute the scheduled castes.

Formal educational credentials were rare among the older women, though a few had been to secondary school in Africa and could converse in and write English. None of them finished their Senior Cambridge 'O' levels. By 1986, three of the older women had retired. One had taken early retirement and had used her redundancy money to buy a post office which she now runs with her young son.

Of the eighteen younger women, fifteen were employed in office jobs as clerks, secretaries, etc. and three were professional women. None of the younger women were employed in factories on assembly-line work. Women who are under thirty-five and who at present work in factories, are mostly direct migrants whose command over English is insufficient for them to get office jobs.[5] Most of them had initially applied for these jobs and had been unsuccessful, hence the move into manual or unskilled work.

In the following section I will refer to specific cases which have been selected because they represent particular patterns of employment even though individual circumstances differ. I am also interested in the following questions: How has the extension of women's networks that now go beyond *rhistedhari* – the kinship group – affect their perceptions of their roles within the household and also their rights? How does the access to information through their daily interaction with women of other castes and classes and ethnicities at the workplace influence their modes of operation within the domestic domain? How has the patriarchal unit of the past with the dominant wage-earning males been affected by migration and women's control over cash? How has this influenced kinship organisation?

CASE 1 MOTHERS AND DAUGHTERS: CHANGE IN THE DOMESTIC UNIT

Mrs N. Kaur and Harjinder

Mrs N. Kaur came directly from India immediately after her marriage, though she lived for a short period of five years in East Africa. Her husband worked for the railways as a station master, before moving first to the Punjab and thence to the UK in 1966. She arrived in 1968 with three children, all under the age of ten. Her fourth child, now aged sixteen, was born here.

Upon arrival, she did home-sewing because her children were still young. A few years later, when her youngest child was old enough to go to playgroup, she started work in a cells/batteries factory, a job she got through the help of her mother's brother's son's wife. Whilst working there, she got her younger sister employed in the same section as her own. After a year, she moved to the ice-cream factory, which is closer to her house. Her oldest daughter, who is now married, works there as a clerk-secretary. She found this job with the help of a Punjabi neighbour who had also worked in the cell-making factory. She did not much care for this job, so soon after she got another job with Scandanavian Airlines in the catering section. Her husband's friend's wife who also worked here let her know of the vacancy. She has for the past fourteen years remained in this job, packing food trays for the aircraft. She now gets discount airline tickets, a perk of the airline jobs which are extremely popular in West London with both men and women.

The reason it was possible to change jobs so frequently until the mid-1970s is that jobs were plentiful and news of vacancies spread rapidly through the Punjabi networks. Women left jobs frequently, because as one informant said, 'there was always another job ready the very next day'. The same women interviewed in 1986 present a very different picture – of increased unemployment and difficulties in finding employment not for themselves, because they have settled down in permanent jobs, but also for younger women who are frequently more highly educated but cannot find any sort of waged work. There is at present a much greater expectation from employers of fluency in English.

Another reason the older women have retained specific jobs is that their employment experiences have taught them the benefits of longer term service, for example, reduced airline tickets, pension funds, work incentives accrued through length of service, etc. This is knowledge they have acquired through job experience and through their trade unions – i.e. through '*Kaam Dhi Dhunia*', the 'World of Work'.

N. Kaur's daughter, Harjinder, was nine-and-a-half years old when she came to Britain. She did all her secondary and some of her primary schooling here. She had five CSEs, three of which dealt with office and secretarial skills. She worked initially for the Gas Board before moving to the ice-cream factory's offices after her marriage. She has a three-year-old daughter who is looked after by her grandmother when she has a night shift and can be free during the day and by her husband (Mohinder) at other times.

Her husband migrated directly from India five years ago. Initially he had a job, but for the past two years he has been unemployed. He is a skilled carpenter and has learnt to install central heating systems from his father-in-law; this he does unofficially with his mates. His time is more flexible, which is why the responsibility of childcare during the day is borne by him. His mother-in-law cannot always help because she also goes out to work.

Mohinder comes from a household in Ludhiana in the Punjab, in which there is a clear division of labour by sex, the men run the business which manufactures ball-bearings and the women are responsible for household tasks. The men are not involved in any childcare or in household tasks. The women have never entered the labour force as wage earners in the past, nor have they done so in the 1980s. This applies to younger women as well within his extended kin group. His paternal family resides in a joint household which has a shared economic base and a clear hierarchy. His father, being the oldest brother, is in charge because even though the grandfather is around he is old and not active in running the business. His mother being the oldest daughter-in-law (the *jathani* to the younger daughters-in-law, the *duranis*, who are the wives of the younger brothers) is in charge of the household budget, being the most senior female and also the authority figure in control of the finances generated by the men. Her mother-in-law, who died fifteen years ago, was responsible for household expenditure in the past.

Mohinder came from a household in the Punjab which increasingly represents the present urban joint family in India and also to an extent, the type of family organization that most of the Sikh women in the British labour market belonged to, prior to migration. His own household situation after marriage has changed completely because his employment situation is much more unstable than his wife's, who has a permanent job and has been in the labour market since the age of seventeen, five years ahead of him.

His wife's mother, Mrs N. Kaur, belonged to a similar type of household, though from the more rural parts of Ludhiana – a village five miles outside this city. She was responsible to her mother-in-law who controlled the tasks she did, her movements, and the amount of money that was reserved for her, for both her personal and her children's expenditure, from her husband's salary. Mrs N. Kaur says that even though she entered Britain with young children and she missed the company of other younger women in the extended family, who all lived close by and helped with childcare, especially in the early difficult stages of settlement in London, she was really pleased to be on her own with her husband in their own separate household. There were no '*sianay*' (senior elders) around to defer to, to avoid, and to serve (for *seva karan*). She had got tired of all this as her marriage matured.

The lack of seniors in the household here has also meant she has had easier access to her husband, who helped her not only with the household tasks in Britain but also with the children and the cooking. On her arrival in Britain, for the first time in thirteen years of marriage, they made key decisions concerning their children and their lives jointly. In the past, her husband had deferred to both his own mother and father and was never involved in domestic tasks. The situation changed completely in Britain, especially the childcare dimension, because she herself went out to work, forcing her husband to be more involved in the domestic domain. In the past, as migrants, men had been involved in running their own households, especially in the early stages of migration to Britain when they lived in bachelor households (Ballard 1976). But they had never been in charge of childcare and the household for long periods of the day as they are now. In the past, childcare was the exclusive concern of women both in India (Sharma 1980; De Souza 1980; Caplan 1978, 1985; Vatuk 1972) and in Africa prior to migration.

Mrs N. Kaur frequently refers to these changes and to her own money from *apni kamai* (her own job), with which she can do as she likes. She is responsible for most of the daily household expenses, though her husband pays utility bills and the mortgage. She uses any of the money left over for herself. Her husband also contributes to her personal expenses now and again. Whereas in the past she used to do her own sewing, her Punjabi suits are now made for her by a local dressmaker whom she pays out of her own salary. If she has a lump sum or a tax rebate, she buys gold jewellery for her daughters. All these items in the past would have had to come out of the male income or be taken out of the mother-in-law's expenditure budget. Twice every year, she has *langar* and a *satsung* (a religious function where food is provided as at almost every temple-related event), the money for which comes from her own pocket. This is a common pattern for women – funded religious events which are increasingly frequent both at the temples and in homes.

It is clear that changes in household have emerged as a result of migration and the woman's entry into wage earning: decision making has become much more equal, both because of Mrs N. Kaur's command over earnings and because of the establishment of a separate household unit without seniors. The husband's role within the domestic domain in relation to task sharing has increased, especially in those spheres that were in the past considered 'a woman's job' – '*bibi dhay kaam*'. There is an increase in religious rituals and also wedding ceremonies connected with women (Bhachu 1985), which are often financed entirely by women themselves.

This case also shows the different (occupational) niches occupied by the mother and the mainly British-educated daughter. The shift from factory production and unskilled employment to white collar work is almost a universal pattern amongst the younger East African woman.

CASE 2 BEYOND KINSHIP AND CASTE

Inder Kaur

Inder Kaur came to UK in 1972 in her late 40s as a widow with a young son of fourteen years. She was born in East Africa in 1925, and belongs to the first generation of local born Asians, in Africa. She went to a Secondary School but never entered for her 'Senior Cambridge' ('O' levels) because she was, in common with other women in her peer group, withdrawn from school for an early marriage at seventeen years. She can write in English and speak it, though not fluently. She was more educated than the other Asian women in her factory in her age set.

Her husband, who worked for a government department, died soon after the birth of her second child when she was in her mid 30s. She survived on the money he left her and her widow's pension until she moved to Britain. By this stage, her older daughter who trained as a teacher was married, her education paid for by her husband's brother who also helped with the marriage expenses.

Until three years before moving to Britain, Inder Kaur had lived with her parents-in-law. Although she had her own money, her father-in-law was the person in charge of the household in Kenya. In Britain she got a job in a small electrical firm with the help of her *Jathani* (husband's elder brother's wife) who also worked in the same place. She lived in rented accommodation at first before moving to West London, where she bought her own two-bedroomed flat with the help of a Sikh insurance agent who helped her raise the mortgage. By this stage she had moved to a sausage-making factory in Southall, in the packing section. Her brother's son's wife helped her find this job, from which she retired last year. Her retirement as the first Asian women from this factory was celebrated by the predominantly Indian labour force and the white management with great enthusiasm. She was presented with £400 in cash and two gold bangles amongst other gifts collected by her colleagues and workmates. She said, 'I got more from my colleagues (*kaam wallian*) then from my *Sauras*' (affinal kin) both in terms of companionship, emotional support, and gifts.

Her position in her affinal home as a widow was weaker than that of the other daughters-in-law (who were not resident with her parents-in-law and were not widows). She also frequently states that she 'has learnt a lot more about life in the past ten years after starting work than ever in the past'. She emphasizes that trade unions have taught her about her rights, something she had not considered seriously before.

Whereas in Africa she had lived in a small town where the movement of daughters-in-law were monitored – they only went out of the house infrequently and then only to the temple or to visit kinsmen – the situation has changed completely in Britain. She goes out to work every day where she meets *Churis*, *Chamaris*, *Chieris*, *Jatis*, *Khatranis*, *Hindis*, and *Muslmanis* – women of other caste and religious groups, most of whom are from the subcontinent, plus whites and Afro-Caribbeans. Although she did meet Indians of other ethnicities and castes in Africa, this contact was much more infrequent. At the workplace, in London, she interacts with them daily, eats with them, and visits their homes frequently at marriages, engagements, and other life-cycle rituals.

Hence, although initially she found it difficult to work for long hours every day for fixed periods[6] this extension of her non-kin network helped her to develop a friendship network through work that provides emotional support. Women from work and their families do endless tasks for her that she cannot manage on her own, and drop in on her at home frequently.

It was through this network that she arranged her husband's brother's daughter's marriage to an accountant. The groom's mother's brother's wife worked with Inder Kaur, which is how she heard about the accountant when a match was being looked out for. Her husband's brother's daughter is also an accountant. This is a caste endogamous marriage that met all the necessary criteria for marriage arrangement (see Bhachu 1985).

In this case, entry into the labour market helped Inder Kaur to establish her own household, thus breaking her dependence on her affines. She entered the labour market at a later stage in the developmental cycle, which meant that childcare problems were absent for her, giving her time to explore her work network much more than women with younger children, who are more restricted in the time they can be spared for socializing outside work hours. Her friendships outside the kinship network have given her exposure to a whole set of experiences that she did not have when she was restricted to the household and to the extended kin group in Kenya.

She emphasizes that it is the 'World of work' (*Kaam dhi dhunia*) that has taught her her *haaq* (rights), especially from trade union activity at work and the knowledge that all tasks can have a price attached to them and that women should get this price paid to them for work they perform. She said, 'They (her work mates) would never pack more trays than they could reasonably manage. If any more work was expected, then they would go on strike'. At home, 'You keep working and no one cares how much you do even if you are *bone-tired*'. She says, she is no longer afraid of doing what she wants to, she doesn't feel beholden to people nor does she feel that she has to seek approval for decisions she makes herself which previously she would refer to a senior kinsmen or women in the extended family. 'Going to work' has increased her confidence to manage her own life according to her own desires. She says: I does as *I* pleases' – '*Apni marzi kardhi*'.

Inder Kaur's situation as a widow made her household position weak before migration. However, the vulnerability of such women has decreased in relation to their increased financial independence. This is frequently referred to as a by-product of earning. Entry into the labour market has given women stronger levers to negotiate their position within the household through skills, knowledge, and products acquired from their direct relationship with production.

CASE 3   FACTORY FLOOR TO MANAGEMENT

Barinder Kaur
Barinder had been resident in West London for eight years with her husband who worked as a mechanic for Ford before moving to Birmingham to go into the rag-trade. She had a BA degree from Punjab University but she could not get an office job here because her Indian qualifications were not recognized in Britain and her spoken English was poor. She worked in a potato crisp factory for five years before moving to Birmingham.

Mr B. Singh (her husband) decided to give up his job in Ford Motors because he said '*naukeri* (paid employment) doesn't pay a decent wage'. He started a blouse- and skirt-making factory with a school friend from the Punjab six years ago. As the business flourished his wife gave up her London job and moved to Bimingham but only after the business had proven itself viable. Also at this stage she had her youngest daughter and didn't want to go out to work.

They have now both set up a separate factory, in which she herself works as a supervisor and is the 'expert at labour relations' according to her husband, because she organizes work targets and 'hires and fires' the women who work there, who are mostly Sikhs of lower caste groups than her. Her husband says that it helped to have her employed with a stable income in the early stages of the business because of the security it provided and her skills are useful for running the present business.

Her own view is that she misses her own independent income and her circle of friends even though there is more money around because the factory is now profitable. Also, she doesn't much care 'for having him [her husband] around all the time'. She does not receive a separate wage but has an allowance, and uses whatever other money is available for her own and her daughters' requirements.

This pattern, of women helping to set up a business and actually helping in it once established, is a strong trend within the Sikh community (cf. Westwood, this volume). Women have helped to establish businesses, mostly retail outlets but also some manufacturing concerns as the one described above, because of the stability of an income whilst one spouse takes the entrepreneurial risk. Women's earnings also help with the initial capital accumulation because they bear the basic household expenses that would have come out of the husband's income.

CASE 4 ENTREPRENEURSHIP AND WOMEN'S WORK

Gurinder Kaur
Gurinder works as a secretary in a local electrical firm. Her husband Satwant worked for London Transport before taking voluntary redundancy after twenty years of service as a bus conductor. This couple came to Britain in 1965, soon after their marriage. Both their children, who have now grown up, were born here. Their daughter Simi recently got a computer programmer's job in an office after studying for her diploma in Business Studies. Their son is studying for 'A' levels.

They had both wanted to 'go into business' earlier but had no capital to do so until two years ago, when they used Satwant's redundancy money and their own savings to buy a sports shop. They did this because Gurinder's mother's brother's son is also in this line of business and is more experienced in the sports goods retailing field. They tapped his expertise and experience.

Gurinder was educated in Africa. She had five 'O' levels and acquired secretarial skills prior to migration. She never worked in factories though; her mother, who migrated a year after she did, worked in a hospital laundry ironing sheets before retiring four years ago. Gurinder and Satwant lived with her parents-in-law before migrating to Britain. They jointly bought their present house on arriving here. Since both her children were born here, childcare was difficult for her especially as there was no mother-in-law (because she stayed behind in Kenya) around to help and her own mother had a full-time job. She had to continue to work full time and use a childminder on a part-time basis.

Her husband did the evening shifts mostly, so that he could be around to fetch the children from school and care for them before she returned from work. They both could not have managed if she had taken up a part-time job. Her salary was, and is, crucial to the maintenance of the household.

They have started a business because they say 'most of our friends who come to Britain with us have also taken up post offices/supermarkets or some other shop business because there is more money in it than in a regular job. Also, our children have grown up and need us less, in fact they help in the shop all the time in their spare time'. The business has not yet become profitable, though it pays for itself. Gurinder cannot stop work because she says 'it's too risky just yet'.

In this couple's case, both were urban migrants and came to Britain whilst still in their 20s. Their children were born here and they established their own household in Britain away from the husband's joint family. They had to rely on each other for childcare because even though senior women like her mother were around, these older women were in the labour market, and unable to help with childcare. This would not have been the case in East Africa because a large number of Gurinder's friends at that time (the early 1960s), were in office and secretarial jobs in Africa. Their children were the responsibility of the joint family if they resided in one or they could employ a baby minder (an *ayah*) within their own homes if the extended kin group was not around to help out.

Gurinder says Satwant her husband had to help her with childcare even though he was reluctant to do so initially, because his other Indian friends did not always do so.

'The other women were not working then, there were fewer women going out to work in those days. In fact, there were fewer women around and those around did factory jobs in Southall, or sewed at home or had older children with them and younger ones at home in India. There weren't many educated women in office work until East Africans arrived five or six years after we came. I have worked for nearly twenty-two years and I am only still forty-five.'

Gurinder, being younger and better educated, did not enter factory production and has been in the labour market for almost the whole period of her settlement in Britain. However, their entry into business has only been possible because both of them had been earning for twenty years before they could accumulate the initial capital to start. Gurinder still runs the household, till the business starts to pay. She has had to remain in the labour market to support this enterprise which initially started because of her contribution to their joint savings. She also works in it after her own work hours and at weekends. She complains that her workload has not decreased as she has got older because the space and time reserved for her children in the past now has to be devoted to the business. She is resentful of this because for her there has been no time for herself ever, in her life. 'It's rush, rush, rush', she says. But, she also feels that her mother could never have done what she is doing and be more independent financially. Her father 'used to drink a lot and not give her any money to spend. I would never put up with it. I have helped my husband with money and not asked for it'.

This couple also represents an example of settlers who have established their own household at an early stage in Britain after migration. Hence, they have not had to renegotiate gender roles and the sexual divisions of labour but have formulated these in Britain since settlement.

Female wages: household changes

A consequence of women's entry into the labour market has been the impact of wage earning on power relations within the family and the structure of the domestic domain. Whereas, in the past, prior to migration, 'patrilineality' and the seniority of older members of the household was much more defined because they had a 'monopoly of authority' (Saifullah Khan 1976b: 225)[7] this is much less the case now.

Households since migration have become more egalitarian, with a decrease in sex segregation and increased contact between women and their husbands. In fact, older people within the community attribute the increase in divorce within the community to increased contact between the younger men and women and to the fact that women do not visit their *peke* (maternal home) enough and keep out of the way of the menfolk. In British homes they say, 'the husband and the wife are on top of each other too much, and also women are *azad* (free).'[8]

In the past, even when senior kinsmen were not around to mediate between the masculine and feminine spheres, and even when couples lived in nuclear households, men were much less available, maintaining a circuit of work- and club-related male friends or as Vatuk (1972: 140) states they 'interacted with agnatic kin of the local patrilineage'.

The situation has changed in Britain, though it also reflects a continuation of the pattern established in urban India in which 'Households which contain only one married couple, sometimes also a younger relative of the husband or wife, allow greater leeway in structuring interpersonal relationships' and also allow for a more 'relaxed relationship between the husband and wife' (Vatuk 1972: 122, 123).

I have referred to the urban household in the subcontinent to demonstrate that changes in authority structures, and the re-establishment of the masculine and feminine roles, are related for British Punjabis not only to migration to Britain and to women's increased control over economic resources, but also to the general process of urbanization, and to the move from rural to urban India and Britain and from Africa to urban Britain. Hence, changes in British Asian households represent a continuum of development, a process that had begun for a number of settler families in the subcontinent and also in East Africa, where Asians resided in predominantly urban areas due to the restrictive policies of the British in Colonial Africa (Ghai 1965) which reserved rural areas for Africans and Europeans.

However, it should be emphasized that some of the features described above related to changes in gender roles and family structure are accentuated in Britain, because women's control over productive resources has given them greater power in determining their modes of interaction and in using their resources to initiate changes in the structure of kinship organization. For example, in my West London sample, 18 out of 31 households were nuclear ones in the late 1970s compared to 23 out of 31 households in 1986.

Separate households are much more difficult to establish if women do not have a direct relationship with the productive process. This, of course, does not apply to the wives of some of the businessmen and high-earning professional men like the travel agent, the car agent, and the accountant in my sample. However, it does apply to joint households in my sample, in which three brothers, their wives (none of whom are involved in waged work) their children, and their parents-in-law all reside together. They live in two adjoining houses, with the central wall of the living room removed to create one large, common house.

The daughters-in-law have never been employed in waged work, even though one of them was educated here, because there is no tradition of women in this household entering the labour market.

This family has a business in East Africa which is at present being managed by the eldest son. The three brothers here have all gone into public sector work. They pool their salaries and each daughter-in-law gets an allowance for herself and her children and any other money needed for major expenses. There is a strong ethos of maintaining the family under one roof and sharing economic resources i.e. of *kath nabana*. The parents-in-law have maintained this family ideology by ensuring that their sons married women who have never entered waged labour and had not thus had exposure to the public world of work, prior to their marriages. The mother-in-law herself did not enter the labour market in Britain, though her kinswomen resident locally have nearly all done so.

All the daughters-in-law said that they would have preferred to work but their parents-in-law had forbidden it. They emphasized constantly that their husbands, like themselves, did not have a separate cash pool to invest in a house.[9] The eldest son recently bought a house, close to the joint household, and has moved out with his family after ten years of joint residence. The brothers' families have expanded and their present home has become too small for the needs of three young growing families. In this case it has taken a much longer period for a nuclear residence to be established. A number of households started off as this one did, especially in the early stages of settlement, but the situation changed rapidly soon after women began to generate a separate income.

This is especially the case among the young newly married couples who live with the groom's parents for a couple of years before buying their own homes. The couples in my wedding sample followed this pattern unless the groom already owned a house or was a higher earner, in which case a nuclear residence was established straight after marriage. The latter was fairly common, a 'propertied' groom increased his prestige in the marriage market, especially if he already possessed a house before the engagement.

The point that I want to emphasize is that women's earning capacities facilitate both the establishment of a separate nuclear household and its maintenance. By doing this, they have, through their own earnings, reduced the dominance of their husbands, as key decision makers and controllers of economic resources. Women's access to money had reduced the patrilaterality of the household and also the kinship group itself, which could only be sustained if authority was restricted to the seniors. Control over cash has allowed women to be more assertive about their own areas of operation and personal rights than ever before, when in the past economic resources were almost exclusively monopolized by the men (see Sharma 1980: 39, 1984: 66; Kapur 1970: 141; De Souza 1980: 22).

All this has led to the increase in women's decision-making powers within the household. The women I interviewed emphasized that they felt more confident about voicing their opinions about important issues to do with the management of the house, because of their lack of fear of the consequences of their assertiveness and their knowledge of the world outside.

One woman, Kuldeep Kaur, who works in the sausage factory, said:

'I told my husband that he has to help me in the house because I can't manage with a full time job. I too go out to do work [*kamai*] just like him. I am just as tired when I come home as he is. I don't expect him to cook and clean for me but I do expect him to listen to what I have to say. My take home pay is almost as much as his, we couldn't manage without it.'

This is typical of remarks made by the younger women with children whose working day is long – very much the double day. Women's control over cash has not necessarily led to the reversal of roles but to a recognition by women that they have a right to assert their opinions about household management and to negotiate more favourable positions for themselves vis-à-vis their menfolk. While most of the household tasks are still done by women, there is a blurring of the distinction between what were considered to be exclusive masculine and feminine roles. Thus, there *is* a change in their status, making them more equal to the husband than they were before they entered the labour market. For this reason, the asymmetry of marriage (Whitehead 1976: 184) has been revised.

Another dimension of the more egalitarian households, since migration and women's entry into paid work, is that whereas in the past women did not control the distribution of goods within the household, especially at the earlier stages of the developmental cycle, because this was the area reserved for the senior women,[10] at present this situation has been radically revised. The establishment of separate nuclear households and women's personal earnings under their own control has meant that women manage household expenditure and the gift exchange system at a much earlier stage, before reaching seniority. Since they help to produce wealth, they also expect to be able to control and redistribute it.[11] The moral authority of the elders no longer holds with their loss of control over economic goods. Since the reproductive unit has its own resources which are independent of the extended unit and generated by the husband and wife together, there is also an expectation that these commodities will be managed according to the couple's desires, not those of the wider kin group.

All these factors have led to the renegotiation of the sexual division of labour or at least, the desire, especially by women, to share domestic chores with men particularly those related to childcare and decision making. Men are forced into helping with childcare, especially where there is no help from senior kinswomen who are themselves working grandmothers. For example, my landlady worked on the night shift, leaving home around 7 p.m. and returning at 7 a.m. to get the children off to school. Her husband worked during the daytime and was at home when his wife was away at work. This type of arrangement is commonest among the younger couples with children in West London as a strategy for managing reproductive tasks, especially in households with women in full-time employment. I have stated earlier that women in the later stages of the developmental cycle did not have such childcare problems because their children were older on arrival in Britain, but then their husbands did not help with such activities, which were the exclusive domain of the women who had been resident in much more male-dominated homes in their countries of origin. Thus although the latter category of women have had greater access to cash through the labour market and have as a result, increased their personal autonomy and expenditure power, they have not, unlike the younger women, been able to establish more equal roles within the household vis-à-vis their husbands. Nor have the older women been able to get their menfolk to help with 'feminine tasks' in the domestic domain. This is not to say that their decision-making powers have not increased – they have – but that the sexual division of labour has not been reallocated as in the case of younger couples. The roles of the older couples had already got well defined before migration and before the entry of the women into labour markets. One fifty-five-year-old woman who works in the ice-cream factory said:

'Look at my son, he changes the baby's nappy and feeds him every day. He also cooks sometimes for his son and wife. He was even present at the birth of his son. My daughter-in-law just expects him to do all of these things. I would not have dreamed of asking my husband even to fetch a glass of water or take care of the children when they were babies, not even when they were ill. My mother and sister helped then, not him.'

Female wages: commercial enterprise

I have already referred to the increase in small businesses within the Sikh community which either involve female earnings or require the woman (or sometimes the male spouse) to remain in waged employment for either the stability of the reproductive unit or as security against an unsuccessful business venture (see Gurinder Kaur's and Barinder Kaur's cases described earlier). This trend has also been documented by Sallie Westwood for the Gujaratis in Leicester.

In the case of Punjabi Sikhs, an interesting dimension of this development, especially related to caste, is that commercial entrepreneurship among Sikhs is relatively new on this scale; it does not reflect the ethos of the community, especially for Sikhs who have migrated from East Africa who are predominantly public sector workers of the Ramgarhia caste – the artisans, and were even more so in the past (Bhachu 1984, 1985), and for those from the Indian subcontinent, who are mainly Jats – predominantly agriculturalists (Helweg 1979; Pettigrew 1972). This is not to suggest that Punjabi Sikhs have not been businessmen in the past and for generations, because Khatri and Arora Sikhs – the urban mercantile castes – have always had a monopoly over education and trading activities (McLeod 1976: 103), but that this trend in Britain towards small-scale entrepreneurship among families who have never been involved in it the past is a relatively new one. It is new in both the types of couple-orientated businesses (mostly in the retail trade) that have been started, and also in the involvement of female labour and the use of women's wages to help perpetuate both the reproductive unit and the business. However, it is also a response to the racism which has catalysed their entry into commercial enterprises. Common reasons cited for 'starting a business' include the 'ceiling to promotion' and lack of opportunity experienced by informants in 'going up the hierarchy in places of work because of discrimination' and in the desire to exercize greater control over 'our destiny and future without whites telling us what to do', as the sports shop owner in my sample suggested.

The businesses are mostly small – for example, a sports shop, post offices combined with groceries (these are the most popular), supermarkets, motor spares shops, Punjabi suit fabric and sari shops, electrical goods stores, etc. In the Midlands, there has been a rapid growth of enterprises in the rag trade. Other ventures include carpentry, building contracting firms, small hotels, supermarkets, and pharmacies. Wives, older daughters, and daughters-in-law are involved in such businesses as receptionists and administrators. The larger enterprises in which the women are not involved are those that had already been in existence in East Africa and the subcontinent, and which have been further reproduced here. These were initiated with a larger capital base and expertise established prior to migration. They include the travel and car agencies and the larger building contracting firms.

I will not detail cases here because I have already selected the case of the sports shop owner (Case 4, Gurinder and Satwant) to emphasize the importance of female earnings in initiating the capital and later in maintaining the domestic unit. This pattern applied also to the electrical goods shops, the motor spares shop, the post office/mini-supermarket, and the car repair garages. All the wives of these businessmen had worked for anything up to a decade before entering the business as helpers 'on the counter', though in the case of the sports shop, the wife, Gurinder, has carried on in the labour market as have the husbands of the women running the post offices, electrical goods, and motor spares shops. In the latter two cases, the men have not given up their jobs but have only been able to set up the businesses with the help of their women folk because neither of them had a family history of commerce or of inherited capital to invest in their enterprises.

In the cases of women who have given up waged employment to participate in the running of the business, few get a separate wage packet, even though there is an increase in the money available for domestic expenditure. By giving up work, these women not only lose an independent source of income, and a large network of often female colleagues, but also find themselves sucked back into the kinship system which emphasizes patrilaterality. Whereas patriarchal relationships were dented by women entering the waged economy, commercial ventures are in fact returning women to units of organizations where gender relationships follow the more traditional lines of male dominance through control over economic resources i.e. that women re-enter the kinship group which has a strong ethos of male dominance. This gets reinforced by women's loss of individual earnings out of an economic system which is not kinship controlled and goes beyond the kindred of cooperation (Mayer 1960). Hence, women's withdrawal from the labour market results, in most cases, in their assumption of more subordinate positions in relation to the gender division of labour because of their loss of a direct relationship with the productive process. All this reinforces the patriarchy within the reproductive unit which had been temporarily diluted or disturbed by migration and women's entry into the labour market.

Conclusion

The discussion above of the consequences of women's entry into the wage economy should have demonstrated that even though women do the majority of dirty and low-paid jobs (Harris 1972: 169; Phizacklea 1982, 1983), nonetheless their control over wages has in the case of Punjabi women had a strong impact on the domestic domain.

It should be emphasized that forces governing women's economic position have not changed. Punjabi women, in common with women in general, remain subordinate. However, waged work in which women's input is measured in terms of money gives them a strong lever to create a powerbase both within the household and the wider kin group. It is their use of economic resources that has given them a stronger position within the reproductive unit especially vis-à-vis their men (Morokvasic 1983; Foner 1986).

Even though the clearest areas of change for the older Punjabi women are within the domestic domain, the situation for younger Asian women is changing as they diversify into a wider range of occupations. The class positions of younger Punjabi women have also shifted with their occupations from those of their mothers' mainly working class and subordinate positions within employment sectors. Despite the increased command over mainstream skills of the younger settler women (many of whom are increasingly British born and educated) and their increased earnings, this has not led in their case to the abolition of traditional values as a result of settlement in Britain. The latter is reflected in the expansion of the dowry system in the case of younger women and in the increase in gift exchanges and ritual elaboration, through the re-establishment of non-compulsory ceremonial activity, which is almost entirely woman-focused in the case of older earning women (Bhachu 1985, 1986).

All this has resulted in more than just the increase in women's personal autonomy and decision-making powers. It has resulted in changes in culturally defined notions of 'female' and 'male' roles and duties and also in the social fabric of Punjabi society itself, which is becoming more loosely organized and increasingly bilateral due to shifts in household patterns, a move away from the stronger patrilaterility prior to migration. Through their earnings, women have negotiated a strong position in it and a wider power base to establish cultural patterns over which they exercize greater control. Hence, the social construction of cultural values which underpin Punjabi social organization have indeed been modified and have undergone radical changes due to the articulation of the cultural and the economic as a result of both migration and women's direct access to the productive process. This is in opposition to the emphasis in the literature on the *lack* of change in such features.[12] Punjabi social mores and the matrix of society have neither remained static nor followed a single path of change in the case of the female spheres because of the dynamic relationship between the household, women's position in it, the economy, and the culture. In a constant and complex process of both the maintenance of the traditional though changing values, and the establishment of 'British Punjabi' social patterns, women's economic position and increased command over resources monopolized prior to migration by the men, have been and are crucial.

Notes

This paper is a revised version of a paper delivered at the Second Sikh Studies Conference, University of California, Berkeley, February 1987. I am grateful to Sallie Westwood for comments on the paper.

1 This paper draws on fieldwork which was mostly carried out within the East African Sikh community in West London in 1977–78 and within the general Sikh community, i.e. direct migrants from the subcontinent and 'twice migrants' from East Africa, between 1981 and 1983. I updated the material by conducting further interviews with some of the women in my sample in 1985 and 1986, especially because employment conditions have changed since the late 1970s and early 1980s, with unemployment higher than ever in the past. This has affected the men in particular, especially those resident in the Midlands. Hence, although the paper focuses on the East African Sikhs, where relevant, I shall refer to cases of the directly migrant women, the majority of whom have come from rural Punjab to urban Britain, unlike the East Africans who have moved from urban Africa to metropolitan Britain.

2 See Phizacklea 1983; West 1983; Saifullah Khan 1979; Westwood 1984 and this volume.

3 In comparison with white indigenous women born in the UK who are economically active, a higher proportion of Afro-Caribbean and non-Muslim women (including Sikh women) are in the labour market in full-time employment. Of women between the ages of 25 and 44 years, 66 per

cent of white indigenous women are economically active, as are 77 per cent of those of West Indian origin. Sixty-two per cent of those of Indian origin are economically active but only 17 per cent of those of Pakistani/Bangledeshi origin. Asian women of East African origin, with whom this article is primarily concerned, have a higher rate (at 67 per cent) than both white indigenous women and Indian and Indian Pakistani/Bangladeshi women from the subcontinent (Labour Force Survey 1984 – reported in the *Employment Gazette*, December 1985).

4 Even though nuclear households are common in urban India and existed in urban Africa, women did not in the past and still often do not have access to economic resources which increase their decision-making powers within the home. Their access to their husbands increases dramatically as a result of this type of organization, but not their control over expenditure which chiefly remains in the husband's hands.

5 Fluency in English language is cited as an important feature in gaining employment. For example, the PSI study (Brown 1984) states that 'Economic activity among Asian women is related very strongly to fluency in English. Fifty-six per cent of those who spoke English fluently are in the labour market, compared with 29 per cent of those who speak English only slightly and 8 per cent of those who speak no English.'

6 Abadan-Unat (1977: 31) describes a similar situation for Turkish women in West Germany who were not used to the discipline of work routine: 'Countless Turkish women entered urban jobs without knowing what constituted city life, highly disciplined working hours, or production norms.'

7 This stronghold of authority by elder kinsmen is also mentioned by Sharma 1980, 1978: 265; Caplan 1985: 52; Vatuk 1972: 140; De Souza 1980: 21; and Pettigrew 1975: 52, describing urban and rural households in the subcontinent.

8 This trend towards egalitarian family relationships, the increase in divorces which are becoming common among Punjabi Sikhs, the establishment of nuclear households, and the fragmentation of extended families has also been documented for other migrants by, for example, Morokvasic (1983) for Yugoslav women, Abadan Unat (1977) for Turkish women in West Germany, Foner (1975, 1986) for Jamaican women in London and New York, Brettell (1982) for Portuguese women in France.

9 Vatuk (1972: 116–17) and Sharma (1984: 64) describe a similar situation where junior men defer to senior men who control the expenditure, leaving even the younger men of the household without personal resources. Hence, both men and female juniors were/are subservient to the elders.

10 Sharma (1984: 64–5) refers to the lack of women's control over productive property, especially the junior women. For example

'The bride herself will have very little say in what happens to her dowry once it leaves her parents home. . . . Where household goods and items of clothing are concerned, it is likely to be the bride's mother-in-law who has the greatest say in how these items are distributed. This is partly by virtue of her position of seniority, but also relates to her position as *senior woman*.'

Amrit Wilson (1978: 119) describes a similar process for the case of Gujarati women in Britain whose husband and eldest sister-in-law expect to take control of her earnings. This situation was not in existence in any of the families I came across.

11 All the Sikh women in my sample kept and controlled their earnings. This is not to suggest that they spent their wages on themselves because they constituted a crucial part of the household budget but that their paypackets are/were not handed over to senior male or female kin for redistribution. They used their earnings for everyday expenses: the income was not just pin money, but resources that were essential for the maintenance of the reproductive unit.

12 Hilary Standing (1985: 234) describing the urban Bengali household (in the subcontinent) and women's employment says that their earnings have not enhanced their ability 'to determine the conditions of their own lives'. She states:

.my data show that many employed women do control at least some of their incomes in this narrow sense. But the social matrix within which decisions are taken is underpinned by culturally constructed notions of needs and rights which overwhelmingly militate against personal accumulation or personal expenditure on the part of women, while such categories may be fully sanctioned for men. Indeed, it is difficult to see how 'personal autonomy' in respect of women could be defined at all within existing family decision-making processes.

References

Abadan-Unat, N. (1977) 'Implications of migration on the emancipation and pseudo emancipation of Turkish Women', *International Migration Review* **11**: 31–57.

Allen, S. (1980) 'Perhaps a seventh person', *Women's Studies International Quarterly* **3**: 325–38.

Amos, V. (1982) *Black Women in Britain: A Bibliographic Essay*, London: Race Relations Abstracts, Sage Publications.

Anwar, M. (1976) *Between Two Cultures: A Study of the Relationship Between the Generations in the Asian Community in Britain*, London: Commission for Racial Equality.

—— (1979) *The Myth of Return: Pakistanis in Britain*, London: Heinemann.

Ballard, R. and Ballard, C. (1977), 'The Sikhs: the Development of South Asian settlements in Britain', in J.L. Watson (ed.) *Between Two Cultures: Migrants and Minorities in Britain*, Oxford: Basil Blackwell.

Bhachu, P.K. (1981) 'Marriage and dowry among selected East African Sikh families in the United Kingdom', unpublished PhD dissertation, London University.

—— (1984) 'East African Sikhs in Britain: experienced settlers with traditionalistic values', *Immigrants and Minorities* **3**: 276–95.

—— (1985) *Twice Migrants: East African Sikh Settlers in Britain*, London and New York: Tavistock Publications.

—— (1986) 'Work, dowry and marriage among East African Sikh women in the United Kingdom', in R.J. Simon and C.B. Brettell (eds) *International Migration: The Female Experience*, Totowa, New Jersey: Rowman Allanheld.

Brettell, C.B. (1982) *We have Already Cried Many Tears: The Story of Three Portuguese Migrant Women*, Cambridge: Cambridge, Mass.: Schenkman Publishing Co.

Brown, C. (1984) *Black and White Britain: The Third PSI Survey*, London: Policy Studies Institute and Heinemann.

Brown, P. Macintyre, M., Morpeth, R., and Prendergast, S. (1981) 'A daughter: a thing to be given away', *Women in Society: Interdisciplinary Essays*, The Cambridge Women's Studies Group, London: Virago.

Caplan, P. (1985) *Class and Gender in India. Women and their Organizations in a South Indian City*, London and New York: Tavistock Publications.

Community Relations Commission (1975) *Who Minds: A Study of Working Mothers and Child Minding in Ethnic Minority Communities*, London: Community Relations Commission.

Caplan, P. and Bujra, J.M. (eds) (1978) *Women United, Women Divided. Cross cultural perspectives on female solidarity*, London: Tavistock Publications.

Crishna, S. (1975) *Girls of Asian Origin in Britain*, London: YMCA.

Dahya, B (1973) 'Pakistanis in Britain: transients or settlers?', *Race* **14**: 246–77.

Dahya, Z. (1965) 'Pakistanis in Britain', *Race* **6**: 311–321.

De Souza, A. (1980) *Women in Contemporary India and South Asia*, India: Monohar New Delhi.

De Souza, V.S. (1980) 'Family states and female work participation', in De Souza (ed.) *Women in Contemporary India and South Asia*, India: Monohar New Delhi.

Dhondy, M.J. (1974) 'The Strike at Imperial Typewriters', *Race Today* **6**: 201–05.

Eglar, Z. (1960) *A Punjabi Village in Pakistan*, New York: Columbia University Press.

Employment Gazette (1985) 'Ethnic origin and economic status' by Ann Barber, December.

Foner, N. (1975) 'Women, work and migration: Jamaicans in London', *Urban Anthropology* **4**: 229–49.

—— (1978) *Jamaica Farewell: Jamaican Migrants in London*, London: Routledge & Kegan Paul.

—— (1986) 'Sex roles and sensibilities: Jamaican women in New York and London', in R.J. Simon and C.B. Brettell (eds) *International Migration The Female Experience*, Totowa, New Jersey: Rowman & Allanheld.

Ghai, G.P. (1965) *Portrait of a Minority: Asians in East Africa*, Nairobi: Oxford University Press.

—— (1970) *Portrait of a Minority, Asians in East Africa*, second edition Nairobi: Oxford University Press.

Harris, H. (1972) 'Black women and work. The body politic', *London Stage* 1: 166–74.

Helweg, A.W. (1979) *Sikhs in England: The Development of a Migrant Community*, Delhi: Oxford University Press.

Hoel, B. (1982) 'Contemporary clothing "sweatshops". Asian female labour and collective organization', in J. West (ed.) *Work, Women and the Labour Market*, London: Routledge & Kegan Paul.

Kapur, P. (1970) *Marriage and the Working Woman in India*, New Delhi: Vikas Publications.

Karve, I. (1953) *Kinship Organization in India*, Poona: Deccan College Monograph Series II.

Lamphere, L. (1986) 'Working mothers and family strategies: Portugese and Columbian women in a New England community', in R.J. Simon and C.B. Brettell (eds) *International Migration: The Female Experience*.

Mayer, A. (1960) *Caste and Kinship in Central India*, Berkeley and Los Angeles: University of California Press.

McLeod, W.H. (1968) *Guru Narak and the Sikh Religion*, Oxford: Clarendon Press.

—— (1976) *The Evolution of The Sikh Community*, Oxford: Clarendon Press.

Morokvasic, M. (1983) 'Women in migration: Beyond the reductionist outlook', in Annie Phizacklea (ed.) *One Way Ticket: Migration and Female Labour*, London: Routledge & Kegan Paul.

—— (1984) 'Birds of passage are also women', *International Migration Review* **XVIII** (4).

Lewis, O. (1958) *Village Life in Northern India: Studies in a Delhi Village*, Urbana: University of Illinois Press.

Madan, T.N. (1973) 'Structural implications of marriage in North India: wife givers and wife takers among the Pandits of Kashmir', *Contributions to Indian Sociology* **9**: 217–43 (n.s.).

Parmar, P. (1982) 'Gender, race, and class: Asian women in resistance', in *Centre for Contemporary Cultural Studies, The Empire Strikes Back: Race and Racism in 70s Britain*, London: Hutchinson.

Pettigrew, J. (1972) 'Some notes on the social system of the Sikh Jats', *New Community*, Vol. 1(5): 354–63.

—— (1975) *Robber Nobelmen: A Study of the Political System of the Sikh Jats*, London and Boston: Routledge & Kegan Paul.

Phizacklea, A. (1982) 'Migrant women and wage labour: the case of West Indian women in Britain', in J. West (ed.) *Work, Women and the Labour Market*, London: Routledge & Kegan Paul.

—— (1983) *One Way Ticket: Migration and Female Labour*, London: Routledge & Kegan Paul.

Pocock, D.F. (1972) *Kanbi and Patidar: A Study of the Patidar Community of Gujerat*, Oxford: Clarendon Press.

Saifullah Khan, V. (1976a) 'Pakistani Women in Britain', *New Community* 5: 99–108.

—— (1976b) 'Perceptions of a Population: Pakistanis in Britain', *New Community* 5: 222–9.

—— (1977) 'The Pakistanis: Mirpuri villagers at home in Bradford', in J.L. Watson (ed.) *Between Two Cultures: Migrants and Minorities in Britain*, Oxford: Basil Blackwell.

—— (1979) 'Work and network: South Asian women in South London', in S. Wallman (ed.) *Ethnicity at Work*, London: Macmillan.

Shah, S. (1975) *Immigrants and Employment in the Clothing Industry: The Rag Trade in London's East End*, London: Runnymede Trust.

Sharma, U. (1978) 'Segregation and its consequences in India', in P. Caplan and J. Bujra (eds) *Women United, Women Divided: Cross-Cultural Perspectives on Female Solidarity*, London: Tavistock Publications.

—— (1980) *Women, Work, and Property in North-West India*, London and New York: Tavistock Publications.

—— (1984) 'Dowry in North India: its consequences for women', in R. Hirschon (ed.) *Women and Property – Women as Property*, London and Canberra: Croom Helm.

Sidhu, G.S. (1977) *The Sikh Woman*, Gravesend, Kent: The Sikh Missionary Society.

Singh, K. (1953) *The Sikhs*, London: Allen & Unwin.

Standing, H. (1985) 'Resources, wages and power: the impact of women's employment on the urban Bengali household', in H. Afshar (ed.) *Women, Work and Ideology in the Third World*, London and New York: Tavistock Publications.

Uberoi, S. (1965) 'Sikh Women in Southall', *Race* 6: 33–40.

Vatuk, S. (1972) *Kinship and Urbanization: White Collar Migrants in North India*, Berkeley and Los Angeles: University of California Press.

West, J. (ed.) (1983) *Women, Work and the Labour Market*, London: Routledge & Kegan Paul.

Westwood, S. (1984) *All Day Every Day. Factory and Family in the making of Women's Lives*, London and Sydney: Pluto Press.

Whitehead, A. (1976) 'Sexual antagonism in Herefordshire', in D.L. Barker and S. Allen (eds) *Dependence and Exploitation in Work and Marriage*, London and New York: Longman.

Wilson, A. (1978) *Finding a Voice: Asian Women in Britain*, London: Virago.

6 Workers and wives: continuities and discontinuities in the lives of Gujarati women

Sallie Westwood

Introduction

> Having indirectly and inadvertently brought Asian women to
> Britain, the racism of the state and racism of British society now
> defines the wider position of Asian women in this country – as the
> lowest paid and most exploited workers, or as the wives and
> daughters of such workers – an unstable and unacceptable
> situation full of conflicts and contradictions. Inside their families,
> too, their roles are in a state of flux, with the past, the peasant
> past, the tribal past and the colonial past each with its own
> particular prescriptions for the woman's role constantly intruding
> on the present. Out of these multiple fields of conflict the future of
> Asian women in Britain is being resolved.
>
> (Wilson 1978: 15)

Amrit Wilson's comment reminds us that however we understand
cultural diversity and ethnicity these are part of a larger pattern of
relations founded upon capitalism, colonialism, and patriarchy. The
starting point of this paper on the working lives of Gujarati women
must therefore situate the ethnography within these relations. As
Miles has cogently argued, ethnic relations cannot be abstracted
from production relations and the ideology of racism which pervades
the state and civil society of Britain (Miles 1982: 44–71). In
addition, feminists have insisted upon the importance of gender
relations, understood to have a material base that sustains the
subordination of women.[1] These are large issues and I cannot begin
in one paper to unravel their complexities, but it is important to
raise them, because it is these relations that are brought into focus
through my study of Gujarati women, which begins in the factory.

The questions with which I am concerned can be usefully divided
in relation to the two key areas of women's lives: production and the
world of work outside the home, and reproduction and the world of

unpaid labour in the domestic unit.[2] In another language, I am concerned with the relationship between capitalism and patriarchy, but as the life of the factory made clear the articulation between the two means that patriarchal relations are as much a part of the factory as of the domestic unit. Given that these are key areas of discussion and ones that will be pursued in the pages that follow the question to be asked is: How far does being a worker, positioned within the production process as a class member, cut across racial and ethnic diversity and generate collectivity and solidarity on the shopfloor? This is one major part of this paper. The issues invoked by this discussion are complex given the history of racism in Britain generally and among the white working class in particular.

Racism is a key component in our understanding of the life of the shopfloor and although it is not easily amenable to definition Annie Phizacklea and Robert Miles have attempted one which allows us to situate the practices which form racist abuses. They write:

> We use racism to refer to those negative beliefs held by one group which identify and set apart another by attributing significance to some biological or other 'inherent' characteristic(s) which it is said to possess, and which deterministically associate that characteristic(s) with some other (negatively evaluated) feature(s) or action(s). The possession of these supposed characteristic(s) is then used as justification for denying that group equal access to material and other resources and/or political rights.
>
> (Phizacklea and Miles 1980: 22)

The question then becomes: How far does racism divide the working class and sustain hostility and division? There are many examples of the ways in which racism has affected the lives of South Asian women and the ways in which they have fought against it. One way is through the generation of solidarity among culturally and ethnically diverse groups, with the emphasis placed upon the shared experience of racial discrimination in Britain. To this end black writers have used the term 'black' to emphasize unity, but in ways that also recognize cultural diversity. This view is clearly expressed by Valerie Amos and Pratibha Parmar when they write:

> We are aware that many differences exist in the cultures, languages and religions not only between Afro-Caribbean and Asian communities but between these two groups. We do not see our cultural differences as operating antagonistically because we recognise the autonomy of our separate cultures. By working together, we have developed a common understanding of our

oppression and from this basis we build our solidarity. The black struggle is a political one and it is important that we fight our oppression together.

(1981: 130)

The women in the study presented here used the term 'black' to describe themselves if they were Afro-Caribbean or black British women; the South Asian women rarely used the term, preferring instead the designation 'Indian' as a means of distinguishing themselves from other women in the workplace. I have followed their usage in this paper.

Being a worker, and one within a society where workers are racialized, is one aspect of being a member of a working class that is stratified by skill, 'race', and gender. Consequently, the experience of being a worker is powerfully modified according to whether a worker is skilled or unskilled, black or white, a woman or a man. Indian women are placed in a stratified working class and the ways in which they have forged commonalities within the working class as a whole or within particular sections of it, is a substantive issue. But being a woman worker has other implications, as I have suggested: the production relations within which our working lives are situated are articulated with the relations of reproduction which situate the lives of women in the home, as wives, mothers, daughters, and domestic labourers. Consequently, the second part of the discussion is to consider the ways in which being a woman (on the basis of a patriarchal definition of womanhood which is securely tied to the home and motherhood) provides the basis for unity and continuity between the lives of black and white women. The complexities of the articulation between these two areas (production and reproduction) and the relevance of cultural diversity within and between them generate a kaleidoscopic picture in which it is essential to hold both similarity and difference together, and to avoid abstracting relations from the complexity of the whole.

One way in which these complex relations came together in the factory that I studied was in the generation and sustenance of a powerfully creative shopfloor culture made and guarded by the women. Initially, of course, this was a culture generated in the workplace by white, working-class women in resistance and opposition to production imperatives, but which also provided a powerful celebration of the culture of femininity. Indian women over the last decade have become part of this culture and have shown in this factory, as they have elsewhere, that they too can generate a powerful resistance to work discipline and the exploitation of capitalist relations. The union clearly has a role to play in this and the paper discusses the relations between the union and women workers.

Throughout my writing I have called the city Needletown and the factory StitchCo and I will continue to do so in this paper. I start with a brief overview of the labour process including the authority relations in the factory and the way in which they demonstrate not only capitalist management imperatives, but patriarchal relations as well. The women situated in this labour process, who are the subjects of this paper, play out the drama of shopfloor life with all its ramifications for class solidarity and sisterhood among women workers. These issues are further explored in relation to the forms of resistance expressed by the women in the elaborate ritual and gift giving that accompany the change in status from daughter to bride, or young woman to mother. The bride and the mother are potent symbols of womanhood which are offered to all members of the shopfloor and resonate across cultural diversity, but which are concretized in specific ways. Consequently, motherhood is most crucially about the way in which the biological and social are articulated in the lives of women and the way in which the cultural moment intervenes directly in this interrelationship.

In concluding the paper I want to generate a discussion of the implications of the processes of workplace politics and culture for the wider gender and class struggles beyond the workplace and in the home in relation to Gujarati women. They have become, in some situations, a powerful and militant group of women committed to a struggle against racist practices and capitalist exploitation – how does this relate to the prevailing ideologies generated and sustained within the ethnic communities of which they are a part?

To sum up: this paper examines the working lives in the workplace and the home of Gujarati women employed in the hosiery industry in the East Midlands. The discussion necessarily involves an attempt to deal with the complexities of the interrelationship between class, gender, and racism. In attempting this analysis I want to concentrate upon the cross-cutting axis between production relations, which situate women as workers and class members, and relations of reproduction, which situate women as wives and mothers. These two axes come together in the factory and most dramatically in the elaborate shopfloor culture which is generated and sustained by the women at work. The crucial questions to which the paper is addressed then become:

1 How far are class relations the overriding context for culturally

diverse women promoting the commonality of being a worker and a member of the working class as the major experience of life on the shopfloor?

2 Do the symbols of the bride and mother which are central to the culture of women on the shopfloor offer all women a basis for shared experiences? And do these symbols resonate with the actualities of domestic life for wives who are also wage labourers?

3 How fare does the 'proletarianization' of Gujarati women in the factory set up contradictions with the ideologies that characterize the communities of which they are a part?

It is to an exploration of these themes that I now turn.

The factory setting

The factory where I carried out my research during 1980–81 employed over 2,000 workers at its main site in Needletown and women made up over two-thirds of the workforce – a situation typical of the hosiery industry nationally.[3] The gender division of labour was replicated at StitchCo: men were knitters, mechanics, dyers, and top managers, while women worked in the finishing processes, as they had traditionally always done, and in white-collar personnel work. The company, like the city, was ethnically diverse, but the largest group were South Asian workers who had come to the city in the last decade or so, following earlier immigrants from Poland, Eastern Europe, and the Caribbean.[4]

Generally, men and women worked separately in large departments which were a consequence of the technical division of labour in the industry. The factory was, therefore, an example of the gender segregation at work explored by Catherine Hakim which shows clearly that very few workplaces are places where men and women work alongside one another or together (Hakim 1981). The department where I conducted my research was the fashion make-up department where the production process was finalized. Here, the fabric that had been knitted in the knitting department, dyed and rolled in the dyehouse, and cut and trimmed in the cutting and trim shops, arrived in pattern pieces to be turned, finally, into the clothes designed by the design department.[5]

The statistical bases of the department were highly problematic because the size and composition of the workforce was constantly changing (labour turnover ran at 40 per cent during my year on the shopfloor). Of an average 285 women working in the department, 43 per cent were under twenty-five and 35 per cent were over forty. Women in their thirties were under-represented (11 per cent) because the company did not offer part-time work. Sixty per cent of the women were married and most had children, 20 per cent had three children and more. Most of the women (82 per cent) had been at StitchCo for less than ten years, 53 per cent for less than five years, and 25 per cent for less than two years. The women in the department were culturally and ethnically diverse and they included a very small number of Irish and Polish women alongside the South Asian and Afro-Caribbean women who together made up 43 per cent of the workforce, 38 per cent were South Asian women and there were also four young black women who had been born in Britain.

Neither the Caribbean nor the South Asian women were entirely homogenous groups. Black women from the Caribbean came from Jamaica and the smaller islands of Barbados, St Kitts, and Antigua and the South Asian women included two Sikh women and a woman from Guyana whose family originated in South India. But the great majority of Indian women were Gujaratis and among them Patel was the most common 'surname'.[6] Among the Gujarati women there was a clear network based on familial ties which provided information on jobs in the factory and which brought mothers and daughters, sisters, and sisters-in-law into the factory and the department (see Brooks and Singh 1979). In addition there was also a network among friends, young women who had been to school together and who had started work at the same time and who widened the circle of women to whom information was relayed. The Gujarati women were not alone in having networks like these, many of the white women had also come into the factory through familial interventions and they continued to bring their daughters to the department.

The labour process

All women coming into social production sell their labour power under conditions they do not make. They share a production process and its demands upon them as workers, and they respond to the labour process both as a set of technical relations and as a set of social and power relations (for a more extended discussion see Westwood 1984: 13–38).

Women worked in units of up to forty individuals, and each unit was organized with machinery, skills, and workers for one or two specific items of clothing. Certain units worked on the same type of garment for long periods of time, which meant that the women became very proficient and earned high bonuses while other units were shifted from style to style which meant low, or no, bonuses. This, of course, encouraged internal competition between the units and discouraged solidarity among the women.

The machinists were supervised by female supervisors and their assistants, or on the larger units by two supervisors. It was their responsibility to maintain a steady flow of production by keeping the unit supplied with work and by dividing the production process in the most efficient way. They were an experienced and skilled group of women who covered the whole age range and who included three South Asian women – one from Guyana, one Sikh woman, and one young Gujarati woman who had been to school locally. Amita was the youngest supervisor and was very popular: she was often presented as one of the Indian women in the department who 'is just like us, really' by the English women. Unlike Satwant, the Sikh woman, Amita was not accused of favouritism towards Indian women by white women. These accusations were one example of racial tension on the shopfloor. As far as I was able to ascertain the accusations were unfounded. The assistant supervisors were not on a promotion ladder but were 'run arounds' for the units and because of this most of them were young women, including two Gujaratis. Older white supervisors had fewer Indian women on their units than the younger or Indian supervisors. This might have been an attempt to minimize conflict between different groups of women, but this was unclear. Management had no overt or express policy for dividing the women, the rationale was manifestly their skills and where they were needed. But it is interesting to note, and later section of the paper will show, that the most militant group of Indian women were all part of the unit with the highest proportion of Indian women to white women.

The supervisors occupied a deeply contradictory position in relation to the women on the shopfloor. At one level they were women who joined in the celebrations and life of the department while at another they were involved in the supervision and control of women in the workplace. They too had been machinists and they still held some sympathy with the women, but management demanded that they were the final stage of the management hierarchy. The tensions in the situation were enormous and were often discussed by the supervisors, as Amita pointed out:

'Being a supervisor is a really difficult job because you are in the

middle. The girls want you to be for them and management insist
you are part of them. It gives me a real headache. I go home some
days so worried because I, haven't done my job right. I'm not
kidding.'

The work was hard, as many of the supervisors and machinists
attested. The complicated, measured day-work system in operation
at the factory meant that the women were stratified by grades and
each grade had a set target which produced a guaranteed weekly
wage.[7] Black and white women showed a very similar profile in
relation to the grades with a slightly higher proportion of Indian
women in the higher grades. Wages were low, an average £60 per
week (which was an average for women workers in the industry)
with a highest wage of £80 for a star grade machinist with bonuses.
These rewards represented only one half to two-thirds of the wages
earned by male knitters in the industry. For wages such as these the
women would sit at machines eight hours a day sewing side seams
week in and week out, with aching backs and sore fingers. But it did
not stop the steady flow of gossip and jokes, the witty comments and
lively banter that characterized the shopfloor.

In another area of the department ironers and pressers pressed
clothes before they went to the examiners and packers and finally
into the lorries for the shops. They were better paid (£90) for the
pain of standing all day in the heat and the steam of the irons. Most
of the workers in this section were black women from the Caribbean
who had worked for the company for a decade or more and there
was, in addition, the 'grandmother' of the Gujarati women. Close to
retirement, she spoke very little English still, but always managed to
communicate with those with whom she worked. Champa had
started work when she came to Britain with her husband in the
Uganda exodus, a woman then in her fifties and now in her sixties
who had walked off a plane into a refugee camp and then into a
factory.

The examiners worked close by, standing under strip lighting
looking for faults which meant clothes were sent back to the units,
much to the annoyance of the machinists. The packers counted
clothes, put them in polythene, and marked their disappearance
from the factory. A lively group of younger women worked here
alongside a couple of 'old hands'. The young women were women
the company had decided to keep on when they showed no aptitude ,
for sewing at high speeds. Finally, the clothes were wheeled into the,
vans by three lads, two white and one black, whose major
preoccupation was to stay away from the department as long as

possible – every job was stretched to its limits. They could do this because they were mobile, which most of the women were not. When I was working I usually worked in the packing area where I had some mobility and where the most minimal skills were required. The woman who sewed, pressed, examined, and packed clothes were at the bottom of the hierarchy in the department. John, the manager, was at the apex of the pyramid. There were three production managers, all of whom were white women, and a younger white woman personnel officer. The women directly in control of the women on the shopfloor were the supervisors. This was a woman's world but for the male manager at the top and the six mechanics, all white men, who were responsible for maintaining the machinery. Technical work in this and other departments was men's not women's work and there was no opportunity for women to train for the job.

The mechanics were very important because if a machine went wrong they had to be called and a woman was dependent upon their arrival before she could carry on working and, therefore, make her production target or her bonus. Men thus had power over the earning capacities of women. Men (and they were white men) controlled knowledge and skills which gave them power over the lives and earning capacities of women. This fact was not lost on the women, who referred to the male manager as 'Father' and who had constant battles with the mechanics.

The organization of production both united and divided the women. They were united by their position as workers on the shopfloor against the authority structure and the demands of the bonus scheme, but divided because the units and grades were differentiated. However, the labour process that divided them also united them because they were dependent upon one another and they protested about the production targets individually and collectively through the culture of the shopfloor.

Shopfloor culture

In my account, cultures are understood to be composite entities generated and sustained by collectivities which promote dynamism and contradictions within the overall social formation. Culture is not viewed as fixed or static, but as multi-faceted, embracing most simply a way of life with specific symbols that define membership and resonate with the lived experiences of people. But rituals add to this and confirm and underline cultural elements in the commonsense world. Common sense, however, is shot through with contradictions and offers partial understandings that become 'the practical ideologies' through which people make sense of their world.[8] The culture of the shopfloor is a stunning example of contradictions writ large because it both fiercely opposes the capitalist labour process and those who exercise authority and surveillance as management, and celebrates the collectivity of women through an ideology of femininity which reorganizes women's life experiences and further integrates them into domesticity and an image of themselves as wives and mothers.[9] The complexities of this situation are developed in the pages that follow but it is important to understand that the origins of this shopfloor culture lie in the history of white working-class women in Britain; it is ethnically and historically specific, and yet it is offered to all women, and all women, black and white, are inducted into the rituals and language of the shopfloor with its attendant excitement and creativity. Does this mean, therefore, that the Gujarati women, especially those arriving from East Africa and Gujarat, are outside this culture? Clearly, they bring their own cultures and life experiences but by following the life of the shopfloor it is possible to see the ways in which Gujarati women take hold of life in the factory and reappropriate it to make it their own.

Resistance

All women who came into the factory as new workers would be formally inducted into the life of the factory via the training line, but this ended when they moved on to the units where they would start to learn the shopfloor way of getting things done. They would learn from the other women the 'tricks of the trade', like working slowly when they were timed, and how to respond to the production targets set by the workstudy team. Gujarati women learned these things as effectively as any one else and it was not long before they, too, understood that there was a battle fought between management and workers over what was produced in the department and in what way.

The production targets given out to the women were fiercely contested as part of the general opposition to management's definition of 'a fair day's work'. Instead, the women promoted their own version of this, disciplining anyone who was accused of rate busting. Women who tried to work through tea breaks or lunch were stigmatized by the other women. The shopfloor enforced its own rules as a means of defending the interests of workers against management. Theirs was a collective struggle against the erosion of their control over production processes. These aspects of shopfloor culture were oppositional and collective in inspiration and were expressed in a variety of ways. Some of the fiercest resistance was generated and sustained by Gujarati women who would contest the targets they had been given, call the union, and walk off the job if they felt unjustly treated. They acted from the premise expressed by Lata: 'This company is not nice, they try to cheat us'.

On one memorable occasion the unit with the largest proportion of Gujarati women walked off the job in protest against what they considered to be unreasonable production targets. The women united because the targets were so high that they could not reach them, let alone earn a bonus. The Gujarati women also used their ethnicity as a resource in this encounter with management. When Hansa, an older woman, was given a written account of her target and how the work was to be done she pushed it away with a grand gesture and then refused to acknowledge that she understood any English. Turning away from her machine, she sat with arms folded, exuding rage. Asha in front of her burst into tears and dashed towards the lavatory while the younger women shouted 'We'll go on strike . . . we're not accepting this'. The women were united on the issue and the matter was never resolved. Instead, the baby clothes that were the centre of the row stopped coming into the department and on to the unit. Hansa admitted that she did understand the instructions she had been given, but that it was one way to resist them. It was a strategy that Indian women used whenever it seemed appropriate. In this incident Gujarati women led the revolt and the small number of white women who worked on the unit joined in and together all the women maintained a high level of solidarity in the face of management pressure.

The collectivism of the shopfloor and the way that the women would come together in defence of their perceived interests was demonstrated again when management suggested that redundancies might be necessary at the factory. At the departmental meeting when the issue was raised the women (an ethnically diverse group) who represented each unit objected to any job losses and they opted, should it prove necessary, for short-time working for all rather than have any individual lose her job. They also suggested that management might sacrifice their company cars and subsidized lunches in an effort to cut costs. The women drew upon their own experience and offered an analysis that suggested the interests of the company and the workers were not the same despite the company's appeal to the notion of the 'family' firm, which was founded on the ideological assumption of common interests within a family. For the women there was no fair bargain to be struck between workers and management, 'they' meaning management always wanted more without increasing wages. Part of the women's opposition was also located in the attempt to defend their skills. Although the women were classified and paid as semi-skilled workers they saw themselves as skilled workers, but who were in the process of being deskilled by the measured day work scheme.[10] In trying to defend their skills the women set up an opposition between quantity, which the company wanted, and quality which they produced as skilled workers, and speed, which the company demanded, and skill, which was their possession. The constant discussion of skill belies any suggestion that women workers are not concerned with skill.

The opposition sustained and generated by the women in relation to issues of time, effort, and skill were directly related to their position as workers in the production process and in this they showed a keen awareness of their class position and the way in which profits are generated within capitalism.

'The union makes us strong'

As workers, therefore, Gujarati women came together with other women in defence of what they perceived to be their shared interests as wage labourers who sold their labour power in the market. Indian women were often very militant and they called upon the union to assist them. All women were paid-up members of the union and they called the union representatives to support them in disputes connected with the production targets and bonus and wages system.[11] But although they called the union they had little faith in its ability to act for, or with, the membership. The union was seen as an adjunct to management, part of the hierarchy and the world of men. That this should be so is not surprising given that the two reps were paid by the company and the union was well integrated into the factory (like other unions in similarly large companies). The union's lack of credibility was not related to any specific group of women. When I asked Amina if the union helped Indian women her response was swift and to the point: 'Indian, English – its all the same. They are useless.'

In fact, the woman representative, Annie, understood and sympathized with shopfloor discontent. She recognized that the union was mainly concerned with skilled white men and she had fought long and hard for the cause of 'semi-skilled' women. She also understood that the situation of Indian women required specific responses from the union and she encouraged the union to have Gujarati representatives, both men and women, in the departments throughout the factory. But she saw the major problem within the union as the way in which it was geared to the male knitters, the craftsworkers of the industry who must be protected at the cost of higher wages and better maternity leave for women. All the women in the department supported Annie and if there were disputes that required the union rep it was Annie they called for rather than Bill, whom they mistrusted for being smooth, white, and managerial.

Despite the militancy of some of the Gujarati women in connection with issues of pay and production targets Annie was conscious that trade unions and their history in Britain were a largely unknown quantity for the Indian women generally, and the problems this raised were often left to the departmental representative whose knowledge was not much greater than the women she represented. Shanta was young and spoke Gujarati and English fluently, but the union did not try to induct her into its history or struggles so that she might better understand the role of trade unions in working-class history. Instead, she had to deal with situations where the women were already alienated from the union both from the out-of-work context of the ideologies held within the Gujarati communities (which I will discuss further in the conclusion), and because they were women on the shopfloor.

Indian women tried, through Shanta, to reassert their ethnicity and gain space for their own culture. Consequently, Shanta was asked by the older women if she would raise the freedom to wear sarees at work, which was disallowed by the company on the basis of safety. The younger women did not want sarees to be legitimate because they preferred to experiment with Western dress, but the older women felt undignified in their trousers and tops and diminished as Indian women. They asked Shanta to raise this issue and another, the festival of Diwali which they celebrated at work by bringing food to eat, but they wanted to have an official, paid day off for Diwali 'Because it is our Christmas', and because the burden of cooking and domestic work at this time was enormous. Shanta relayed the request but it did not receive the backing of the union and she had little success. Her lack of success on these matters convinced some of the Indian women that the union was 'no good'. Shanta battled constantly with threats, especially from the older women, that they would leave the union. She also tried to educate the women into seeing the importance of unions in the struggles by workers, pointing to the Grunwick strike as an example of the way that South Asian workers have struggled to have a union. Her task was very difficult and it was fraught with the contradictions of her situation because as a young unmarried woman she was seen as a daughter by the older women, with the lack of power and the status this implied.

Ritual and celebration

The collective resistance expressed by the women as workers in the production process was complemented by the opposition conveyed in other elements of shopfloor culture which were essentially concerned with the world of women and the home. The factory was domesticated by the women introducing a culture of femininity symbolized by the slippers and the aprons (made from company material) that they wore. More importantly, shopfloor culture celebrated the major life-cycle events of women's lives – marriage and motherhood – in ways that romanticized both on a western model which was offered to all women irrespective of the cultural context. The insertion of reproductive roles and 'femininity' into the heart of the production process was both an act of resistance and, simultaneously, one of collusion because the models which inspired this femininity were located in patriarchal definitions of women's roles as wives, mothers, and sex objects. These deeply contradictory elements were played out in a situation of cultural diversity and the women were conscious of this diversity. Young women, for example, are all daughters subject to familial authority. But the context of this authority is variable, constructed in relation to the cultural moment which intervenes and contours the materials with which women fashion their lives.

The celebrations which surrounded birthdays, brides, motherhood, and retirement wrested space and time from the production process and offered the women the opportunity to act collectively in a celebration of women's lives. Birthday lists were kept on all the units and sweets were bought and passed around by the woman whose birthday was celebrated, with cards and gifts from her close friends.

Shopfloor creativity peaked in relation to the importance of marriage in women's lives and produced a celebration of the bride enacted through a powerful and contradictory ritual, which divorced the bride from any cultural context and presented her as a symbol in which all could share. Indian women on the shopfloor connected with this and intervened to make the bride their own while they encouraged their white friends to take part in their traditional wedding celebrations. The ritual, as I saw it repeated many times during my year at the factory, has a largely unrecorded history but it is clear that similar events take place in the potteries and in other factories where there are numbers of women in the workforce.

When the wedding date is determined the friends and women who work on the same unit as the bride-to-be start to collect materials and discuss ideas for the costume they will make for her. The materials and the time in which to make the fancy dress are company time appropriated by the women. Designs are decided in relation to the young woman, how *risqué* the outfit should be or how gentle and romantic – this seemed to figure more often in the case of young Gujarati women unless it was known that an Indian woman would not be offended by sexual innuendoes. One of the most popular costumes was that of the sexually alert schoolgirl, which young white and black women wore. All costumes had hats to match, tall hats, bonnets with streamers, tinsel, and ribbons flowing from them. These creations were works of great skill and thought. When the young woman arrived at work she would be greeted with one of these and would then disappear to put it on and parade throughout the department for all to see. Units competed with one another to produce more and more extravagant creations, while they cooperated in finding materials and producing the garments.

The bride-to-be brought food to work and set up in the coffee bar with sticky cakes and pop, which was consumed by friends and well-wishers throughout the morning, thereby disrupting production on most of the units until lunchtime, when the costumed woman would be taken off to the local pub and plied with alcohol (unless she was known to be a non-drinker, as many of the Gujarati women were). The lunch break was extended to take account of the pub and what followed. Flushed with drink and/or excitement the bride-to-be was hurried out of the pub and towards a lamp-post close to a busy road where her friends, armed with binding from the department, and often a chain as well, proceeded to tie the woman to the lamp-post while she wailed and begged to be set free. Once she was securely tied and sufficiently upset everyone disappeared, leaving her with the task of extricating herself from the knots and lengths of binding. It was a difficult and uncomfortable task which left her a dishevelled wreck. When she finally reappeared in the department she was ready to leave for home and often did after more coffee and tears in the coffee bar.

Later in the day the celebration was extended through a 'hen party' which involved white women in a stagger around the pubs and clubs of the cities, especially those that offered concessions or drinks to groups of women. In some of these clubs the brides-to-be were paraded for the eyes of the men in the clubs as a form of cheap and highly exploited entertainment. Gujarati women are rarely to be seen on these jaunts around town which mark the presence of women in the public sphere in ways not acceptable in either culture (Leonard 1980). Instead, Gujarati brides spent their evenings at home with their families, well-wishers, and relatives who had come for the wedding, listening to wedding songs and being a bride teased about her innocence in a warm and good humoured way which offered her support and affection before she embarked upon one of the biggest moments of her life.

The ritual enacted on the shopfloor in relation to the bride is a *rite de passage* which marks the change in status from girl to woman, with all its contradictions so clearly portrayed in the binding of the bride and her struggle for freedom. In some respects the ritual is like the passing out ceremonies that characterize the passage of the apprentice to craftsman. But in the bride's ritual, it is not a type of worker who is hailed but a gendered subject.

Motherhood, like marriage, was a cause for great celebration on the shopfloor, and a pregnant woman became a celebrity. The attention she received signalled general approval for her ability to collaborate with Nature and it rewarded her for tying herself securely to her 'feminine destiny'. Pregnancy also drew from the women in the department a stock of knowledge on the processes of motherhood: how to have an easy birth, which hospitals to avoid, what to eat, and where to obtain cheap baby clothes and equipment. Mothers would accompany their daughters to the hospitals, offer guidance, and look after the new mother when the baby arrived. Gujarati women did not always have their mothers on hand to assist, and drew their support from other female relatives.

Beyond the factory Gujarati women were offered advice and rules about behaviour appropriate to pregnant women, like which foods to eat and avoid. Some of these strictures the women followed, others they did not, choosing instead to follow the advice of health care professionals or to make up their own minds. At the hospitals Gujarati women had to cope with a health service that refused to acknowledge the cultural context of the body and pregnancy, or the different ways of reporting health and well-being.[12] As Marsha, a young black woman, commented: 'Because I'm an unmarried *black* woman they give me shit'. The Indian women were less vocal in their response, but no less perturbed. The important point for all the women was that the medicalization of birth and pregnancy undermined the power that they felt in their own bodies and they would come together in the department to complain about their treatment.[13] Issues of class, gender, and ethnicity were interwoven in the processes.

There was another side to this unity, however, in which racism undercut the shared experiences of motherhood. One example of this was when Flo, an older white woman, was commenting upon the number of pregnancies in the department, 'Twenty-seven at the last count, it's all these coloured, they breed like rabbits'. Trying to contest Flo's views proved fruitless and her friends supported her views. Neither Flo nor her friends worked alongside Gujarati women, but with a small group of younger white women. They were the most overtly racist women in the department.

When a pregnant woman left the department she carried good wishes and gifts from her friends. Babies and motherhood were celebrated and romanticized as the final moments in the process of womanhood, postnatal depression was glossed over, and little was said about the isolation of mothers with small children, or the impoverishment attendant upon a single wage, or the fact that many of the women who thought they were leaving paid work for good would be back on the factory floor within a year feeling guilty about leaving their children with childminders, many of whom were of uncertain quality. The shopfloor generally supported the view that a child needed her biological mother until she was five. This, of course, reinforced the traditional view of women as home-makers and mothers, but it also emphasized the importance that the women themselves attached to motherhood and mothering and the lack of adequate childcare facilities. Some Gujarati women had mothers-in-law who cared for their children, but increasingly they have to look to childminders in the city for care. All the women were conscious that they had a crucial role in wage earning which sat uneasily with an ideology that supported stay-at-home mothers. Gujarati women were as conscious of this as their white counterparts and like them they also supported having fewer children. They were anxious to control their own fertility and the shopfloor was a valuable source of information on this.

Workers and wives

It is clear from the preceding account that ethnically diverse women came together in relation to their role in social production despite racism and the divisive nature of the labour process. In many ways the women were a militant and adventurous group who understood and used the premise that workers together are a powerful force. The solidarity of women as class members subject to the same 'proletarian condition' demonstrates the intricacies of the relationship between class, gender, and racism, but the complexities are exemplified in relation to the lives of Gujarati women.

When the world of the factory is juxtaposed with the world of the home the contradictions in the lives of South Asian women who are both workers and wives becomes increasingly apparent. Like their white counterparts they have a network of contacts which propels them towards the factory gate. Following the Uganda exodus the links between the women and the factory were often managed by a series of male brokers, a situation documented for other migrant groups in cities through Britain. Now, brothers and husbands come to collect their sisters and wives and the wages they have earned during the week. Most men regard the factory and women's work within it in an instrumental way (apart from their qualms about the corrupting influence of the factory). Women are viewed not only as wives and mothers but also as wage earners who can contribute towards the household budget and to family projects like business ventures. This is a very important understanding because it views waged work for women as an extension of familial roles, *not* as a source of independence for women. Although the outcomes are clearly contradictory, women's earnings are a crucial factor in the material underpinning for entrepreneurial ventures undertaken by men, that may then require a further commitment from women in terms of a move away from factory work and into the family business. These processes are crucial to the reproduction of the petit bourgeois ideologies which characterize the communities of which Gujarati women are a part. Consequently, women are reproducing both petit bourgeois ideologies and relations while they are economically and ideologically centrally placed in the working class.

The very large numbers of Gujarati women currently employed in factories in Needletown constitute a section of the community who, because of their class position, share only some part of the petit bourgeois ideologies that they help to sustain. Despite the fact that many of the women were married to men in manual work in other industries or in the hosiery industry, the commitment within Gujarati culture to entrepreneurship is very strong.[14] Trade, profit, self-employment, and business acumen are all important features of an ideology that is central to the way in which Gujarati men, especially, conceive of themselves. This is not just an observation made during the course of my fieldwork. Tambs Lyche, in his study of the London Patidar, presented a number of accounts of situations where the commercial ethic was being reproduced through the relations of men. These accounts suggest that 'masculinity' was socially constructed in relation to enterprise, trade, profit, and abilities in the world of business (Tambs Lyche 1982). Enterprises are often termed 'family businesses', invoking both a familial ideology and its practices in terms of commanding resources held within the family. In fact, the enterprises that mark Gujarati communities in Britain are clearly bound to men and male strategies in relation to the household, and women may have no part in the decision making surrounding business and commercial ventures (see Annie Phizacklea's and Parminder Bhachu's papers in this volume), although women take great pride in the family enterprises, referring to 'our shop' or 'our business' in ways that express their commitment.

The important interplay between working class women and petit bourgeois ideologies shows that the ideological moment has a relative autonomy which allows it to act in relation to the economic. But the ideology does not exist of and by itself, it has a material base. There are plenty of examples of entrepreneurship and business acumen, some of them on a large scale, that support the vision of the community it holds up to itself. But, as the so-called 'myth of the Melton Road' has made clear, many businesses are often small-scale enterprises existing at the margins and serving local needs.[15] The corner shop, for example, stays open long hours as a way of generating sufficient income and it may well be underpinned by the wage labour of other household members (rather than labour power). As I have pointed out this may be women's wages from factory work. Some of the women in the factory were married to men who were shopkeepers; some of them were successful like the saree shop owner, the video shop owner, or the estate agent. One woman was married to an Indian-trained doctor who was trying to gain access to posts in the National Health Service, another was married to the a production manager. In none of these cases were their husbands viewed as sympathetic to trade unionism or shopfloor collectivism by the women, and men who were manual workers often hoped that they would be able to start a business with assistance from family members who were usually brothers, fathers, or uncles (see Miles 1982: 181).

The discussion, thus far, shows the ways in which the factory amplified the gender divisions in the lives of Gujarati men and women discussed by Maureen Michaelson and implied in so much of the research (see Michaelson 1983: 185–94). The men, as I pointed out, are fearful of the corrupting influence of factory life on their wives and daughters. 'Factory girls' have always had a bad press, have been accused of 'loose' morals, or crude language and an unhealthy interest in sex and bawdy jokes. It is also the case, as the paper has shown, that through the culture they develop women in factories come to know something of their own strength and power. The life of the shopfloor is a major factor in this and in the dislike of factory work expressed by the husbands, fathers, and brothers of the women I knew. If the men had known more of the working lives of the women they would have been able to see the contradictions exposed by shopfloor culture. Although it offered women a vision of strength and solidarity, the potent symbols of the bride and the mother were at the centre of shopfloor celebrations. The roles they celebrated were constructed in relation to the world of reproduction in the household and the family and they idealized a womanhood that was securely tied to domesticity. The idealization of the bride (or the mother) meant that the symbol could be abstracted from the concrete historical and cultural context and offered as a unifying experience for all women, thereby generating sympathy and solidarity among culturally diverse women.

Becoming a bride is, however, a culturally specific process for Gujarati women and one that many of the young women felt strongly about. Although many of the younger women would have preferred more control over whom they married, and thereby the type of household in which they lived, most of them were involved in arranged marriages. The processes involved emphasized the importance of caste endogamy in the Gujarati communities and the subordination of daughters within the power structure of the family. It is not the object of this paper to discuss in detail either the ritual processes surrounding marriage or the role of arranged marriages in caste endogamy. But it is important to reiterate the point made by H.S. Morris that 'Gujarat is pre-eminently a land of castes, and in no other part of India are the divisions so minute' (see Michaelson 1983; Pocock 1972; Morris 1968: 45; Lannoy 1971). The importance of maintaining caste distinctions is juxtaposed with the importance of increasing status through hypergamy and the process of marrying daughters upwards. The complex interactions involved bring together the worlds of status, marriage, and money through the importance of the dowry, despite its having been outlawed in India. The Patidar are famous for their involvement in these processes, for their dowries and elaborate weddings. Pocock's study showed the size dowries had reached in the 1950s and Amrit Wilson suggests that wealth generated in East Africa contributed to the rise in the size of dowries (Pocock 1972; Wilson 1978: 11–12). Alongside the importance of dowry has been the maintenance of the marriage circles – particular villages that exchanged brides which brought some of them to Britain, or, alternatively, generated husbands for young women already here. Changes in the immigration rules have constrained the viability of the marriage circles. For young women coming to Britain, or for some British Asians, the issue of dowry has become enmeshed with the notion of the bride as a wage labourer capable of realizing wages through the exchange of labour power in the market. Consequently, becoming a wife and becoming a paid worker may happen simultaneously.

To return to the life of the factory, it was clear that Gujarati women could connect with the symbolism of the shopfloor and with the romance that surrounded the bride and the mother. It is also clear that, like their white counterparts, they understood some part of the contradictions that lay behind the romance. Marriage brings together the ideologies that surround and underpin the family and the economic relations sustained by the household. Consequently, marriage is crucially bound to the material circumstances of women's lives. As daughters women live in the family unit and are expected to remain there until they marry, but if they wanted to live away from home they would find it very difficult because they do not have the economic means to do so. Women, black and white, do not earn living wages. In order to leave the parental home, therefore, they are bound to join with a male wage and thereby create the opportunity to control a domestic domain of their own. Gujarati women wanted to live with their husbands as a couple and not with their parents-in-law, for the freedom it offered and the fact that the burden of domestic work in a large household is enormous. This in no way signalled a diminished commitment to family. Marriage looks, in this setting, not like a constraint on women but like a freedom, and this view was reinforced by the status it offered young women and the potential access to power and resources controlled by men. For young white women marriage meant the possibility of council housing, a possibility enhanced by a baby. Gujarati women are much less likely to live in public housing, but it is a growing phenomenon among poorer sections of the community and there were a number of women in the department living on estates close to the main South Asian areas of the city. Most of the women lived in terraced houses in a lively inner-city area. These houses were a major form of property held within the family nexus. The rights that women had to this property were bound to the position that they occupied within the family. They had access to housing and, therefore, possession *as wives*, but rarely did they claim or exercise rights as women.

If Gujarati women could connect with the powerful symbol of the bride generated within white working-class culture they could also share the experience of being a wife within a socioeconomic system which imposes the major burden of reproductive tasks on women, as domestic labourers, in the home. Gujarati women had the same burden of shopping, washing, cooking, cleaning, and childcare as other women on the shopfloor. Some of the younger women took on their own domestic tasks with tremendous enthusiasm and energy and complained very little, although they often cooked and cleaned for large numbers of people. Those who were not living with their parents-in-law saw this as a major freedom which allowed them to develop their own domestic scene and control it in ways that would not have been possible in a joint household. The point to be emphasized here is that Gujarati women are as much a part of the double shift as any other group of women.

The difficulties of 'fixing' and thereby reifying the household as a unit of analysis is underlined when treating the household as a single unit in terms of the generation and allocation of resources. To do so does not allow for the differential access that men and women, adults and children have to household resources, nor does it alert the analysis to the important sources of both support and conflict that exist within and beyond the household. The varieties of forms of the household in which Gujarati women lived were differentiated in relation to three major patterns: a household of parents and children; the more common pattern of a three generational household; and a joint household formed by brothers with or without parents. Household composition was not fixed, it could be fluid and grow or diminish in relation to a pattern of visiting and staying with relatives in other parts of the country. A model based on notions of a core group with a peripheral and much more fluid outer circle described the household composition of many of the families that I knew. This situation gave people access to resources in other households within an overall distributive context which was the family. However, the work of servicing the household, shifting or otherwise, remained with women, who also made a major contribution to the resource base. While women in the factory tried to negotiate the level of their effort in relation to their wages, negotiations were more difficult in the domestic sphere. Women cooked and cleaned, and men did not, and they started this work before they went to the factory and resumed when they returned home. Some were fortunate to have sisters-in-law with whom to share the burden of domestic work and others had older female relatives who guided and assisted them, especially in households where mothers-in-law were absent. Some women coped alone in an extended household where they were expected to carry the major burden of domestic work. A fiction was maintained that life continued as it would have done had the women in the household not been wage workers. In all cases the burden of work was not diminished in relation to the number of hours spent in the factory – the unpaid labour of women was appropriated by other household members. While factory work added immeasurably to the amount of work in their lives most of the younger women guarded their right to work outside the home, for the sense of independence it gave them, the good friends they made and the fun they had at work despite the production targets. I am not, however, suggesting that factory work is in any simple sense a 'liberating' experience for Gujarati women.

The reproductive work done by women as domestic labourers is matched by the importance of biological reproduction and the shopfloor echoed this in its celebration of motherhood. Again, this symbol of womanhood and the women's response to it points to the continuities and discontinuities in the lives of Gujarati women. The mother is idealized and revered in Hindu culture and in Gujarat the mother goddess, Amba Mata is one of the most popular. A woman with sons has respect and the possibility of power over a domestic domain based on the joint family. For many of the generation of women who have come to Britain this is not a real possibility and the contradictions and stresses imposed upon them and their relations with their sons, daughters, and daughters-in-law are in the process of being worked through in the cities of Britain.

Young mothers suffer the same constraints as other women – where to find adequate childcare while they are at work and how to be a 'good' mother and a worker, as Shrikala Warrier's paper has made clear. Again, the cultural moment intervenes to construct notions of motherhood and mothering and to set the specific context for Gujarati women's lives.[16] This context was reinterpreted by the health service, which, while it denied all women the power of their own bodies and kept them locked out of the processes institutionalized by the hospitals, through the medicalization of pregnancy and birth, reserved its racism for women whose cultural specificity was subjected to scrutiny and denied or abused by both ignorance and prejudice. Women try to exercize control over their fertility in the same was as they attempt to intervene in the household and family relationships, and the results of these interventions are various and subject to circumstances. It was quite clear that the combined effort of factory and domestic labour depressed women's desires for children. They were conscious of the cost and energy required to nurture two or three children and few women wanted more than this.

The patterns of family decision making and family investment strategies, whether this was educating children, buying houses, or starting a business, were the preserve of men. Many of the women felt that they were ill qualified to make decisions in these areas although their contributions were crucial to any strategy through their work both as domestic labourers and as wage earners. It is difficult to know precisely, because I asked for accounts of decisions made and was not privy to the processes that generated a decision. The male version was that women controlled the domestic sphere and all that happened within this domain, but in some cases the power attributed to women was exercized within parameters set by men. If men controlled the finances and gave women 'housekeeping' women were bound by this and allocated only those roles, in relation to money, that were involved in cash transactions and immediate consumption. The patterns varied within households. Where a husband and wife lived as a conjugal unit and pooled their income there was some discussion about major purchases and savings, but the houses that the women occupied had often been bought prior to their marriages by their husbands using family finances, so that debts were built into the marriage relationship. The division of labour over who paid the bills, etc. often followed one working-class pattern where men were in charge of public utilities and women of domestic affairs. Further along in the life-cycle of the domestic group the pattern might change and in three-generational households a mother-in-law often controlled the domestic income allocated from a pool of all family members' earnings, which younger men in the family controlled in consultation with their father (although he may have little power in reality).

Decision making and the exercise of control is also related to consumption within the domestic unit and there was a discernible pattern of joint decision-making over consumer durables and the purchase of commodities/services by married couples. Women tried, in households where their money was pooled and they had to request money for personal consumption, to find ways of keeping some of their money for their own use, or for savings of their own, e.g. using the catalogues at the factory (see Parminder Bhachu's paper for an alternative account). It could be argued that the material circumstances of Gujarati women's lives are set within the context of an entrepreneurial, petit bourgeois ideology which makes of women's wages another factor in enterprise strategies bringing together the ideological and cultural moments.

In concluding an all too brief discussion it is possible to bring elements of this together in the proposition that all women share a subordinate status and that as both workers and wives there are deep resonances which echo across their lives and are played out through shopfloor culture, in relation to their roles both in production and in reproduction. Yet, there is an intervention by the cultural moment which affects the way in which subordination is contoured and contexted and the mechanism of resistance available to women.

I am indebted to all the women whose lives are presented here and who made the research possible. I am also grateful to Ali Rattansi and Parminder Bhachu for comments on an earlier draft of this paper and to Maureen Cottrell for word processing.

Notes

1 For the debate surrounding patriarchy see, V. Beechey (1979), 'On patriarchy', *Feminist Review* **3**: 66–82. My use of patriarchy rests upon the following definition offered by Heidi Hartmann:

> We can usefully define patriarchy as a set of social relations between men, which have a material base, and which, though hierarchical, establish or create interdependence and solidarity among men that enable them to dominate women. . . .
> The material base upon which patriarchy rests lies most fundamentally in men's control over women's labour power. Men maintain this control by excluding women from access to some essential productive resources (in capitalist societies, for example, jobs that pay living wages) and by restricting women's sexuality. Monogamous heterosexual marriage is one relatively recent and efficient form that seems to allow men to control both these areas.

from Heidi Hartmann, 'The Unhappy Marriage of Marxism and Feminism', in Lydia Sargent (ed.), *Women and Revolution: A Discussion of the Unhappy Marriage of Marxism and Feminism* (Pluto Press: 1981) pp. 14–15.

2 The confusions and contradictions in the use of 'reproduction' have been discussed by Felicity Edholm, Olivia Harris, and Kate Young 'Conceptualising Women', *Critique of Anthropology* Vol. 3, No. 9–10, (1977), pp. 101–30, and by Michele Barrett, *Women's Oppression Today. Problems in Marxist Feminist Analysis* (N.L.B. 1980) pp. 19–29.

In this paper reproduction encompasses biological reproduction, the reproduction of labour power, and the area of social reproduction concerned with the induction of new members into the dominant ideologies held by the social formation. The first two forms of reproduction are most especially the preserve of women's work. Under capitalism the reproduction is secured through the wage form – but it is women's work that turns wages into goods and services in the home for consumption by the family.

3 Employment opportunities in the city and in the East Midlands more widely, have for decades revolved around a number of industries: hosiery, boot and shoe, engineering, and food production. All these industries have employed migrant labour and have historically been a source of work outside the home for women. The hosiery industry with which this paper is concerned has always employed women as semi-skilled labour. But the industry, like its sister the textile industry, is in decline and thousands of jobs have been lost in these industries and the allied footwear industry. The statistics paint a dramatic picture (I am grateful to David Ashton for supplying the following statistics):

	Clothing and footwear		*Textiles*	
	women	*men*	*women*	*men*
1970	321,000	109,000	302,000	331,000
1983	193,000	60,000	108,000	153,000

The industry and the workforce have shrunk dramatically and among those who have suffered have been many black and Asian workers employed as cheap labour in industries working on low profit margins. It now seems cheaper and easier to import goods from the free trade zone, with the consequence that South Asian women in Sri Lanka compete with South Asian women in the East Midlands for jobs.

The women in this study worked for a paternalistic company, StitchCo, which had a good reputation locally and, in terms of the hosiery, which was separated from the crudely exploitative homeworking sector or the clothing sweatshops both of which involve large numbers of South Asian women.

4 The city in which this study was conducted, Needletown, has a population of nearly 300,000 of whom an estimated 25 per cent are Asian. Since the Second World War the city has housed migrants and refugees from Poland and Eastern Europe alongside a thriving Irish community. Black migrants started to arrive in the 1950s and the black population has grown in the last decade following the arrival of the East African Asian.

5 Women working in the hosiery industry are working in an industry based on mechanized knitting and a large variety of machines make knitwear, socks, tights, and stockings. Due to the problems of mechanization the industry was slow to industrialize and move from the

home base into the factory. In the home the stockingers at the frames were men and the knitters of the present industry are also men. It is protected, skilled work which in the home was supported by the labour of women and children. When the men moved into the factories the women and children came too and became sock turners and machinists because it is not only 'hose' in all its forms which is manufactured in the industry. Today vast circular machines make jerseyknit fabric which becomes T-shirts and underwear. This cloth is not woven as it would be in the textile industry, it is knitted on the same site as socks and sweaters. Once knitted the fabric is dyed, rolled, trimmed, and cut into pattern pieces where upon it moves to the department and the machinists who are the subjects of this paper. See, Wells (1972).

6 In so far as this paper is concerned with detailing and discussing the ethnic and cultural specificities of the Gujarati population in Britain I am guided by the work of earlier writers including Pocock (1972); Morris (1968); Michaelson (1979; 1983).

7 Measured Day Work: MDW is a system where pay is fixed in relation to a specified performance. See Powell (1976) and Westwood (1984).

8 The term 'practical ideologies' is borrowed from Louis Althusser as a way of emphasizing the concrete, lived experience of ideologies rather than the abstract, theoretical level. See Althusser (1971).

9 See Hoare and G. Nowell-Smith (eds) (1971). There is also a very large secondary literature on Gramsci's work see, for example Mouffe (1979) and an introduction to his work by R. Simon (1982). Gramsci insists that 'commonsense' is a complex combination of knowledge born out of the experience of working class lives with ruling class ideas which legitimate the status quo.

10 The issue of skill is a complex one. See Braverman (1974) and a collection in response to the debate generated by Braverman, S. Wood (ed.) (1982), Phillips and Taylor (1980); Coyle 1982.

11 For a more extended discussion see Westwood (1984).

12 Concern has been expressed by certain sections of the medical profession for the health and wellbeing of South Asian mothers and their babies. See, for example, Pearson (1983).

13 See Oakley (1981) for an extended discussion and study of the management of birth among a sample of white women.

14 In writing of Gujarati culture I would not wish to present this as a simple unity – it is a complex phenomenon located both in Gujarat as a place and the Gujarati language and its transformations within the East African context. Gujarat has a major emphasis upon trade and enterprise evidenced in the position of the Vania castes and the level of entrepreneurship in Gujarat and East Africa alongside the power of Gujarat business in Bombay. Alongside is the Gandhian influence which has promoted paternalism and the coop movement in Gujarat which is very successful. It has also meant that Gujarat is dry. While the Hindu elements of Gujarati culture are emphasized especially in this paper it is important to emphasize that Gujarat has a large Muslim minority. The

130 *Enterprising Women*

religious division coexists with the urban/rural division in Gujarat itself
and in the backgrounds of the women who migrated.

15 There is, of course, an articulation to be explored among the white
working class between petit bourgeois ideologies that emphasize the
'freedom' of self-employment against the routine and control of factory
discipline. Ideologies are complex entities and I am drawing maps
rather than complete pictures of the terrain.

16 For the ceremonies and rituals surrounding pregnancy and birth among
the Patidar see Pocock 1972: 113–19 and for a more general discussion
see Lannoy 102–12.

References

Althusser, L. (1971) 'Ideology and ideological state apparatuses: notes
towards an investigation', in *Lenin and Philosophy and Other Essays*, London:
New Left Books.

Amos, V. and Parmar, P. (1981) 'Resistances and responses: the
experiences of black girls in Britain', in A. McRobbie and T. McCabe
(eds) *Feminism for Girls: an Adventure Story*, London: Routledge & Kegan
Paul.

Barrett, M. (1980) *Women's Oppression Today: Problems in Marxist Feminist
Analysis*, London: New Left Books.

Braverman, A. (1974) *Labour and Monopoly Capital: The Degradation of Work in
the Twentieth Century*: Monthly Review Press.

Brooks, D. and Singh, K. (1979) 'Pivots and presents: Asian brokers in
British foundaries', in S. Wallman (ed.) *Ethnicity at Work*, London:
Macmillan.

Coyle, A. (1982) 'Sex and skill in the organization of the clothing industry',
in J. West (ed.) *Women, Work and the Labour Market*, London: Routledge &
Kegan Paul.

Edholm, F., Harris, O., and Young, K. (1977) 'Conceptualizing women',
Critique of Anthropology 3 (9–10): 101–30.

Hakim, C. (1981) 'Job segregation: trends in the 1970s', *Employment Gazette*,
December, London: HMSO.

Hartmann, H. (1981) 'The unhappy marriage of Marxism and feminism',
in L. Sargent (ed.) *Women and Revolution: a Discussion of the Unhappy
Marriage of Marxism and Feminism*, London: Pluto Press.

Hoare, Q. and Nowell-Smith, G. (eds) (1971) *Selections from the Prison
Notebooks of Antonio Gramsci*, London: Lawrence & Wishart.

Lannoy, R. (1971) *The Speaking Tree: A Study of Indian Culture and Society*,
London: Oxford University Press.

Leonard, D. (1980) *Sex and Generation: A Study of Courtship and Weddings*,
London: Tavistock.

Michaelson, M. (1979) 'The relevance of caste among East African
Gujaratis in Britain', *New Community* 3: 350–60.

Michaelson, M. (1983) *Caste, Kinship and Marriage*.

Miles, R. (1982) *Racism and Migrant Labour*, London: Routledge & Kegan Paul.

Morris, H.S. (1968) *The Indians of Uganda*, London: Weidenfeld & Nicolson.

Mouffe, C. (1979) 'Hegemony and ideology', in C. Mouffe (ed.) *Gramsci and Marxist Theory*, London: Routledge & Kegan Paul.

—— (1983) 'Caste, kinship, and marriage: Two Gujarati trading castes in Britain', PhD Thesis, University of London.

Oakley, A. (1981) *From Here to Maternity: Becoming a Mother*, Harmondsworth: Penguin.

Pearson, M. (1983) 'A brief review of research and publications on antenatal care for ethnic minorities', Bradford: Centre for Ethnic Minority Health Studies.

Phillips, A. and Taylor, B. (1980) 'Sex and skill: notes towards a feminist economics', *Feminist Review* 6: 79–88.

Phizacklea, A. and Miles, R. (1980) *Labour and Racism*, London: Routledge & Kegan Paul.

Pocock, D.F. (1972) *Kanbi and Patidar: A Study of the Patidar Community of Gujarat*, Oxford: Clarendon Press.

Powell, J. (1976) *Work Study: How to Beat the Con*, London: Arrow Books.

Simon, R. (1982) *Gramsci's Political Thought*, London: Lawrence & Wishart.

Tambs Lyche, H. (1982) *The London Patidar*, London: Macmillan.

Wells, F.A. (1972) *The British Knitwear and Hosiery Industry: Its History and Organization*, London: Allen & Unwin.

Westwood, S. (1984) *All Day, Every Day: Factory and Family in the Making of Women's Lives*, London: Pluto.

Wilson, A. (1978) *Finding a Voice: Asian Women in Britain*, London: Virago.

Wood, S. (1982) *The Degradation of Work? Skill, Deskilling and the Labour Process*, London: Macmillan.

7 Marriage, maternity, and female economic activity: Gujarati mothers in Britain

Shrikala Warrier

Introduction

'For Asian women', writes Amrit Wilson, 'wage labour is a new experience, both baffling and exciting. Baffling because it is all so new and strange, and exciting because it brings the first hint, the first distant suggestion that for women an independent economic identity is possible' (1978). Although a large proportion of migrant-settlers come from societies where women, especially those belonging to the lower strata, have traditionally contributed in various ways to the household economy, the unreliability of employment statistics and the very concepts used to define female economic activity in their countries of origin mask the true extent of women's participation in the field of employment or of their problems and disabilities.

The customary underestimation of women's economic contributions both in and out of the labour market is largely due to the fact that many women in rural Punjab, Gujarat, Pakistan, and Bangladesh work only intermittently and often without pay. For these women, familial and economic roles are usually complementary, since both may centre around the home, family farm, or business. Economic activity in these situations is not necessarily an alternative but rather a normal and natural extension of a woman's domestic responsibilities and contributes both directly and indirectly to the maintenance and renewal of male labour power and to the creation of surplus value.

The 'labour force' concept excludes much of the informal economic activity carried out by women within the household, such as the processing or manufacturing of food items and various consumer articles for sale in markets or in the streets. The income derived from such activity supplements the wages earned by their menfolk and is often essential for the day-to-day maintenance of the household. Thus, what is novel about many Asian women's situation in Britain is the experience of working for wages outside the home in non-agrarian industrial enterprises in a society where women comprise a significant section of the labour force.

Throughout the world, women have entered the formal workforce in unprecedented numbers during the past three decades and since 1975, the International Labour Office reports that the general upward trend has become even more pronounced. In the early stages of industrialization, the wage-earning female labour force was composed mainly of single, unmarried women for whom family responsibilities were minimal. Since the Second World War, however, married women have been the fastest growing segment of the paid work force in most industrial countries.

The movement of women into the world of employment is generally associated with the postwar shift towards the service sector and the decline of many manufacturing industries. Smaller families and the tendency to complete childbearing in the early years of marriage, as well as the application of modern technology to housework to lighten some of its physical burden, are also cited as factors that have 'pulled' women into the labour force.

Outweighing these positive factors, however, is the economic need experienced by many families. This is repeatedly emphasized by a number of studies to be the most influential factor propelling married women into the workforce. While a distinction is often made between working out of financial *necessity* and the need to *improve* the family's standard of living, high inflation, the drop in real incomes, and rising male unemployment, as well as a perceived need to spread the family's risks, have led to a greater reliance on the wage-earning activities of the female members of the family.

Though women now have greater access to the job market, the range of employment opportunities open to them has remained surprisingly narrow. Throughout the world, the labour market is dichotomized into stereotypically 'masculine' and 'feminine' jobs and women's work generally follows the lines of their traditional household occupations. Thus, as the Department of Employment statistics and researchers such as Oakley (1974) Mackie and Patullo (1977), Sharpe (1984), and others point out, in the industrial sector, women are mainly employed in factories producing textiles, garments, footwear, and processed food. In the service sector, they are concentrated in childcare, clerical and secretarial work, the distributive trades, domestic and miscellaneous services such as laundries, catering, and hairdressing. The overwhelming majority of female professionals are teachers in primary and secondary schools and nurses, and in nearly every profession, the number of women in high-paying prestigious positions is insignificant.

Within this restricted field of opportunities, various research studies reveal that migrant-settler women occupy a subordinate position in the labour force and are typically confined to specific niches in the labour market. The Labour Force survey (1984) indicated that among working women aged 25–44 in Britain generally, 66 per cent of indigenous where women were economically active compared with 77 per cent of West Indian origins and 62 per cent of Indian origins.

More recent studies, such as those by Phizacklea and Miles (1980) Hoel (1982), reveal that racism is a crucial context for the lives of black and ethnic minority women in Britain. Migrant women are seen to be a cheap and flexible source of labour and they continue to be over-represented in jobs that are characterized by low pay, low status, and little opportunity for advancement. Since their menfolk tend to be located in a similarly disadvantaged position within the British workforce, the income which migrant women bring into the family often spells the difference between poverty and a fairly reasonable standard of living.

Even as women generally have been drawn into the labour market in response to a combination of both positive and negative factors, of compulsion and choice, the allocation of duties and responsibilities within the domestic sphere continue to be shaped by patriarchal notions of gender roles. Men are regarded as the 'breadwinners', while the management of the household, domestic chores, and the physical care and psychological well being of their children are firmly identified as the wife-mother's responsibility. Female preoccupation with childcare in particular is thought to have greatly structured women's position in relation to the labour market.

Whilst other papers in this book explore more generally the complex relationship between gender, race, and class, this paper addresses a more specific issue, namely the implications of racially and culturally constructed gender roles for motherhood and the more technical questions of childcare and childminding. In order to demonstrate the way in which the theoretical connections between paid work, domestic responsibilities, and childcare are actually experienced in the lives of Asian migrant-settler women in Britain, I shall be drawing extensively upon material from my study of a Gujarati community in London.[1]

The normative values attached to motherhood

Women, as Sue Sharpe (1984) notes, have a variety of experiences and responses to motherhood. Yet it is almost universally assumed that motherhood will feature prominently in a girl's future and preparation for this role tends to be the hallmark of the female socialization experience. The close identification of mothers and daughters, for which there is some suggestible anthropological evidence, implies that 'motherhood' and 'maternal role' activities are readily observable in the world about her and consequently become an essential component of a girl's gender identity.

While the structure of a woman's body determines her childbearing function, psychoanalytic theory sees maternity as the keynote of feminine psychosexual development (Lidz 1968; Lundberg and Farnham 1947). The whole weight of sex-role training and interaction from childhood onwards creates in women the expectation that childbearing and childrearing are the areas in which the greatest life-satisfactions are to be found. Motherhood thus becomes a major life-goal and women's role in childcare and reproduction provides the basis for their power and sense of personal value.

The significance of motherhood must be seen in the broader context of its societal importance. In every society, the renewal of the species is a primary requirement and the main function of a stabilized marriage union, according to traditional anthropological theory, is to provide a secure setting for procreation. Many marriage ceremonies, as Westermarck (1926) wrote, are practised with a view to making the bride fruitful or the mother of male offspring, and in almost every society, conception, pregnancy, and childbirth are surrounded by complex ritual observances to ensure a safe and satisfactory outcome.

Within the patricentred Hindu family system, for instance, the position of women is founded in their maternity. Brides enter patrilocal households as strangers and legitimize their place through the birth of children. Sons are especially valued since they not only guarantee the continuation of the generations but also assure the mother social dignity and status and the promise of considerable power in the later stages of her life-cycle.

Whilst motherhood confers status and secures a women's place within her conjugal household, the obverse is equally true. Terms such as 'barren' and 'childless' have been used to negate the very essence of femininity and the inability to bear children was recognized by the ancient law givers as valid grounds for the supersession of the wife. Though attitudes may be less extreme today and higher education and the rising aspirations of women may lead to a postponement of motherhood, the desire to have children is a positive and enduring one and for most women bearing and rearing children continue to be the most satisfying experience of their lives (Rao 1965; Mahajan 1966; Goldstein 1972).

The renewal of the species is unquestionably the fundamental requirement of all human societies. Nevertheless, any culture's continued viability also depends upon properly socialized individuals. In view of their prolonged period of immaturity and dependence the human young require constant care and supervision and the mother is generally regarded as the ideal person for this task. Nurturing and rearing children and producing well-adjusted individuals is seen to be a natural extension of the bond established between mother and offspring at birth. Mothers who choose to work instead of caring for their children on a full-time basis are thus perceived to be sabotaging their children's chances for a happy and normal life.

The twin beliefs that all women need to be mothers and that all children need their mothers have, as Ann Oakley (1974) points out, combined effectively to confirm that a woman's 'rightful' place is at home. It is therefore not surprising that women's labour force participation has usually been characterized by two peaks: one in the early years before childbearing and one after the youngest child has become self-sufficient. Exceptions to this general pattern tend to be either professionally qualified women who are committed to a career (Rapoport and Rapoport 1976) immigrant women, single parents, and other hardship cases of severe economic necessity (Hunt 1968; Runnymede Trust Census Project 1973; General Household Survey 1976; Mackie and Patullo 1977; Brown 1984).

With the rising levels of male unemployment and the deepening recession, the extension of women's economic functions from resource management in the household to resource procurement has been taken almost for granted. However, the responsibility for childcare remains a highly emotional and polarizing issue and one which dominates most working mothers' lives, influencing their patterns of employment and the strategies they pursue in attempting to deal with the logistical problems of managing childcare, their households, and their jobs. The rest of this paper will therefore look at the various childcare options available to economically active Asian women and the factors that influence their choice of particular arrangements at different stages of their children's lives. The data that informs this discussion is based on research carried out between 1980–85, in a Gujarati community in north-west London. Fifty families belonging to the Prajapati (potter) caste were interviewed in depth with a view to understanding the impact of changes in women's roles as a result of migration on the structure of family roles and sociability networks. The families in the sample were from East Africa and when fieldwork commenced in mid-1980, had been resident in Britain for nearly a decade. The majority tended to see their stay in Britain as being more or less permanent, at least in the foreseeable future.

'Working mothers'

Of the fifty married women in the sample, thirty-nine (i.e. 78 per cent) were employed at the time of the field investigation and all but five of them had children. The majority of working mothers (87 per cent) were in full-time employment (i.e. thirty or more hours a week were worked) and only two of the women had worked before coming to Britain.

The research findings appeared to be more or less consistent with the general trend noted for black and South Asian women in Britain. As Table 7.1 indicates, the overwhelming majority of the working women in the sample (74 per cent) were between the ages of 25 and 40, i.e., during the active motherhood period, with roughly one third of the sample falling within the 35–39-year age group. In the higher age groups the proportion of employed women in the sample showed a tendency to decline and very few women beyond the age of forty-eight were employed.

Table 7.1 *Age distribution of working women sample*

age	number of employed married women	%
20–24	5	13
25–29	8	21
30–34	4	10
35–39	13	33
40–44	4	10
45–49	5	13
N =	39	100

Of the thirty women in full-time or part-time employment, nine had worked for a period of 5 to 7 years; sixteen had worked for 4 to 5 years; ten had worked for 2 to 3 years, and of the remaining four, one had worked for less than six months at the time of being interviewed. Less than 30 per cent of the sample, however, had been in continuous regular employment.

The pattern of female economic activity suggests that women tend, on the whole, to enter and re-enter the labour force according to the stages in their family formation and their own life-cycle. Thus, four out of the nine women in the 40–49-year age group who had been in continuous regular employment, had started working only after their youngest child had attained self-sufficiency. In seven other cases, living in a joint family household had made it possible for the women to remain at work during pregnancy and the infancy of their children.

The nature of women's work: sectoral distribution

With the exception of one professionally qualified woman who was self-employed, the women in the sample appeared for the most part to be confined to a limited range of jobs in the 'feminized' sector of the economy. As Table 7.2 indicates, over half the number of women working outside the home were employed in manufacturing industries. Eleven women were employed in the service sector and three women helped in the family business. One woman who had been a self-employed seamstress in Kenya did outwork intermittently since coming to Britain.

Table 7.2 *The sectoral distribution of working women*

sector of employment	numbers employed
professional	1
family business	3
manufacturing	23
service	11
outworker	1
N =	39

Office work carried relatively greater prestige and was generally preferred by the younger women in the sample, i.e. those in the 20–30-year age group, who also tended to have some of the social and linguistic skills of the indigenous population. Office workers also had higher educational qualifications than the rest of the sample. One woman who had worked as a teacher in East Africa, was unable to get a similar job in London and had therefore taken up clerical work instead. Another woman who was employed as a shop assistant at the time of the interview expressed the intention of joining a government-sponsored training course (TOPS course) in order to pick up some office skills.

The older women in the sample who had no previous vocational training or experience, proportionately lower educational qualifications, and relatively less fluency in the use of the English language, were mainly employed as machinists and in more menial jobs in the service sector. Without exception, however, these women hoped that their daughters and daughters-in-law would secure white collar work in offices.

The tendency among women workers to slide from one industry to another at different points in their working lives is revealed in both government statistics and in the work of other researchers (Thompson and Finlayson 1963; Mackie and Patullo 1977). Of the twenty-eight women in the present sample whose employment patterns appeared to be punctuated by spells of economic inactivity, six returned each time to their previous place of employment; seventeen returned to the same sector of employment but in a different place each time, and five tended to take any job that was available at the time and which fitted in with their family commitments. The professional woman, who also fell into this category of intermittent employment, always returned to her profession, although the hours worked tended to vary at different periods in the family life-cycle.

A comparison of the husband's and wife's occupations revealed that in approximately 18 per cent of cases, there was a high level of consistency. Of this category, one was the professionally qualified woman, whose husband was also a professional; three women worked in the family business; two were office workers whose husbands were similarly employed, and in one case, both husband and wife were semi-skilled workers in the manufacturing sector. In all other cases, wives in the sample tended to be in jobs of lower status and earned less than their husbands. Not only did the occupational prestige of the male head of household determine the status of the entire family, but nearly every woman in the sample tended to see the husband as the principal 'provider' and his job or career as being more important than her own.

The majority of women in the sample gave economic reasons for working. However the research findings suggested that the emphasis placed upon financial necessity has undergone significant reduction over the years. Of the twenty-two women in the 35–50-year age group, seventeen pointed out that in the early 1970s, East African Asian women had been propelled into the labour market out of dire economic necessity. Most families arrived from Uganda with only £50 in their pockets and had been forced to seek help from relatives who had arrived earlier and who were already settled. However, as the refugees were anxious to achieve self-sufficiency in the shortest possible time, women were drafted into the workforce. Ten years later, when the present study was carried out, most families in the sample were on a more secure financial basis, although most couples continued to feel the necessity for two incomes to support a home. Over 60 per cent of the women in the sample made a clear distinction between working out of financial necessity and the fact that they worked in order to *improve* the family's standard of living. The wife's income was generally considered to be 'supplementary' to that earned by the husband and in about 72 per cent of cases, a part of the income earned by her was kept aside as savings or spent on expensive consumer durables. Seven women who were working in order to purchase a house were all, at the time of the interview, living in joint family households. (The houses were owned by the husband's father or were the joint property of brothers.) In all these cases, the woman's earnings were not 'pooled' into the family's common fund but were kept separately as part of the couple's savings.

Although the need to earn money appeared to be the most influential factor in the decision to go out to work, over 50 per cent of the sample indicated other reasons as well. The most frequently expressed non-financial reason was what may broadly be termed a 'social' one, i.e. the need to escape from boredom and loneliness at home. It is significant that in the case of two women in the 40–50-year age group, this factor appeared to be even more important than the economic reasons. Both women had grown-up children, i.e. the youngest child was above the age of twelve, and in one case, a married son and his wife were also living in the same household. At the time of the interviews, the women had been working for about five years. One of them was employed as a packer in a factory manufacturing garments; the other was employed as a machinist in a clothing factory. Although both women said they found it hard at times to go out in the cold and rain to a job that was not intrinsically interesting, nevertheless, the alternative of staying at home did not appeal to either of them. These women intended to work as long as they could and both emphasized the friendships they had made at work.

Although most women had been full-time housewives in East Africa, few had experienced a sense of isolation as a strong and effective social network operated amongst the women, which frequently cut across the boundaries of caste and kin. Neighbours tended to be part of the effective social network and several women in the sample mentioned the practice of a group of neighbourhood women (often unrelated) getting together to cook special dishes, and to exchange news and gossip. The tedium of the working day was also punctuated by the return of husbands and children at lunchtime so that, on the whole, the total number of hours a woman spent on her own during a working day was limited to about five, and for much of that time she would be occupied with domestic chores. Eight women who had lived in joint family households in East Africa pointed out that the problem of loneliness had never existed for them there.

In Britain, on the other hand, the separation of households and the distances separating friends and close relatives, prevented women from meeting during the day when housewives usually have more time and relatively greater control over domestic space. The cold climate, moreover, tended to restrict the mobility of women, especially since the majority did not have independent means of transport. (Only four women in the entire sample of fifty had the use of a car.) Women who stayed at home under such circumstances generally found it very lonely, depressing, and isolating.

Housework itself has been reorganized since the women have come to Britain. Most women reported doing routine chores like cleaning the house only once or twice a week and much of the physical burden of housework has been lightened by modern technology. Nevertheless, as Ann Oakley (1976) and several others have pointed out, the net effect of household technology on women's domestic workloads is rather difficult to gauge. Despite having washing machines, vacuum cleaners, and other appliances to improve their productivity, over 80 per cent of married women in the sample continued to put in several hours in the household every evening after returning from work and on weekends. Although most women found it tiring to cope with housework at the end of the working day, over 60 per cent said they would have found it equally difficult to spend their time at home during the day. In short, although housework is still regarded as a chore and primarily a woman's responsibility, the need to get away from the loneliness and isolation of the home had tilted the balance in the favour of paid employment outside the home. Few women in the sample, however, regarded paid work as a liberating experience and the income they earned was in most cases utilized for the benefit of their husbands and children.

Working mothers: arrangements for childcare

The thirty-nine working women in the sample were by no means a homogeneous group. Their needs, aspirations, and values tended to differ, as did the nature of the work they did, the period and hours they worked and the ways in which their earnings were utilized. Though the decision to go out to work in each case was influenced by a unique combination of economic, social, and personal reasons, the data on the whole suggested that factors such as household size and structure had a considerable impact on female economic activity patterns. It is to the analysis of this crucial common denominator that I now turn.

Of the thirty-nine married women in the sample, all except five had children. Fifty-six per cent of the women had small families, i.e. one or two children. Twenty-three women had at least one child below the age of twelve and of these there were nine cases where the youngest child was of pre-school age (see Table 7.3). The issue of suitable childcare arrangements was thus highly pertinent to the majority of women in the sample.

Table 7.3 *Labour force participation according to age of youngest child and household structure*

		household type	
age of youngest child	*number of working mothers*	*joint*	*nuclear*
pre-school	9 (26%)	7	2
5–12 years	14 (41%)	—	14
12 years and over	11 (32%)	4	7
N =	34	11	23

The findings from a number of studies suggest that employed mothers, irrespective of their ethnic affiliations, find themselves caught between two pressures: on the one hand is the perceived need for more than one income to support a home, and on the other, the pressing logistical problems of fulfilling work-role obligations as well as domestic responsibilities, including childcare (Rapoport, Rapoport, and Bumstead 1974; Saifullah Khan 1979; Oakley 1982; Gowler and Legge 1982; Sharpe 1984; Westwood 1984). Though in most cases the income earned by a wife is a valued contribution to the total financial resources of a family, her employment outside the home is accepted only as long as it does not interfere with her culturally defined responsibility for the management of the household and care of her children and husband. Women who go out to work are thus faced with the major problem of finding suitable alternative childminding facilities.

The extreme paucity of childcare facilities for employed mothers in Britain has been well documented in a number of studies. 'Local authorities', write Mackie and Patullo (1977), 'vary considerably in their commitment to the provision of pre-school care', and the findings of researchers like Simpson (1978); Freeman (1982) and Sharpe (1984) indicate that the issue of providing suitable care for school-age children in the interval between the end of the school day and the return of a parent from work, and during school holidays, had been completely ignored by the DHSS, educational authorities, and employers.

Surveys such as those undertaken by the Community Relations Commission (1975) reveal that ethnic minority women experience greater difficulties in gaining access to the day-care provision they desire, despite the fact that such families are over-represented in the low-income category and mothers with pre-school children are more likely to be at work than indigeneous women. Caught between the pressures of having to earn an income in order to support a home, their culturally defined responsibilities for caring for their children, and the oppressive force of institutional racism which denies them access to suitable childminding provisions, such women are forced to create their own 'informal' childcare arrangements.

Data from the present study suggested that the twenty-three mothers who had at least one child below the age of twelve had resorted to a wide variety of childcare arrangements. All these women when interviewed appeared to be satisfied with the arrangements they had and several pointed out that had they been unable to make suitable provision for the care of their children, they would not have gone out to work.

The preferred alternative in most cases was to leave pre-school children in the care of grandmothers and for the seven women who lived in joint family households this was easily accomplished. However, in the case of the two women in this sub-sample who lived in nuclear households, such a facility was not readily available, and the mothers worked only part-time. One of these women was the self-employed professional whose work schedule dovetailed with that of her husband, so that she was free to work in the evenings when her husband was at home with the children.

Part-time work was also preferred by three other women in the sample whose youngest child was below the age of twelve. Of these, one lived in a joint family household but was unable to work full-time, as her mother-in-law's health prevented her from taking care of the children, who ranged from pre-school to school-going age.

In the majority of cases, women with younger children in the age range 6–12 were able to work full-time, even though they were living in nuclear households, because the younger children could be left in the care of older siblings when they returned from school and during school holidays. Eight women in this sub-sample generally took their annual holidays during the school summer holidays so that they could be at home with their children during part of this period.

No specific arrangements for childminding were made by mothers of children aged ten and above. In all these cases the mothers worked full-time and had resorted to a 'latch-key' pattern.

Leaving children in the care of relatives other than grandparents who lived in the same household was not a favoured course of action for the majority of women in the sample. Working mothers who lived in nuclear households generally left younger children in the care of older ones or preferred not to work if this was not possible. There were only three cases in the sample where relatives other than grandparents had helped with childminding. All three women lived in joint family households and the caretaking relative in two cases was a temporary substitute.

None of the women in the sample had ever used the services of registered child-minders, state-run or private nurseries, day-care centres, or crèches. However, there were two women who relied on a neighbour to help with the care of a school-going child. The arrangement did not involve the exchange of money but as the description below indicates, covered a range of mutual-aid activities.

Case 1

At the time of the interview Mr and Mrs PM and their six-year-old daughter had only recently moved from his parents' house to a home of their own. In order to help with the mortgage repayments, Mrs PM had decided to take up paid work, but the care of the little girl was a major issue for which a solution had to be found. Initially, the couple had decided that Mrs PM should only work part-time, but the difficulties in finding suitable work, which fitted in with school hours, forced her to take up a full-time job.

The couple could not afford to hire a babysitter nor could they depend upon Mr PM's parents as the latter lived at a considerable distance. They had to rely upon an English neighbour, whose child went to the same school, to look after their daughter in the period between the end of the school day and Mrs PM's return from work at 5 pm.

During most school holidays the child stayed with the

neighbour all day, although Mrs PM planned to take her annual leave during the school summer break so that she could be at home with her child.

In return for the neighbour's services, Mrs PM would babysit whenever the former wished to go out in the evenings with her husband. Reciprocity also took the form of expensive gifts on the occasion of birthdays and at Christmas. The PMs also looked after the neighbour's cat when the family went on holiday.

Despite the idealization of women's maternal role, as Dally points out (1982), motherhood for working women today has become full of uncertainty and paradox, fraught with dilemmas at all stages. The uneasy balance between the costs and benefits of paid employment becomes particularly apparent in critical situations such as when children fall ill. All but one woman in the sample had actually experienced such a situation and the interview responses suggested that it was usually dealt with in the traditional mode, ie. the mother, as the parent responsible for the child's wellbeing, would take time off from work when the child fell ill.

Women who lived in joint family households generally relied upon their mothers-in-law if the child's illness was not of a serious nature. There was only one woman in this category who *always* took time off from work on such occasions, since she believed very strongly that it was her responsibility to look after a sick child. 'It's very worrying – going out to work when children don't feel well . . . I know my mother-in-law will look after my children . . . Still it's not the same . . . I mean, I'm the mother, it's my responsibility, isn't it? You can't expect other people to look after your children in the same way.' Children above the age of twelve were usually expected to take care of themselves in the case of minor ailments, such as colds and 'flu. But in every case, the mother had arranged for leave of absence when the illness had been more serious.

The firm identification of infant and childcare as part of the mother's responsibility became quite clear when the case of the full-time housewives was considered. In a society where the workplace is physically separate from the home, childcare appeared to acquire a concrete opportunity cost which had to be evaluated in terms of the total familial, social, and economic circumstances of the parents. When confronted with the choice between maternity and withdrawal from the labour force, it appeared that many women in the sample chose the latter, especially if young children, i.e. those below the age of twelve, were involved, and if the support of elderly female relatives such as a mother-in-law could not be counted upon.

Characteristics of 'non-working mothers'

Of the total sample of fifty women, there were eleven who were not in paid employment at the time of the interviews. All of them had children and in approximately half of the cases the youngest child was of pre-school age. Four women had at least one child in the 6–12-year age group.

The only woman in the sample who had no child below the age of 12, was between 45–49 years of age and considered herself to be too old to find a job. Table 7.4 shows the age-distribution of the 'housewife' sample.

Table 7.4 *Age distribution of the housewives*

age range	numbers	%
20–24	1	9
25–29	3	27
30–34	4	36
35–39	1	9
40–44	1	9
45–49	1	9
N =	11	99

Four of the women lived in joint family households and of them, two had worked before the birth of their youngest child. In both cases, the mother-in-law's ill-health made it difficult for them to resume their employment immediately after the birth of the youngest child. Both women, however, intended to take up paid employment when the child reached school-going age.

Another woman who lived in a joint family household, and who had never been employed, did not take up paid employment but had, instead, offered to look after her husband's brother's children so that his wife could retain her well paid job. Of the seven women living in nuclear households, four had at least one pre-school child. Two of these women had stopped working when their youngest child was born. The inability to make suitable provision for childcare was a major factor hindering their re-entry into the labour force.

None of the eleven women in the sample disapproved of women working but they all believed that mothers of pre-school children should go out to work only if the family was facing acute financial crisis. None of these women approved of leaving their children with childminders, as they felt that such people could not be trusted to take 'proper' care of the child, besides being very expensive. In every case, the husbands also disapproved of leaving pre-school children with professional childminders. There was only one woman in the sample who had no desire to work, although her youngest child was of school-going age. This woman, the mother of three children, aged from 6–13, had worked for several years when both her older children were of pre-school age. However, after the birth of the youngest child the family's financial situation had become more secure, which made it unnecessary for her to continue working. This woman also believed quite firmly that the employment of mothers is incompatible with satisfactory family life and with the healthy emotional development of children.

'I think my place is at home with my children . . . I couldn't help it (going to work, I mean) when the older two were small – I mean, we needed the money you see . . . But I felt it was wrong not to be at home when they came back from school. Now we don't need the money so much . . . If you have children, you must spend time with them.'

Of the seven women living in nuclear households, there were two mothers of pre-school children who intended to work once the child reached school-going age. One of them, who had worked until the birth of the youngest child, was keen to return to work because she found her housebound existence extremely isolating and very depressing. Two other women in the sample, both living in nuclear households and mothers of school-going children, intended to take up employment if they could find a part-time job that coincided with school hours. One of these women pointed out in the interview that her husband had been against her working when the children were younger, but when the youngest had also reached school-going age, he was 'less opposed' to her intentions of taking up employment.

The process of decision-making

The evidence from the study suggested very clearly that a woman's decision to go out to work or to stay at home depended upon the complex interplay of several factors, including the particular stage in the family's life-cycle, the economic circumstances of the family, the composition of the domestic group, and personal, idiosyncratic factors.

In every case, the issue of the wife's employment had been decided jointly by the husband and wife. The question of acceptable childcare arrangements appeared to be of equal concern to both parents and in the overwhelming majority of cases, husbands believed that the wife's job should not interfere with her maternal role-responsibilities. Thus, in four cases, the wife's decision to work only part-time had been greatly influenced by her husband and in the case of two full-time housewives, the husband's disapproval prevented the wife from seeking employment.

Significantly, more husbands than wives in the sample believed that female economic activity could generate strains in the marital relationship. However, none of the twenty-seven husbands in the sample who lived in nuclear households believed that their own roles as 'breadwinners' and the head of the family were in any way threatened by their wives working. Although the extra income was useful, it was only 'supplementary' to that earned by the man and except for one case (where the wife was professionally qualified), the men usually tended to see their wives' employment as a short-term arrangement.

The case of the professionally qualified woman was exceptional in that her husband both supported her career and assumed considerable responsibility for childcare.

Couples who lived in joint family households generally consulted other members, such as the husband's parents or brothers, before deciding whether the wife should go out to work or not. Seven women who worked could only do so because their mothers-in-law, or a female relative in the same household, were willing to help with the care of pre-school children. When such assistance was not forthcoming, the wife generally stayed at home.

Concluding discussion

The women in the sample were in no way exceptional and as such represented the paradigmatic situation of all Asian women for whom the opportunity to work and earn a regular wage has been one of the most significant aspects of the migration to Britain. The primary reasons given for seeking work outside the home were economic; however, the reason did not appear to remain unchanged and static in any individual case. Family circumstances and needs changed over time and these had considerable bearing upon women's motivations to enter the labour force, the hours they worked, and the ways in which the income they earned was utilized.

The evidence from this study and others suggests that the search for paid work is largely prompted by economic considerations. Asian women work primarily in order to supplement the incomes earned by their husbands and, in most cases, they enter the workforce at a stage in the family life-cycle when domestic responsibilities and expenses are at their heaviest. On the other hand, women in the older age-groups, i.e. in the 45 + age-group, who in most cases also have grown-up children who are themselves contributing to the family's financial resources, work not only because a job brings in an additional income, but also because it 'helps to pass the time'.

The research findings make it possible to draw certain conclusions of general interest about the relationship between female economic activity rates, maternity, and household structure. A detailed analysis of the working women sample revealed that while it is now customary for married women of all ages to work, entry into the labour force and resumption of paid employment are influenced to a considerable extent by the number and age of dependent children and the availability of traditional support structures. Thus, most mothers of pre-school children in the sample were able to work because they lived in joint family households and the children could be left in the care of grandmothers. On the other hand, women with at least one child below the age of 10 were less likely to work full-time if they lived in nuclear households and if there were no older children in the family who could be trusted to look after younger siblings.

The phenomenal increase in the number of Asian women working to support their families has prompted a number of social scientists to conclude that this pattern of female economic activity is likely to lead to fundamental reformulations of the traditional reciprocities built into the structure of relationships in Asian families.

Thus, Michael Banton (1979) writes:

> Asian groups enter Britain with a distinctive culture and mode of organization that makes it possible for them to organize as groups and compete more effectively with members of the majority in the economic sphere. Part of their strength derives from structures of group property rights which confer power on the senior generations by enabling them to control the marriages of their juniors.
>
> In Britain, this power is greatly weakened; new opportunities are open to the women, which they seize, and as an unintended consequence, gender roles change.

The threat posed by the widespread availability of wage work for women to the structure of patriarchal authority, is also emphasized by both Dhanjal (1976) and Ballard (1982).

From the data gathered in the course of this investigation it was evident that although many men in the sample were ambivalent about their wives working, the majority perceived a real need for the additional income which could be converted into tangible, material benefits for the entire family. Few women in the sample, however, regarded paid work as a liberating experience. Working and contributing to the total financial resources of the family, moreover, had not diminished the mothers' ultimate responsibility for childcare.

Before drawing any conclusions about the net impact of female wage earning upon gender-role structuring within migrant families, it is necessary to take account of the perceived importance of the wage-earning role in relation to the traditional wife-mother role of women, the criteria used (by both men and women) to evaluate female contributions to the financial status of the family and the degree of control exercised by women over the incomes they earn. Moreover, as Sallie Westwood (1984) has argued, any analysis of the impact of female economic activity upon the structure of the family and on women's status must also take account of the intervention by the cultural moment to construct notions of 'proper' wifely conduct and mothering and the specific socioeconomic and political structures within which Asian women are obliged to sell their labour power.

Note

1 The research findings on which this paper is based are elaborated in my unpublished PhD thesis, 'Family roles and sociability networks in a Gujarati community in London, with special reference to changes in women's roles' (University of London, 1986).

References

Ballard, R. (1982) South Asian families. In Rapoport *et al.* (eds) *Families in Britain*, London: Routledge & Kegan Paul.

Banton, M. (1979) 'Gender roles and ethnic relations', *New Community* **7** (3): 323–32.

Brown, C. (1984) *Black and White Britain: The Third PSI Survey*, London: Heinemann.

Community Relations Commission (1975) *Who Minds? A Study of Working Mothers and Childminding in Ethnic Minority Communities.*

Dally, A. (1982) *Inventing Motherhood: The Consequences of an Ideal*, London: Burnett Books.

Department of Employment (1984) *The Labour Force Survey*, London: HMSO.

Dhanjal, B. (1976) 'Sikh women in Southall', *New Community* 5 (1–2): 109–14.

Freeman, C. (1982) 'The understanding employer', in J. West (ed.) *Work, Women and the Labour Market*, London: Routledge & Kegan Paul.

General Household Survey (1976), London: Office of Population Censuses and Surveys.

Goldstein, R.L. (1972) *Indian Women in Transition: A Bangalore Case Study*, New York: Scarecrow Press, Inc.

Gowler, D. and Legge, K. (1982) 'Dual worker families', in Rapoport *et al.* (eds) *Families in Britain*, London: Routledge & Kegan Paul.

Hoel, B. (1982) 'Contemporary clothing sweatshops: Asian female labour and collective organization', in J. West (ed.) *Work, Women and the Labour Market*, London: Routledge & Kegan Paul.

Hunt, A. (1968) *A Survey of Women's Employment*, Department of Employment, London: HMSO.

Lidz, T. (1968) *The Person: His Development Throughout the Life Cycle*, New York: Basic Books.

Lundberg, F. and Farnham, N. (1947) *Modern Woman: The Lost Sex*, New York: Harper & Brothers.

Mackie, L. and Patullo, P. (1977) *Women and Work*, London: Tavistock Publications.

Mahajan, A. (1966) 'Women's two roles: the study of role conflicts', *Indian Journal of Social Work*, January: 377–80.

Oakley, A. (1974) *The Sociology of Housework*, London: Martin Robertson.

—— (1976) *Housewife*, Harmondsworth: Pelican.

—— (1982) 'Conventional families', in Rapoport *et al.* (eds) *Families in Britain*, London: Routledge & Kegan Paul.

Phizacklea, A. and Miles, R. (1980) *Labour and Racism*, London: Routledge & Kegan Paul.

Rao, G. (1965) 'Emerging role patterns of women in the family', *Indian Journal of Social Work*, October 239–42.

Rapoport, R. and Rapoport, R.N. (1976) *Dual Career Families Re-examined*, London: Martin Robertson.

Rapoport, R., Rapoport R.N., and Bumstead, J. (eds) (1974) *Working Couples*, London: Routledge & Kegan Paul.

Runymede Trust (1973) Census Project.

Saifullah Khan, V. (1979) 'Migration and social stress: Mirpuris in Bradford', in V. Saifullah Khan (ed.) *Minority Families in Britain*. London: Macmillan.

Sharpe, S. (1984) *Double Identity: The Lives of Working Mothers*, Harmondsworth: Pelican.

Simpson, R. (1978) *Daycare for Schoolage Children*, Manchester: Equal Opportunities Commission.

Smith, D.J. (1977) *Racial Disadvantage: The PEP Report*, Harmondsworth: Penguin.

Thompson, B. and Finlayson, A. (1963) 'Married women who work in early motherhood', *British Journal of Sociology* 14 (2): 150–67.

Westermarck, E. (1926) *A Short History of Marriage*, London: Macmillan.

Westwood, S (1984) *All Day, Every Day: Factory and Family in the Making of Women's Lives*, London: Pluto.

8 Narrow definitions of culture: the case of early motherhood

Ann Phoenix

The 1960s restrictions on black adult workers' entry to Britain meant that a large proportion of new black migrants were the children and spouses of workers who were already resident. New migrants were permitted entry to Britain for the purposes of 'family reunification' (Phizacklea 1983), if it could be proved that the proposed entrant was economically dependent on the resident worker and could be supported by them.

These increasingly stringent immigration controls have meant that a growing proportion of black adults in Britain have either been born here or have lived most of their lives here. They are not therefore faced with the task of settling in Britain and coping with the migration process. Rather, they are black people who have been through the British education system and are familiar with a range of British cultures and institutions. For the majority of them there is no question of 'returning' to the countries in which their parents grew up. These black adults are not 'between two cultures' (Watson 1977) as has been commonly believed. Instead they are situated in their social networks as well as in the wider society, and in that sense are clearly British.

This paper argues that concentration on cultural differences between black people and white people has frequently obscured the fact that cultural beliefs, identities, and practices necessarily embody the structural forces that affect people's lives, and that culture itself is dynamic rather than static. In particular, analyses of class, race,[1] and gender are crucial to the understanding of British society and of individual behaviours, since the intersection of these structural forces serves to locate individuals in their social positions and also to produce social constructions of beliefs and identities. Much of the discussion would be equally relevant to black people of South Asian origin. However, this paper concentrates on black people of Afro-Caribbean origin because literature on early motherhood (discussed here) has focused on black women who are 'West Indian' rather than South Asian.

The first part of the paper is concerned with reasons why

simplistic views of cultural influence are inadequate for the understanding of young black women's lives. The second part uses empirical material as a way of exploring how analyses which rely on such simplistic views of culture (referred to in this paper as narrow definitions of culture) obscure the similarities between black women and white women who become pregnant before they are twenty years of age. In order to do so it focuses on the areas of paid employment and mother-daughter relationships. Particular attention is given to class, race, and gender as forces that simultaneously structure young women's lives. Although it is generally thought that race only influences black women, what it means to be 'white' can only be understood in contradistinction from what it means to be 'black'. White women's lives are thus as racially structured as black women's lives (Frankenberg, unpublished), although the effects are of course vastly different. The paper concludes that young black women and young white women become pregnant for the same sorts of reasons, and that this is because they share the same socioeconomic contexts. A more dynamic definition of culture would therefore necessarily include analyses of material factors.

Cultural influence and young black women

Young black women have rarely been the subjects of academic study. The category 'youth' has tended to be applied almost exclusively to young men, both black and white. Similarly the term 'black' has tended to be used as if it were either gender neutral or male. When 'women' have been written about it is almost exclusively white women that have been discussed, yet the term has been used as if it were colour neutral. The net effect of this is to render black women, and young black women in particular, invisible (Hooks 1982).

There are some exceptions to this omission of black women. Over the last decade black women have increasingly documented and theorized their experiences themselves (see for example Parmar 1982; Carby 1982; *Feminist Review* **17**; Hooks 1984; Bryan, Dadzie, and Scafe 1985), and the experiences of young black women (Amos and Parmar 1981). By way of contrast, white academics who have focused on young black women have tended to treat them as if they were pathological. Thus, while black women have frequently been omitted from work which has sought to gain an understanding of 'normal' women, black women have frequently been the focus of research which studies devalued groups.

Studies of 'teenage mothers' provide examples of this negative focus on young black women. These studies frequently either compare black mothers (of African descent in the USA, and of Afro-Caribbean origin in Britain) with white mothers, or concentrate only on black mothers. This focus on black women as 'teenage mothers' occurs within a context in which early motherhood is stigmatized and devalued. 'Young motherhood' has been associated with a variety of negative outcomes both for the women themselves and for their children. These poor outcomes include postnatal depression, poor educational qualifications, and 'welfare dependence' for the women and risks of perinatal mortality, child abuse, and developmental delay for their children (Scott, Field, and Robertson 1981; Butler *et al.* 1981).

The attention given to young black women as members of a devalued group, 'teenage mothers', has to be considered in the context of the routine exclusion of black women from psychological studies which explore the processes of normal child development, and hence concentrate on mother-child interactive processes. That exclusion helps constitute black women as abnormal mothers and means that they are only visible as members of stigmatized groups.

One of the few contexts in which young black women (of Afro-Caribbean origin) are explicitly discussed in this society and in the USA is thus as 'young mothers'. (Young black women of Asian origin become visible in a similar way at the point at which it is thought likely that they will experience 'arranged marriages'. See Brah and Minhas (1985) for discussion of this.) The following section will consider how young black women are socially constructed in the literature on 'teenage mothers'.

Young black women and studies of 'teenage motherhood'

In literature on 'teenage mothers' black 'teenage mothers' are presumed to be different from white 'teenage mothers'. Phipps-Yonas in a 1980 review of American literature pointed out that psychological explanations, to do, for example, with problems in individual mother-daughter relationships, tend to be advanced for the incidence of early motherhood in white, middle-class women. For black, lower-class women however, sociocultural explanations, suggesting that early motherhood occurs for 'cultural reasons', tend to be invoked. Phipps-Yonas suggested that this common approach was unjustified because there was no evidence that black teenagers and white teenagers became pregnant for different reasons or that their families were more accepting of early motherhood than white mothers.

By comparison with the USA, Britain has produced little research on early motherhood. However, the north American model of black 'teenage mothers' and white 'teeange mothers' becoming pregnant for different reasons has been reproduced in British research. Examples of these different types of explanation for early motherhood in black women and in white women are provided by two recent British studies (Skinner 1986; Ineichen 1984/5). Both these papers start by considering whether 'West Indian' cultural patterns account for there being proportionally more black mothers of Afro-Caribbean origin who are under twenty years of age than of white mothers of British origin. To do this both researchers discuss family patterns that have been observed in the Caribbean (in fact almost exclusively in Jamaica).

While Skinner states in her introduction that she found no evidence to support the hypothesis that young black women have children for cultural reasons, she nonetheless makes consistent reference to 'West Indian' family patterns as a means of explaining the behaviour of the black women in her study. Much of the material for the typologies she uses is drawn from Clarke's (1957) study done in Jamaica and Fitzherbert's (1967) work on 'West Indian family patterns'. The implicit assumptions underlying this use of work which is thirty and twenty years old respectively are twofold. They are first, that the behaviour of British people of Afro-Caribbean origin can only be understood by making reference to behaviour in Jamaica (one of many Caribbean countries). This suggests that the British context in which black people live is irrelevant to an understanding of their behaviour. The second assumption is that 'the West Indian family' is timeless and remains unchanged over decades.

Skinner herself recognizes that problems are presented by the use of an explanatory framework that is derived from work which is geographically and historically removed from the black British sample whose behaviour she is trying to explain. She says, for example:

> It would be misleading to describe early pregnancies in the UK black teenagers as being attempts to prove fertility on the grounds that similar behaviour observed in the West Indies has, in the past, been interpreted in this way.

(p. 97)

The recognition of the problematic nature of such explanations does not prevent Skinner from drawing parallels between 'Jamaica and West Indian society in the UK' (p. 99). She does so because this is the usual way of understanding black British people's behaviour in academic writing. In the absence of equally long-established alternative discourses to draw upon, she reverts to these comparisons.

This readiness to draw parallels between the behaviour of black people in the Caribbean and that of black people in Britain is further illustrated by the study done by Ineichen (1984/5). In his study Ineichen claims that:

> the contrasts between these two groups of teenagers (white and black) can best be illustrated by prefacing a consideration of their situation by quoting from recent writers . . . on attitudes to and patterns of youthful fertility in the Caribbean.
>
> (p. 52)

Ineichen then lists eight Caribbean traits which he considers particularly relevant to 'West Indian patterns' of fertility. His black British samples are discussed under the headings provided by these eight traits. The Caribbean traits he identifies (from the literature) thus provide the framework for the analysis of the behaviour of his black British sample.

The first trait on which Ineichen compares his black British sample with Caribbean women is 'frequency of teenage motherhood'. He concludes that:

> This ['teenage motherhood'] appears to be commoner among Afro-Caribbean girls. They formed one-fifth of our sample, but a much smaller proportion of the teenage population of the Bristol Health District, although precise figures are not available.
>
> (Ineichen 1984/5)

It is in fact difficult to establish whether, and if so by how much, black British rates of early motherhood exceed white ones. In the USA the rate is known to be higher among black women than among white women, but because white women are more numerous than black women in the USA, the majority of births to women in their teenage years are to white women. Unlike the USA, Britain does not produce national statistics broken down according to the mother's colour. Very few studies of early motherhood have been done in Britain, and Ineichen and Skinner have so far conducted the only research which has shown a higher rate of early pregnancy in black women than white women. Since national figures are not available, the conclusion that early motherhood is more common among black women than among white women must be a tentative one. However, Ineichen draws this conclusion from a study of only eighteen women of Afro-Caribbean origin (with Afro-Caribbean partners). Why does he feel confident on the basis of such slight evidence?

One reason is probably to do with Ineichen's belief that Caribbean patterns of fertility behaviour are likely to be reproduced in black British women of Afro-Caribbean origin. Any evidence in the correct direction, however slight, is considered to provide confirmation of this hypothesis without it being felt necessary to discuss factors such as class, which influence the incidence of early motherhood (in both black women and white women) and provide the context in which it occurs. The absence of discussion of this sort makes it necessary to question Ineichen's analytical framework and his interpretations of his data.

Problems with explanations of black British behaviour based on comparisons with the Caribbean

This emphasis on the Caribbean as providing the key to understanding young black British women's behaviour is inappropriate for the following four reasons?

1 It excludes black people from the category 'British'

A major implication of this concentration on the Caribbean is that black people of Afro-Caribbean origin are not really British. Their behaviour does not have its roots in Britain and can only be understood by reference back to the Caribbean as their place of origin.

2 It oversimplifies Caribbean cultures

The use of narrow cultural explanations implies that 'West Indian' culture is unitary and static. Class differences and urban/rural divisions in the Caribbean are not given serious consideration. Thus differences in behaviour between the peasantry (on whom much of the work which informs a narrow cultural perspective has been done) and the middle classes are not discussed. Neither are differences between islands addressed, even though they differ greatly in many ways, for example the degree of urbanization and industrialization and the relative proportions of African and Asian people who are nationals. Skinner relies on work that is thirty years old. The assumption here seems to be that lifestyles in the Caribbean are not likely to change with time. Thus the description of Caribbean culture presented is extremely simplistic. Particular elements of behaviour (such as 'pro-fertility values') are singled out as if they were definitive of Caribbean society.

3 It starts from the assumption that all black people are different from all white people

Culture only becomes a primary focus when black women's behaviour is being explained. This helps maintain the social construction of white people as the norm and black people as deviations from that norm, because it emphasizes that only black people's behaviour needs justification. However it also falsely implies that culture does not influence white people's lives as crucially as black people's. White people also have a diversity of cultural backgrounds. The focus on young black women as culturally influenced only by the Caribbean, and young white women as being acultural serves to exaggerate differences and underplay similarities.

4 It confuses colour with culture while ignoring issues of power

Work which is structured around the narrow definition of culture frequently confuses colour and culture. White people are treated as if they were culturally homogeneous and British whatever their ancestry or religion (although there is sometimes an ambivalence about the Irish!). Black people are treated as similar to other black people whose ancestry lies roughly in the same region, but not as British. It is colour not culture which is being represented in such instances (although vague notions of ancestry are included). This is done without any reference being made to the differential social and power positions which black people and white people occupy.

This issue illustrates one way in which power relations permeate social relations. In this case people from the dominant social group (white British) infer the importance of cultural influences for a subordinate social group (black people), without ever asking them how *they* perceive culture to influence them. At the same time they fail to acknowledge cultural influences on their own group's behaviour. This illustrates Freire's (1971) point that it is difficult for people in a position of political dominance to recognize how culture influences their own group's actions. Hence in studies of 'teenage mothers', culture is implicitly accepted as an important influence on young black women, but not on young white women. Class is sometimes recognized as an important influence on white people, but in these cases, white working-class people have frequently been studied (in the sociology of community) as if they were deviant in comparison with white middle-class people.

5 It oversimplifies the notion of culture
Cultures are necessarily dynamic (Saifullah Khan 1982). The culture (as shared systems of meaning) that young black adults now subscribe to has some roots in, but is not precisely that of their parents. Given that the young black women described in the above studies were either born in or have lived most of their lives in Britain, their cultural roots are likely to lie at least as much in British society as in the Caribbean (which most have never visited).

Furthermore, culture is not a discrete entity. It cannot be divorced from its socioeconomic, political, and historical contexts (Westwood 1984). Since all societies have a plurality of socioeconomic groupings it is inaccurate to describe a country as having one culture. The non-unitary nature of culture is particularly relevant for the Caribbean which is composed of dozens of countries, extends 1,500 miles, contains a variety of languages, has a varied mix of ethnic groupings, different musical traditions and cuisine. To speak of 'West Indian culture' is thus rather inaccurate. This inaccuracy is compounded by the fact that many writers generalize from observations made only in Jamaica to people from the whole of the Caribbean.

In so far as the category 'West Indian' has any cultural reality in Britain it demonstrates not only that people in the Caribbean share common histories, but also the dynamic nature of culture (in that people who have previously had very few dealings with one another can relatively quickly form a cultural synthesis). Migration to Britain has meant that structural forces of class stratification and racism force black people to dwell on their commonalities. Experiences of 'outsider' status with respect to white British people serve to unify black people of Afro-Caribbean origin.

The broader meaning of culture

Work which perpetuates the narrow definition of culture has tended to be carried out in isolation from the theoretical advances in cultural studies made for example, by those who have worked in the Centre for Contemporary Cultural Studies. Work of this kind has taken a dynamic, structural view of culture by theorizing it as lived experience, inextricably linked with race, sex, and class, and only having meaning in the context of the society in which it occurs (in this case Britain). Hence everyday features of society and of behaviour like the media, styles of dress and music, as well as what these mean to and for, the groups under study are closely examined.

In this way the notion of culture is broadened to include the idea of 'cultures of resistance', rather than being narrow versions of cultural influence. (See for example Hall and Jefferson 1976; McRobbie 1984; Centre for Contemporary Cultural Studies 1978 and 1982.) It seems likely that white children and young adults from the working classes share more cultural features with their black peers than either do with white children and young adults from the middle classes. Inner city Londons schools in which white working-class children interact with black peers allow the sharing of cultural knowledge and practices. Evidence for this is provided by the pattern of language use in such schools which tend to incorporate elements of both black Afro-Caribbean and white Cockney styles of talk (Hewitt 1986). The cultures that working-class young people share are therefore new, combining features from many groups. This does not mean that they do not also have cultural patterns and identifications that are not shared across black-white groupings, but it does mean that explanations of similar behaviour in young people (early motherhood, for example) should not automatically presume different aetiologies.

The case of early motherhood

The second part of this paper will use data from a longitudinal study, done at the Thomas Coram Research Unit, of women who were between 16 and 19 years of age when they gave birth (between 1983 and 1984).[2] Interviews done when the women were heavily pregnant will be used to illustrate how the presumption that early motherhood in black women is the result of narrowly defined cultural influences obscures the similarities between black women's and white women's reasons for becoming pregnant. It will also explore whether, as would be suggested by narrowly defined cultural explanations, relationships with mothers are different for young black women and young white women. (Because of lack of space the similarities in black women's and white women's relationships with their male partners are not addressed here.) About a quarter of the women in this study were black.

This study was originally designed to compare 'West Indian' women with white women. It quickly became evident during piloting and the early stages of data collection however, that black women and white women responded similarly to questions other than those which expressly dealt with racial discrimination. Partly for this reason it was decided to analyse the data from everyone in the study together rather than dividing the sample into a black 'West Indian' group and a white group. There were two additional reasons for analysing the sample in this way.

First, comparisons between black people and white people tend to construct white people as the norm, and black people as deviant by comparison (see discussion above) but, second, because it is difficult to satisfactorily operationalize the categories 'West Indian' and 'white' as analytical constructs. This is partly because 'West Indian' and 'white' are not equivalent terms in that one describes certain countries of origin, and is used as a shorthand for cultural heritage, while the other describes colour. It is also partly because many people do not in reality fit neatly into these categories. Most of the women in our sample (black and white) for example, were British born (as are most of their age peers), but their parents came from a variety of places, had been in Britain for varied amounts of time, and had different religions. Several respondents had parents who came from different places and/or were different colours. If racial discrimination were the subject of study, these problems would be avoided in that this would not necessitate consideration of countries of origin or cultural differences. However narrow cultural analyses cannot represent that diversity, and in addition require that some respondents be placed in groups which do not adequately represent them.

Thus while some percentages which apply to the sample as a whole are presented here, statistical analyses which divide the sample into groups according to colour are not available. Instead qualitative analyses are used to illustrate what black women and white women actually said. The aim of the analysis section is to give some indication of whether similar factors influence black women's and white women's behaviour.

Why become a mother before twenty?

Current dominant reproductive ideologies would suggest that women who are under twenty years of age should not become pregnant. This is partly because mothers are meant to be indisputably adult, and it is not clear whether or not teenage women are adult (Murcott 1980). It is also partly because marriage is expected to precede motherhood (Busfield 1974), and women who are under twenty years of age are more likely to be single than married when they give birth (63 per cent of mothers under twenty years of age who gave birth in 1985 were single: (Office of

Population Censuses and Surveys 1986)). A third reason is that parents are meant to be economically independent of the state, with mothers and children being dependent on the economic provision fathers make for them. Increasing unemployment has however meant that young people from the working classes are more likely to be reliant on state provision of money and housing than they were in the past. Young women's position as dependants is not therefore new since they have long been expected to be dependent on their male partners. However, as their dependence has been increasingly transferred from male partners to the state, mothers who are under twenty years of age have received more public attention as deviants from social norms.

Given this negative social construction it is important to attempt to understand the reasons why about 3 per cent of women in this age group have become mothers each year of this decade. If simple 'perpetuation of cultural norms' hypotheses are to be confirmed, then black women and white women should become pregnant for different reasons, with black women having more 'pro-natalist tendencies' and being more desirous of having children early in their life course (Ineichen 1984/5). However black women and white women give remarkably similar accounts of reasons for and responses to early pregnancy. The socioeconomic contexts within which they live crucially influence these reasons and responses. These contexts are largely similar for black women and white women who become mothers early in their lives in that the majority come from the working classes.

Pregnant women's orientations to motherhood at the point of conception are usually treated as if they were bipolar. Either they were 'trying' to become pregnant, that is they intended to conceive, or they became pregnant accidentally. However orientations to motherhood are rather more complex than this. Nearly half of the women in the Thomas Coram study either did not mind whether or not they became pregnant, or had not thought about pregnancy as something that might affect them. This challenges two widely held assumptions about the conception of children: first that there is a clear dichotomy between wanting and not wanting a child, and second, that women always make clear and conscious decisions about whether or not to conceive. Asked whether it had been important to them not to become pregnant, this group commonly replied, 'I wasn't bothered'. Those who had no conscious thoughts about conception had just started their sexual careers. They illustrate the clear separation that some women (and no doubt some men) make between sexual intercourse and pregnancy, and motherhood.

Women's feelings about motherhood were influenced by how they thought pregnancy and motherhood would affect their lives. Thus employment and education prospects, relationships with parents as well as with male partners, whether or not they had previously been pregnant, their orientations to contraception, when other people in their social networks tended to give birth as well as their perception of the ideal time to give birth all affected how they felt about motherhood. While women in the study reported here could not be dichotomized into a group which 'planned' its pregnancies and a group for whom pregnancy was 'accidental', they did nonetheless have general views about the best time to have children. The following section will consider this samples's views about the ideal time to conceive.

Ideal time to conceive

Within the narrow version of cultural influence (that it is separable from structural factors so that 'West Indians' can be picked out as automatically different from 'whites') it is expected that black women of Afro-Caribbean origin believe it to be acceptable and ideal to have children early in life, while white women do not share these beliefs. However most of the women in this study, whether black or white, reported that they thought it better to have children earlier rather than later in life. This is aptly illustrated by considering some quotations from white women:

'If you have a baby when you're older you're tied down . . . I'll still be able to do what I want to.'

(Jan, seventeen years old)

'I think they look down on women who don't have a child by 30 but there's no set time for anybody to have a baby by. (*What do you think is the ideal age to have a baby?*) I think about now is all right . . . I don't want to get too old and have children.'

(Mary, nineteen years old)

'Yeah I think I'm young and people say I'm young but I don't think it makes any difference how old you are . . . whether you're thirty or sixteen you can still give it as much love . . . She's twenty-six [R's sister] but she's getting on to have a baby when you think of it. The younger you are the more likely that it's going to be healthier.'

(Alice, seventeen years old)

From what these women say, it is clear that they consider it preferable to have children earlier rather than later in life. Their reasons for this come from prevalent 'common sense' frameworks regarding entry into motherhood. Appeals are made to 'not being tied down', and to beliefs about when is the ideal age to have a child. The argument about not being tied down is one also used by older mothers as a reason for not having had children earlier, while the argument about retaining enough youth to enjoy life after the children are grown up (as well as still being young enough to understand their children) is the converse of what older mothers would argue. They also consider themselves to be physically better able to bear and cope with children than older women are.

This did not mean that all the women in the study considered that theirs was the ideal age at which to reproduce. However only one fifth considered that the ideal age was over twenty-one years. The general feeling was that women should start to have children early in their life course. It could be argued that since the interviews were conducted in late pregnancy, these women's responses about ideal ages are simply post hoc justifications of a situation which is inevitable. However they illuminate the differences between 'insider' and 'outsider' perceptions of early motherhood.

It is also important to note that early motherhood was common rather than unusual in the women's social networks. Nearly half of the sample's mothers had themselves had their first child before they were twenty, as this white respondent illustrates: 'Well me mum had me when she was seventeen. I find I am a bit young to have a baby, but there are some girls here [mother and baby home] who are fifteen years of age' (Sandra, nineteen years old).

In this study it was not the case that attachment to early motherhood was culturally specific to young black women. White women were similar to black women in wanting to have children early in life, and knowing many other women (including their own mothers) who had done similarly. In addition the mothers in this study, both black and white, generally considered that motherhood conferred high status on women and so felt that having a child would improve their social status.

The experience of (un)employment

Women's feelings about the timing of motherhood was influenced by how they anticipated that it would affect other aspects of their lives. Dominant reproductive ideologies suggest a conflictual model of employment and motherhood in which motherhood should be deferred until the employment career is well established. The rationale for this is that mothers ought not to be employed while their children are young. Therefore unless they are well established in their careers, they will be unable to return to the same occupational position.

This deferment of motherhood makes sense only if women have managed to obtain and keep employment which has built-in career progression, and for many women this is not the case. The jobs which women commonly do, in factories, shops, catering, and the health service, give few opportunities for career progression. Less than one quarter of women in this study had at least one 'O' level or equivalent. Their lack of formal qualifications meant that they were not well placed to obtain employment with career prospects. Indeed only 39 per cent of our sample were employed when they became pregnant. A further 6 per cent were on MSC schemes, and 16 per cent were in full-time education. This means that 39 per cent were unemployed at the start of pregnancy.

For women who are unemployed, childbearing does not threaten the current employment career, and may well appear a welcome alternative to unemployment. More than a third of the sample had done more than one job since they started working (one woman had done eight jobs since leaving school). This was either due to redundancy (which some women in the study had experienced more than once in their short employment careers) or because they hoped to get more money or better working conditions in another job. Many women (black and white) had experienced difficulty finding work. This means that for the majority of the sample it was not possible to be continually employed for the necessary two years in order to qualify for statutory maternity leave. This explains why only eight women qualified for maternity leave in late pregnancy. The following examples vividly illustrate how hard it has been for this cohort of women to get established in employment:

'When I was looking for work after I left my job, in the job centre it was all 'eighteen' or 'sixteen with experience', and I couldn't understand that. I know my boyfriend is finding it really hard to get a job.'

(Linda, a white seventeen-year-old)

'I don't know. If you go to the job centre they want people with 'O' levels and CSEs and things like that and you have to be a certain age . . .'

(Ruth, a white seventeen-year-old)

'First of all they say that you need education to get a job and then when – I think you just got to be lucky really . . . When you go they say you haven't got enough – or they want someone with at least two years experience.'

(Fay, a black nineteen-year-old)

'When we went up to look [at the banks] they had given out forms to be filled in, and you just sent off for interviews. I got interviews, but I just didn't get no job. I tried one of those youth schemes, but you had to take a test first and get a certain per cent to pass through it. And I failed it by 3 per cent. It was learning computer work. And I went to a few other factories. Towards the end I was giving up a bit, but my mum wouldn't let me sign on. She said if I did, I wouldn't go out and find work.' (This woman tried for over twenty jobs before getting one in a supermarket where she stayed for three years.)

(Judy, a white nineteen-year-old)

White women and black women alike had difficulty getting jobs because of the general unavailability coupled with their lack of qualifications and youth (which partly signalled lack of experience). However, while prospects were poor for the majority of this group, racial discrimination made the situation worse for black women. This was mostly mentioned by black women, but some white women also commented on it.

'It was only when I got to the interviews and I didn't used to get the job I used to think I was unfairly treated because when I'd leave and they'd turn me down I used to hear that a white person got it and that she didn't have as much going for her like what I did.'

(Joyce, a black nineteen-year-old)

'I think they would rather take on a white person than a black person. I don't know why that is. They just would.'

(Tracey, a white eighteen-year-old)

'They [friends' siblings] say like how it's harder . . . you could have the same qualifications as a white person and you could go in an office and get all their little exams and everything like that and you get a higher score than a white person but because you're black, you just don't get the job.'

(Hayley, a black sixteen-year-old)

These accounts illustrate the intersection of race and class in that while all the sample found it difficult to get jobs because of their class position, black women were less likely than white women to get jobs.

The respondents not only shared certain features of their class position, they were also all women. Some responses to questions about employment illustrated the intersection of class, race, and gender in that black women were also likely to experience difficulties getting jobs in traditionally male occupations: 'Like my twin, she's a qualified motor mechanic and she can't get a job, so I don't know' (Debbie, a black nineteen-year-old).

> 'At [motorcar manufacturers] I passed the interview maths test along with two boys who had done woodwork but not metalwork like I had done. I didn't get it, but I found out when I met the same boys at another interview that they had an offer. I thought [motorcar manufacturers] was nasty because I had metalwork. I think it's because I'm a girl, because I had seven letters of rejection saying that I couldn't be employed because I was a girl . . . My dad was annoyed because he thought they had to accept a certain proportion of girls. My mum couldn't believe it. That was a bit *race* discriminatory' (my emphasis).
>
> (Claudette, a black nineteen-year-old who later qualified as a mechanical fitter when her daughter was one year old.)

In the above examples the women involved were likely to perceive the failure to get jobs to be the result of racial rather than sexual discrimination. Racial discrimination operates both directly and indirectly. In the employment field jobs gained through social network contacts probably provide the clearest example of this indirect discrimination. Many women in this study had obtained jobs through social network contacts.

> 'The friend that worked at the factory, she told me about that job. And when she left, she worked at Jamesons – they wanted someone there – she told me about that one. She knew I wanted to leave so I had that one straight on.'
>
> (Clare, a white seventeen-year-old)

> 'My mum found me a [temporary] job where she worked.'
>
> (Hayley, a black sixteen-year-old)

> 'My nan got me the job.'
>
> (Ruth, a white seventeen-year-old)

> 'Because my mum worked there you see. So she knew there was a job vacant, so I went for it.'
>
> (Tracey, a white eighteen-year-old)

The usefulness of social network contacts probably meant that the 33 per cent of women who had unemployed mothers, and the 23 per cent who had unemployed fathers were at a disadvantage when it came to getting employment. Since black people tend to suffer more from unemployment (Brown 1984) than white people do, it probably also meant that the black women were at a disadvantage in comparison with the white women when it came to finding employment.

In summary, the women in this study were clearly not in occupations which had career progression. Their difficulty in finding (and keeping) jobs meant that few were eligible for maternity leave in late pregnancy. Deferring motherhood would have made little difference to this since the types of employment they were eligible for tended not to be ones which provided career prospects. For these women the intersection of the motherhood career and the employment career does not fit a conflictual model in that childbearing would make little difference to their employment prospects. In the late pregnancy interview it remained to be seen how many women in this group would actually participate in the labour market post birth. Black women's and white women's experiences of the employment market were largely similar. Differences could more readily be attributed to racial discrimination than narrowly defined cultural differences.

Mothers and daughters

A narrowly defined cultural approach to the question of why 'West Indian' women become pregnant early in their life course would suggest that whatever their mothers' initial responses to their pregnancy, they can confidently expect their mothers eventually to accept, and even 'mother', their children. Thus the having of children does not entail that they bear full responsibility. White women would be faced with a rather different, and less accepting reaction. Studies of 'West Indian youth' (usually male) have also suggested that they suffer from pronounced intergenerational conflict as the result of a 'clash of cultures' (West Indian and white British). If these things are true, then black mothers and white mothers should have qualitatively different relationship with their daughters, and react differently to their daughters' pregnancies.

In the Thomas Coram study most women, regardless of colour, were dependent on their parents, particularly mothers, for social support. This was partly because many still lived with their parents.

Forty-seven per cent of the sample were living with their mothers when they became pregnant. A further thirty-one per cent saw their mothers at least weekly. Most of the sample were therefore in frequent contact with their parents, and in addition were more likely to be rated as having a confiding, supportive relationship with their mothers than with their male partners or their fathers.

> 'Any problems or that I could tell her if I feel like I wanted to tell her . . . Most of the time I did tell her . . . We're like sisters really . . . I wouldn't change her for anything in the world. She's a very good mother.'
>
> (Geraldine, a black nineteen-year-old living at home)

> 'Me and my mum were always best friends . . . I never used to go to my dad with my troubles, I always used to go to my mum.'
>
> (Jan, a white seventeen-year-old living with her husband)

> 'Oh fantastic! We were very close, and we talked about everything. Everything.'
>
> (Sandra, a white eighteen-year-old living with parents)

> 'We were like sisters to tell you the truth, even though I had my little brothers and sisters. Because I could talk to my mum.'
>
> (Pamela, a black sixteen-year-old living at home)

Good relationships with mothers were not a universal feature. In late pregnancy 21 per cent of the sample were mainly negative about their relationships with their mothers (compared with 37 per cent who were mainly negative about their relationships with their fathers). While black women and white women in the sample said similar things about their relationships with their mothers, some black women perceived these relationships to be similar to white women's relationships with their mothers, while others saw them as different.

Racism as a structural force means that black people are socially constructed as 'outsiders' with respect to white British society. As a result black people recognize that their situation and experiences are similar to those of other black people but different from those of white people. White people similarly experience themselves as different from black people, and perceive black people (who tend to be focused on in discussions of 'race') as 'being all the same', even though they do not perceive all white people to be the same. These notions of similarity and difference are also emphasized by the media, and by academic work which uses the sorts of narrow cultural definitions described earlier.

Implicit within such descriptions of black groups and white groups are issues of power and solidarity. White society demonstrates its power to construct black people as deviant from its behavioural norms while maintaining solidarity between white people in their difference from black people. In a similar way, black people by concentrating on their similarities with other black people show the solidarity which allows them to exert influence on society by use of collective power. However, as discussed earlier, any comparison of groups serve to highlight differences and obscure similarities between them. Difference does not need to be established or proved, but can be taken for granted.

Such taken-for-granted beliefs in the unitary nature of black people and their difference from white people can lead to the simultaneous holding of contradictory beliefs about how black people compare with white people. When asked directly whether she thought that black mothers treated their daughters differently from white mothers, one respondent replied that she felt they did: 'After speaking to some of my friends I realized it was a thing – all black women were the same in that age group . . . because they all have the same beliefs, and the way they've been brought up.' However she then went on to describe the overlap rather than the differences between black mothers and white mothers:

'Some of them [white mothers] couldn't care two hoots, but some of them – I mean they don't say the same thing, but I mean they hold the same principles as some black people. And some black mothers don't really care two hoots what their daughters do neither.'

(Angela, a black nineteen-year-old)

This respondent illustrates the contradictions which permeate the mother-daughter relationship. She indicates that while she found her mother's restrictions on her social life irksome, she also experienced them as caring. She also perceived black mothers and white mothers to hold similar principles, whether those were caring or otherwise.

White respondents were also asked to compare their relationships with their mothers with those of their age peers. However they tended to report individual, but not group differences. This probably reflects the fact that the prevalence of narrow definitions of culture means that black women are familiar with accounts which are concerned with the 'pathological culture' of black families and so are likely to make comparisons between black families and white families. In contrast white women are unlikely to be familiar with such cultural explanations of their household organizations, and are less likely to compare white families with black families (although in other contexts they may compare black families with white ones).

The causes of friction between mothers and daughters in this study were, perhaps not surprisingly, to do with boyfriends, going out, and helping around the house. Arguments about these issues, and inability to discuss them with parents were common (and not confined to black women, although black 'youth' have frequently been described as having severe intergenerational conflict). The following white respondent sums the reasons up very neatly.

'[We would argue] about silly little things. Washing up and going out . . . things about the house. My friends. What I should be doing at night. Where I should be going. Who I should be going with. What time I should be in and all this.'

(Linda, a white seventeen-year-old)

Although these cannot adequately be discussed here, black parents and white parents were reported to be similar not only in their attitudes to what their daughters should and should not do before conception. They also did not differ in their hopes for, and expectations of their daughters prior to pregnancy, or their reactions to the pregnancy.

Prior to pregnancy many women (both black and white) knew that their parents wanted them to get jobs they liked, and also to enjoy themselves. When they first learned that their daughters were pregnant, the majority of mothers (both black and white) were initially likely to be unhappy, but by late pregnancy they had generally become enthusiastic. Mothers' and fathers' reactions were initially similar, so that in early pregnancy only 27 per cent of mothers were enthusiastic about it, compared with 30 per cent of fathers. By late pregnancy however their responses to their daughters' pregnancies diverged, with mothers being more likely to be perceived to be happy about it. As birth approached 62 per cent of mothers were wholly positive, compared with only 46 per cent of fathers. Most parents did however, have some positive feelings towards the end of the pregnancy with only 8 per cent of mothers and 8 per cent of fathers being wholly negative.

An examination of relationships between mothers and daughters, and maternal responses to a daughter's pregnancy suggests that mother-daughter relationships share many similarities aross black families and white families. This reinforces the point, made earlier, that narrow cultural accounts which explain black women's behaviour by relating it to (often outdated) Caribbean patterns of behaviour are inadequate. Meaningful accounts of young women's behaviour need to take account of the structural influences of sex, race, and class as well as their intersections.

Conclusion

Studies that focus on black British people of Afro-Caribbean origin have frequently used a narrow definition of cultural influence to explain their behaviour. Such explanations are unsatisfactory because they oversimplify cultural influence, and in doing so serve to reinforce the social construction of black people as deviant from the norms of white British behaviour.

Research on women who become pregnant early in their life course has tended to use such narrow definitions of culture to explain why young black women of Afro-Caribbean origin become pregnant, but not why young white women become pregnant. This approach masks the similarities in experiences and perceptions between black mothers and white mothers. Consideration of the accounts given by women who become mothers early in their life course suggests that their shared experiences of being women from the working classes influence their behaviour more than do patterns of behaviour in the countries from which their parents come. Apart from racial discrimination (which only black women in this study reported experiencing, pregnant black women and white women under twenty years of age cannot easily be differentiated in their attitudes to and experiences of pregnancy, employment, or relationships with parents.

This does not mean that culture is irrelevant to the study of young people's behaviour or that it is never legitimate either to focus solely on black people or to compare black people and white people. However, complex (rather than simple) representations of culture need to be used. Such complex definitions encompass structural influences of class, gender, and race, which influence white people's as well as black people's lives. This sort of approach allows the representation of differences in style among young black women and young white women. It also takes account of the common experiences that young black women and young white women share as the result of being of the same sex and of similar class positions. However it also recognizes that racism divides white people from black people and stops them from being aware of their similarities. The narrow representations of cultural influence discussed in this paper cannot portray these complexities, and are therefore inadequate for the explanation of human behaviour.

Notes

1 'Race' is used here to refer to the social construction of black people and white people as belonging to different races. This paper concentrates on black women of Afro-Caribbean origin, and white women, most of whom have been born and brought up in Britain. The term as used here connotes the differential treatment that black people and white people in British society receive. As such it refers to racial discrimination on the basis of colour rather than to cultural differences on the basis of ethnicity

2 The sample was recruited from the ante-natal clinics of two large, inner-city London hospitals. Apart from the age criterion women had to be having the first child they intended to rear themselves. Any woman who met these criteria and agreed to participate was included in the study. Seventy-nine women were given in-depth interviews, and the other 101 women were given shorter interviews. The quotations used here all come from the longer interviews, but some of the percentages given refer to the whole sample. All names used are pseudonyms.

Acknowledgements

Without the women who took part in the Thomas Coram study this paper would not have been possible. To them my grateful thanks. The research was funded by a grant from the Department of Health and Social Security. The project has an advisory group of black women psychologists and sociologists who also have an interest in early motherhood. They have been very helpful throughout this project. My thinking on the issues covered in this paper was greatly sharpened by discussions with them. Their input has been invaluable. As a member of a project team I have benefitted from the help and support that Julia Brannen, Peter Moss, and Ted Melhuish have provided in general, and more specifically with this paper. Thanks also to Barbara Tizard and Charlie Owen who each commented on drafts. The final responsibility for the paper must of course be mine.

References

Amos, V. and Parmar, P. (1981) 'Resistance and responses: the experience of black girls in Britain', in A. McRobbie and T. McCabe (eds) *Feminism for Girls: An Adventure Story*, London: Routledge & Kegan Paul.

Brah, A. and Minhas, R. (1985) 'Structural racism or cultural difference: schooling for Asian girls', in G. Weiner (ed.) *Just a Bunch of Girls*, Open University Press: Milton Keynes.

Brown, C. (1984) *Black and White in Britain: The Third PSI Survey*, London: Heinemann.

Bryan, B, Dadzie, S., and Scafe, S. (1985) *The Heart of the Race*, London: Virago.

Busfield, J. (1974) 'Ideologies and reproduction', in *The Integration of a Child into a Social World*, Cambridge: Cambridge University Press.

Butler, N., Ineichen, B., Taylor, B., and Wadsworth, J. (1981) *Teenage Mothering*, Report to DHSS, University of Bristol.

Carby, H. (1982) 'White woman listen! Black feminism and the boundaries of sisterhood', in Centre for Contemporary Cultural Studies (eds) *The Empire Strikes Back, Race and Racism in 70s Britain*, London: Hutchinson.

Centre for Contemporary Cultural Studies (eds) (1978) *Woman take Issue*, London: Hutchinson.

—— (1982) *The Empire Strikes Back, Race and Racism in 70s British*, London: Hutchinson.

Clarke, E. (1957) *My Mother who Fathered Me*, London: George Allen & Unwin.

Feminist Review 17 (1984) 'Many voices, one chant, black feminist perspectives'.

Fitzherbert, K. (1967) 'West Indian children in London', *Occasional Papers on Social Administration* 19.

Frankenberg, R. (unpublished) 'Growing up white: feminism, racism and the social geography of childhood', History of Consciousness, University of California, Santa Cruz.

Freire, P. (1971) *Pedagogy of the Oppressed*, New York: Herder & Herder.

Hall, S. and Jefferson, T. (eds) (1976) *Resistance through Rituals: Youth Subcultures in Post-War Britain*, London: Hutchinson.

Hewitt, R. (1986) *White Talk Black Talk. Inter-Racial Friendship and Communication amongst Adolescents*, Cambridge: Cambridge University Press.

Hooks, B. (1982) *Ain't I a Woman? Black Women and Feminism*, London: Pluto Press.

Hooks, B. (1984) *Feminist Theory from Margin to Center*, Boston: South End Press.

Ineichen, B. (1984/5) 'Teenage Motherhood in Bristol: The Contrasting Experience of Afro-Caribbean and White Girls', *New Community* 12 (1): 52–8.

McRobbie, A. (1984) 'Dance and social fantasy', in A. McRobbie and M. Nava (eds) *Gender and Generation*. London: Macmillan.

Murcott, A. (1980) 'The social construction of teenage pregnancy', *Sociology of Health and Illness* 2 (1): 1–23.

Office of Population Censuses and Surveys Monitor (1986) FMI 86/2.

Parmar, P. (1982) 'Gender, race and class, Asian women in resistance', in Centre for Contemporary Cultural Studies (eds) *The Empire Strikes Back, Race and Racism in 70s Britain*, London: Hutchinson.

Phipps-Yonas, S. (1980) *Teenage Pregnancy and Motherhood. A Review of the Literature*, American Journal of Orthopsychiatry 50(3): 403–31.

Phizacklea, A. (1983) 'Introduction', in A. Phizacklea (ed.) *One Way Ticket. Migration and Female Labour*, London: Routledge & Kegan Paul.

Phoenix, A. (1987) 'Theories of gender and black families', in G. Weiner and M. Arnot (eds) *Gender Under Scrutiny*, London: Hutchinson.

Saifullah Khan, V. (1982) 'The role of the culture of dominance in structuring the experience of ethnic minorities', in C. Husband (ed.) *Race in Britain*, London: Hutchinson.

Scott, K.G., Field, T., and Robertson, E. (981) *Teenage Parents and their Offspring*, New York: Grune & Stratton.

Skinner, C. (1986) *Elusive Mister Right. The Social and Personal Context of a Young Woman's use of Contraception*, London: Carolina Publications.

Watson, J. (ed.) (1977) *Between Two Cultures, Migrants and Minorities in Britain*, Oxford: Basil Blackwell.

Westwood, S. (1984) *All Day Every Day, Factory and Family in the Making of Women's Lives*, London: Pluto Press.

Wilmott, P. and Young, M. (1960) *Family and Class in a London Suburb*, London: Routledge & Kegan Paul.

9 Taking and giving: working women and female bonds in a Pakistani immigrant neighbourhood[1]

Pnina Werbner

Women-centred networks

The focus on practices of female seclusion and veiling in Islamic societies has sometimes obscured the importance of extra-domestic networks sustained by women within their 'separate world'. Yet such extra-domestic, women-centred networks have important bearings on gender relations, conjugal roles, and the external support women can draw upon. Purdah, as Papanek points out in a seminal paper (Papanek 1973a), is both a system of task allocations and an expression of male and family status. In the latter sense, purdah is non-complementary. It rests on the conception of an active male, an achiever in the public domain, and a passive female, secluded within the domestic domain, the object of male protection. This is purdah in its most extreme manifestation (Jeffery 1979). Women participate vicariously in their husbands' achieved status (Papanek 1973a, 1973b) and are constitutive of this status as passive objects in need of protection.

Once we examine the 'world of women' not simply, however, as a world of domestic chores or idle gossip, but as the complex world of extra-domestic female relationships, we are able to shift from the presentation of purdah as a cultural logic to a sociological analysis of variations in conjugal relations as these obtain in purdah societies. As Rosaldo hypothesized at the outset of the current debate on gender relations:

> 'Women's status will be the lowest in those societies where there is a firm differentiation between domestic and public spheres of activity and where women are isolated from one another and placed under a single man's authority, in the home. Their position is raised when they can challenge those claims to authority, either by taking on men's roles or by establishing social ties, by creating a sense of rank, order and value in a world of their own.'
> (Rosaldo 1974: 36)

In Manchester, Pakistani migrant women living in the central residential enclave initiate and sustain widely ramifying women-centred networks. Through the contacts they forge with other women, they extend the family network, incorporating their husbands into the networks they form.

The nature of participation in extra-domestic networks and the 'shape' of these networks is important to define clearly. Anwar (1979: 50–95) stresses the primacy of kinship ties in the formation of extra-domestic networks amongst Pakistani migrants. Friends, he argues, are assimilated into kin-category networks (1979: 62).

Theoretical discussions of interhousehold female-centred networks have also so far focused on the 'matrilateral bias' characterizing kin networks in urban industrial societies (Yanagisako 1977). The bias expresses itself in the closer ties maintained by female kinswomen (primarily mothers, daughters, and sisters). Yanagisako labels this tendency 'woman-centred *kin* networks' in preference to terms stressing the primacy of the maternal role. The debate thus surrounds the economic and normative basis of kinship in urban industrial societies which gives rise to this affective solidarity among female kin.

Although there is some evidence of a matrilateral bias developing among second-generation female kin, my discussion here is somewhat differently focused: it concerns the formation and implications of women-centred *friendship* networks. In these networks female kinswomen and affines are crucial pivotal points; friendship networks aggregate around the 'solidary core' of female affines or relatives (Yanagisako 1977: 212). This conjunction of friendship and kinship is, I will show, a basis for the achievement of status and reputation within a neighbourhood locality, as well as in the wider community. Moreover, such networks crucially affect the conjugal status and influence of women in the domestic household unit.

It is important to stress the central role of friendship, as *distinct* from kinship, in these networks. Friendship ties, which may be conceived of as 'weak' ties, constitute crucial 'bridging' ties (Granovetter 1973). As such, they facilitate communication between different kin groups and across different strata. They are thus potential points of mobilization and change. New friendships and acquaintances forged by Pakistani migrants extend their horizons and support processes of mobility and social transformation.

A further feature of these friendship-cum-kinship networks needs to be stressed. It relates to the exclusivity of networks and the fundamental idea of purdah as a symbolic shelter. Network exclusivity is clearly related to status considerations. Elite families in

Manchester sustain exclusive networks (Werbner 1981 and under consideration). While women, *qua* women, may share certain predicaments, they rarely form a solidary group. Instead, they tend to 'organize themselves to protect class privileges in activities which complement their husbands' objective positions in the class hierarchy' (Bujra 1978: 16). The 'open' networks of women in the central Pakistani residential enclave are a feature of their low-income status. This openness is the basis for a form of female solidarity uniting women in common predicaments and painful experiences or in the sharing of joyful occasions. Although the establishment of this 'women's world' is not a basis for a feminist consciousness (Bujra 1974), it supports women's status and self-confidence in the domestic sphere. It thus protects women from the more iniquitous consquences of strict purdah, interpreted as physical seclusion and isolation.

Labour migration and changes in female status

To appreciate the full significance of Pakistani women's 'networking' activity, it must be seen from a broader perspective of labour migration and its differing impact on the perceived status of migrant men and women.

Saifullah Khan, commenting on the migration of Mirpuri women to Bradford, presents a picture of radical dislocation. She notes that in Pakistan 'women invariably spend their day in the company of other women' and goes on to argue that 'it is this "women's world" and the encumbent emotional and physical support which is abruptly ended when Asian women move to Britain' (1975: 179). In Bradford Mirpuri women were, she found, 'alone and restricted to the house' and such isolation, she argues may generate considerable anxieties and tension (1976: 104). Moreover, migrant men's work outside the home 'causes Mirpuri women to be subject to a stricter form of purdah than they experienced in the home village . . . [they] contribute less to, and have less control over, the household income in Britain' (1979: 53). This stricter system of purdah is sustained by male networks' based on prior village and kinship connections.

This picture appears to confirm the conception of purdah as a protection from the 'real dangers of a segregated world' (Papanek 1973a: 316). Britain as an unknown and alien environment might well be expected in these terms to generate a more extreme form of purdah. The physical isolation of migrant women in their homes does, indeed, occur in Manchester under some conditions, and I discuss this phenomenon below. For many Pakistani women the move to Britain has meant, however, a move towards greater independence. They have escaped the proverbial domination of older female relatives, the constraints of extreme purdah as symbolized by the *burqa* and the restriction on movement,[2] and the deprivations of extreme financial hardships. Many are able to work and their earnings, unlike those of women in rural Punjab (see Sharma 1980: 107) are their own to do with as they choose. Secluded nevertheless in the domestic world of the neighbourhood, women come into little status-threatening contact with the host society. Non-immigrant women they encounter in the neighbourhood are primarily, like themselves, housewives and mothers.

In contrast to women, migrant men must necessarily examine their status in the wider context of the receiving society. At best, they are members of the working class. At worst, they are members of an underclass, earning lower wages and performing more menial jobs than other workers. Their businesses, if they are self-employed, are usually small and marginal. Moreover, in their jobs, and as legal representatives of their families, they are exposed to discrimination or a sense of cultural incompetence. They must contend with the world of officialdom, with the threat of unemployment, or with the precarious conditions of an economy in recession. Hence they derive their self-esteem in large measure from their position among fellow Pakistanis. Even within the Pakistani community, however, class status is defined by objective criteria – education, wealth, pedigree, and Islamic scholarship.

In contrast to class status, reputation is a function of network centrality. Men are active in voluntary organizations, in the mosque, or in welfare associations. Yet many of these associations are dominated by members of the elite (Werbner 1985). Thus the locus of valued interaction for many Pakistani men is not the public domain of work or association but the inter-domestic domain of kinship, friendship, and neighbourly relations.

In this context men participate vicariously in the statuses built up actively by their wives, just as women participate vicariously in the active statuses their husbands build up. The conjugal 'balance' achieved varies from family to family. The wife of a prominent man, active in public affairs, is herself at the centre of a vast female network (see the case of Hafiza, p. 193). Her contacts and activities support those of her husband, and they mutually strengthen each other's statuses. Her conjugal role is thus *confirmatory*. For a low-income mill worker his wife's extensive network is a source of status for both of them. Her conjugal role is thus an *ascendant* one.

Clearly, extreme female seclusion precludes this kind of active 'networking' on the part of women. It is significant, perhaps, that most migrant men in Manchester look upon such extreme purdah with disapproving amusement.[3]

For Pakistani women the formation of extra-domestic networks is not a novel phenomenon, unique to the urban industrial context. What is novel is the extension of ties with prior strangers. Facilitating this interaction is the flow of customary ceremonial gifting which has been adapted and extended to the Manchester context.

Taking and giving: ceremonial gifting

Women are central to the Punjabi Muslim system of ceremonial exchange. The system, according to Eglar (1960), is anchored in the pivotal role of the daughter as the constant recipient of gifts from her patrikin (p. 107). By extension it is a system of reciprocal exchange between households. Amongst Pakistani migrants in Manchester such interhousehold gifting is known, variably, as *lena dena* (*len den* in Urdu), i.e. 'take give', or as *vartan* (the exchange of goods, barter). The basic rule of *lena dena* is that a gift returned should always exceed the initial gift in value (p. 125), thus perpetuating the relationship. The gifts of *vartan* – cloth, sweets, gold, or money – are known locally as *bhaji* (thus Eglar refers to the system as *vartan bhanji*, 'dealing in sweets', although this conjunction of terms was, according to my inquiries, not used by local migrants). Ceremonial gifting and hospitality takes place primarily on festive and life crisis occasions. In Manchester, trips to Pakistan are a major occasion for hosting departing and returning travellers who receive gifts on their departure, and bring gifts from Pakistan on their return to Britain. Weddings, in particular, are central occasions for *lena dena* transactions.

In Pakistan as in Manchester, *lena dena* is primarily the prerogative of women. They are 'the guardians of *vartan bhanji*, who know to whom and when and how much a family is to give as well as from whom and when and how much it should receive' (Eglar 1960: 138). As in Pakistan, so too in Manchester, *vartan* signals a relationship of mutual help, one in which 'two parties . . . feel free to ask favours of each other' (p. 106). That such a crucial and delicate relationship should be handled by women pinpoints their key role in Punjabi Muslim society.

Although the most valuble gifts and costly hospitality are reserved primarily for close kinsmen, the system extends to include friends, caste members, neighbours, and fellow villagers (p. 117). It is this potential for extension beyond the kin group which makes the system so crucial for the formation of interhousehold networks in Manchester. The proper conduct of *vartan* is a source of honour and prestige, *izzet*, for a woman and her family. Thus Eglar comments that:

> The number and quality of the gifts given and received are indicators of the family's knowledge and ability in dealing with people and provide an index of its status, influence and power and of the breadth of its social circle – all of which mean *izzet*. On all such occasions daughters are crucial to the exchange and hence to the acquisition of *izzet*.

(1960: 111)

In Manchester, migrant women who work use some of their earnings to initiate and extend *lena dena* with neighbours and acquaintances. Their independent incomes have facilitated the building up of locally based friendship networks. Families who remain highly oriented to a return to Pakistan try to avoid extensive ceremonial gifting with local acquaintances: they regard such gifting as wasteful (Werbner 1981). The more 'rooted' Pakistanis are locally and the more involved in the local competition stakes for status and prestige, the more likely they are to engage in *lena dena* with friends made locally.

It would be a mistake, however, to attribute the style of neighbourliness which has evolved locally solely to women's independent incomes. Neighbourly relations bear a striking similarity to those obtaining in the North Indian urban neighbourhood studied by Vatuk (1972: 149–89). There too *len den* and 'open' networks predominated. Yet the women studied by Vatuk did not have independent incomes (1972: 164). It must be stressed, however, that overseas labour migration is an expensive enterprise allowing for little surplus. Women's independent earnings are probably more crucial in this context for the building up of local friendship networks since the highest priority in resource allocation remains, for most migrants, the maintenance of relations with family at home, in Pakistan[4].

The pivotal role fulfilled by women in the formation of interhousehold networks raises the question whether these networks may be regarded as part of the 'domestic' or 'public' domains (cf. Rosaldo 1973; Yanagisako 1977: 222; Bujra 1978). I prefer to regard them as constituting the nexus of the public and domestic, mediating between the more formal context of public activity and the privacy and affectivity of domestic household life. As in other 'honour and shame' societies, for Pakistanis a man's status remains crucially anchored in this inter-domestic realm, in large measure controlled by his wife.

I turn now from this general discussion to a more detailed description of the lifestyle led by Pakistani migrant women in a single Manchester neighbourhood.

Life in the residential enclave

Immigrant ghettos have often been described as places of intense sociability, as 'urban villages', and in Manchester too the village-like characteristics of the central residential cluster are, perhaps, its most marked feature. Yet surprisingly, to anyone passing through the neighbourhood on any grey Manchester morning, the streets would seem virtually deserted. Here and there a woman may be seen walking down the narrow pavements, going shopping or visiting a friend. On market days, women carrying shopping baskets converge at the local market. Here all is colourful excitement, as vendors display a variety of goods, from vegetables and meat to new clothes, handbags, and household utensils. The market is a central place for women to meet their friends and exchange news and gossip, while buying a few household goods and picking up a length of material at a bargain price – another item to hoard for the day when a daughter marries or the long-awaited trip to Pakistan takes place. In the afternoon the streets of the neighbourhood suddenly come to life. Women walk along in twos and threes as they return from school, surrounded by children. Young teenage boys return on bicycles from their high schools. After school some of the children go off to the homes of one or other of the local Koran teachers for an hour or so of Koran instruction. On the long summer evenings children play in the streets, and on weekends one may see families going visiting, dressed in their best. But on the whole, social life takes place in the seclusion of the houses, behind closed doors and drawn curtains. For even in this neighbourhood the homes are fortresses of privacy, the street merely a meeting place for polite greetings and brief exchanges of gossip.

Once in the home, however, sociability with neighbours, friends, and kinsmen occupies a great part of the day. The constant comings and goings of neighbours are belied by the emptiness of the streets. On Sundays, close relatives drop by with children of all ages, crowding into the small semi-detached or terraced houses. Even on weekdays, kinswomen and female friends may spend many hours together, drinking endless cups of tea and attending to babies and young children in each others' company. When alone in the house, women and teenage girls usually work, sewing on industrial sewing machines for local manufacturers. Some women and girls even go out to work as machinists in city factories.

As women go about their daily affairs, cleaning and cooking, shopping and visiting, men are either out working, or asleep if they work on night shifts. During the morning and early afternoon the neighbourhood is the world of women. For men working night shifts only the weekends are spared for sociability. But if they work on other shifts they are quite often home during the daytime. Then a man usually joins his wife and her friends in the back room, in a strikingly informal and relaxed manner. Men make cups of tea for guests, casually and unselfconsciously. Indeed, demonstrations of masculine superiority or of a clear-cut conjugal division of labour in domestic matters are conspicuously absent. The conversation during these daily visits usually flows easily, as people debate momentous topical events and often wax enthusiastic, interrupting each other in loud voices. There is a great deal of joking, gossiping and arguing. The spontaneity and conviviality of relations are clearly distinguished from the formality of behaviour towards strangers. The latter are inevitably ushered into the front room, in the exclusive company of their own sex.

Conversations among friends concern absent family members, events back home, marriages, and deaths. Politics in Pakistan are discussed alongside local politics and the politics of the mosque and other Pakistani associations. Hosts and their guests review their savings in rotating credit associations in endless detail: what they plan to do with the money when they hit the jackpot, why (for example) although they had been planning to use it to go this year to Pakistan, they now think they may hold a wedding instead. Women display their new personal purchases – a piece of material for a *shalwar kamiz* (trouser suit), a pair of gold earrings. New household purchases are also admired – a cassette radio, a new television set, a new set of serving dishes. Friends and neighbours are constantly being updated on the course of minor family sagas, while news of accidents or death passes like wildfire, as does news of any sensational scandal. Indeed, life seems all-eventful, as every little change in the fortunes of individuals is scrutinized and discussed in great detail. Should Aftab go to college or take a job? In what month should Shahnaz get married? What happened when Kishwar's little boy fell and injured his head? Why did the grocery store on the corner, run by local Pakistanis, change hands? People recount their trips to other English cities and tell of developments there – a new restaurant in Bradford, the terrible housing situation in London. They make sure that everyone knows that their uncle the doctor is about to arrive, their cousin the tax collector (an influential post in small villages in Pakistan) has had a baby, their classificatory nephew the magistrate has had a promotion. Since everyone seems to have some relatives in Pakistan who are successful, this is merely an assertion of a family's equal worth; as if to say, we too are members of a big and distinguished family.

This type of casual gossip does have some utilitarian aspects, for it helps women to master or control their immediate environment. Women swap notes on practical matters to do with children's schooling and health care – when to register them, to what school, when to take them to the doctor for a check up, etc. They also pass on information about the availability of bargains or the solution to various welfare problems. So too piece work rates are compared and discussed. Home machinists who are in constant contact with each other know what the 'going' rate is per item or per hour; they are less likely therefore to be exploited by manufacturers. They act, in a sense, like a loose and informal trade union. Isolated women are far more likely to accept unreasonable renumeration for their sewing.

Kinship and friendship

Although most Pakistanis in the neighbourhood – and indeed in Manchester – live as nuclear families in separate houses, a set of brothers in the central cluster often regard themselves as members of a single *ghar*, 'house' (or extended family), and expect to make certain decisions jointly. These pertain mainly to the marriage of children, to investment in Pakistan where they often own a house or land jointly, and to the fortunes of ageing parents. More distant kin, both patrilateral and matrilateral, are regarded as belonging to separate *ghars*, but are of the same *biraderi*. They are *rishtedar* (relations). Caste members from the same home town or village locality are also *biraderi*, and even caste members from other parts of Pakistan are sometimes regarded as *biraderi*.

People of one's own caste and others from the same town or village in Pakistan are talked of and addressed as 'sister' or 'brother', although if they are of different castes they will not, of course, intermarry. Very generally, friends and neighbours in the central residential cluster address each other in honorary kinship terms: *baji* (older sister) between women, or women and men of the same age; *khala ji* (mother's sister) to older women or mothers of friends, and *khalo ji* to their husbands, or *chacha ji* (father's younger brother) to father's close friends. Men are more often addressed by their names with the honorary suffix *ji*.

Friendships in the central cluster, especially between women, may be formed very rapidly. There are few overt pretensions of superiority, and people are outgoing and interested in their neighbours. Women meet in English classes, in factories, in the market, even in the street. They make friends with the mothers of their daughters' school friends, the friendship thus spanning two generations. They make friends with women living elsewhere in the central cluster who are friendly neighbours of their close kinswomen. As a result of this pattern of friendship the extended family – the *ghar* – becomes the focus of a shared social network. At weddings this is demonstrated dramatically, for the guests include friends of all members of the *ghar*, not merely of the parents of the bride and groom. Furthermore, it is whole *ghars* that are invited – a set of brothers, their children and even grandchildren. A family invited may thus comprise 20 or 30 people, including children.

Not everyone in the central residential cluster participates so actively in its social life. Some migrants avoid having too much to do with their neighbours, considering them 'low class' or noisy, and also avoid the intense exchange relations that sociability entails. But these are exceptions; for most people life flows in a relaxed manner, full of small excitements and minor tragedies, events that can be shared with those around them. The pressure on women in particular to take part in the social life of the neighbourhood is difficult for them to withstand. Those who avoid interactions often feel lonely and isolated. In the mundane routine of everyday life in the neighbourhood people are treated as equals, and respect is universally accorded unless there is a cause for offence. This is not to deny the undercurrent of caste ranking, but caste is not the main parameter of friendship.

Although friends are easily made and frequently seen, relations with them are not confused with those between kinsmen or between 'home' people. The 'folk model' of friendship preferences which migrants in the central cluster expressed is that people closest to them are either kinsmen or come from the same area of origin. My own plotting of their circle of friends and their participation in indexical occasions indicates that reliance on kinsmen is very high, with the most exclusive or demanding occasions reserved for them, or for close friends, usually known from Pakistan. Beyond the extended family and people actually known from Pakistan, however, the circle widens to include friends from various areas of Pakistan. Networks are not exclusive and tend to be very large; so much so that it was virtually impossible to construct a full network matrix of migrants' social networks.

Because of the great amount of time they spend socializing, women in the central cluster tend to dominate in the choice of family friends. They share a joint network with their spouses, but it is they who maintain the viability of many of the friendships. An associated feature of this is the fact that the conjugal role relations are often relatively unsegregated, while at the same time women control the domestic sphere. They are extremely influential in decision making, and are consulted on all domestic matters. Men and boys help with the housework and shopping. They are often expected to manage on their own as women go on prolonged visits back home to Pakistan. In their behaviour women are vocal and assertive, vigorous and affectionate. They move within the city freely, without asking permission. They shop as they wish. Indeed, they often seem to rule their families. Networks may therefore be said to be 'women centred' without thereby denying the standing of men who remain the legal guardians and deal with all 'external' matters to do with the authorities. Men are active in associational activities, take an interest in politics, and often attend Friday meetings at the mosque, jobs permitting. Otherwise their time is spent with their families, caught up in their wives' social affairs.

Working, saving, and the domestic economy

The influential position of women in the family and in wider social contexts is related to a number of other factors. The fact that they earn an income gives them a right to decide on its expenditure. It also gives them a measure of independence. Usually, the husband's income – the regular income – covers the mortgage, and expenditure on food and fuel. The woman's income is allocated to incidental and non-recurrent expenses such as house decoration, consumer goods, trips to Pakistan, weddings, gifts, etc. Women control the Pakistani ceremonial exchange system and much of a woman's earnings are devoted to it. In particular, women accumulate vast quantities of cloth which is either given away on trips to Pakistan or at weddings in Manchester. If a woman has daughters she must also collect material for their dowries.

Residents in the central cluster are on the whole not particularly wealthy, and some of the least prosperous Pakistanis live in the neighbourhood. This is also an area where migrants from artisan and other low caste backgrounds may be found in substantial numbers. However, their poor background does not directly affect their income in Manchester for most men have jobs, either unskilled or semi-skilled, and earn somewhat similar incomes. Only the recent rise in unemployment has affected this situation, as migrants who are unskilled or illiterate have difficulty in finding jobs if their factories close down. But most men are semi-skilled workers and there are even a few professionals. The neighbourhood also includes some quite prosperous businessmen, while an increasing number of men, especially of the younger generation, are turning away from wage employment to self-employment. Usually they start off as market traders, but there are also a number of manufacturers and other retailers among them. The garment trade – discussed elsewhere (Werbner 1984) – provides both women and teenage boys with work. For young schoolboys it provides part-time work on weekends and holidays, for women it provides opportunities mainly for home machining. This type of work enables a number of family members to contribute their share to the family budget. Women in 1976 could earn over £35 a week in a machining job if they were fast machinists (by 1987 weekly earnings, calculated on a piecework basis, were said to exceed £90).

Many of the women save in rotating credit associations, together with men with more lucrative incomes. This type of forced saving is found by most migrants to be the only effective way of accumulating substantial sums of money, since families tend to be under constant pressure to spend. There are so many attractive things to buy, weddings to attend, trips to make, and gifts to give that people are always short of cash. By joining rotating credit associations they force themselves, they say, to cut their standard of living. The associations, or *kommitti* as they are known, are often run by focal people in the neighbourhood. I return to this below.

A young man who wants to start off as a market trader has to earn for himself the capital needed to start his business. He would not normally use the money earned by his sisters or his mother for this purpose. Their money is devoted to maintaining the family's social position both in England and in Pakistan – through ceremonial gifting, and by keeping up with the neighbours in the race for consumer items. Women are primarily 'target workers', saving for specific projects: a wedding, a trip to Pakistan, a tractor to be sent back home, a dowry, as well as current gifting and hospitality. In other words, a woman supports those events which bring joy and 'happiness' to the family and are essential for participation in life cycle and religious events focused on the home. These events encourage the formation of close-knit networks within the neighbourhood.

The focal role of domestic rituals

One reason why the position of women in the central cluster is so powerful relates to the consequences of residence in close proximity to other Pakistani families. This, and the large amounts of spare time they have, enables women in the neighbourhood to develop close-knit networks. These are less costly in time to maintain, and are also more persistent than loose-knit networks. Friends are able to keep up with each other indirectly, through mutual friends, even if they do not manage to see each other for some time.

Religiosity in Manchester is expressed not so much through the maintenance of strict purdah, but through an emphasis on prayer and through the convening of domestic religious gatherings such as communal Koran readings. In the central cluster *Khatam Koran* rituals, as they are known, are usually held by women, as are many of the wedding rites. Women are involved in matters of birth, marriage, and death to a far greater extent than their husbands. They also organize birthday parties for younger children. It is usual to invite friendly neighbours to all these events. Some *Khatme Korans*, for example, are conceived to be mainly neighbourhood affairs and outsiders are not called in. In other *Khatme Korans* the opposite occurs: close friends living outside the neighbourhood are invited – in addition to kinsmen – and neighbours are excluded. This is because the size of the congregation would be too unmanageable and the food costs too high if neighbours were invited as well. Neighbours are perceived as a single category, so that to invite one neighbour would mean having to invite all of them. To weddings, however, neighbours are invariably invited, and they also take an active part in the *mhendi* rite before the wedding itself. At funeral wakes and at the *Khatam* rituals following them neighbours play a major role, as they do in all cases of serious illness, helping especially with children.

Ceremonial exchanges in the neighbourhood, while frequent, are not as costly as they are among the more affluent migrants who live outside it. People in the central cluster monitor their resources very carefully, and the meals given at *Khatam* rituals and weddings are scaled to their income. Usually only two wedding ceremonies are held: *mhendi* (which includes the *thel*) and the reception (which includes the *nikah*). People attending the *mhendi* do not receive a full meal, which is given only at the reception. Most people hold the reception in a hired hall, but some hold it in their homes. In this case people come and go during an extended period of the day, as houses are too small to accommodate everyone at the same time. However, in relation to their incomes, which are much lower than those of the Pakistani élite, such expenditures as residents of the central cluster make can be regarded as equally 'excessive', in neighbourhood terms. One woman estimated to me that she spent £10 a week on gifts, dinner parties, etc. The family's income was very low for her husband's job was poorly paid. She supplemented his wages by sewing outfits for local people and teaching the Koran. Her daughter earned about £20 a week as a machinist which she was saving up in a *kommitti*. However, the money she earned was her own and was not intended for ceremonial gifting and entertaining. This woman estimated that a dinner (*dawad*) cost her £10 in meat alone.

While ceremonial gifting is not usually as costly as it is for more wealthy Pakistanis, its value is augmented for the exchange partners by a constant stream of minor acts of reciprocity between neighbours, and by a great deal of mutual aid. Such mutual aid involves giving lifts if one has a car, taking messages if one has a telephone, caring for neighbours' children, putting up neighbours' wedding guests from other towns, taking gifts to Pakistan for neighbours, watching over their houses while they are away, etc. In these circumstances, ceremonial exchanges can be regarded as indicators of a far more complex exchange relationship, and their value cannot be assessed independently of these other exchanges. However, friendly neighbours do sometimes exchange very costly gifts, especially at weddings. Two families I knew gave each other gifts valued at over £100 at the weddings of their respective daughters. Neither family was wealthy, and this represented a major financial burden for both. The two families were not related, did not belong to the same caste, and did not come from the same part of Pakistan. They had become friendly in Manchester, where they had been close neighbours for a number of years.

Although close neighbours often become friends and are then invited to attend ritual and ceremonial events (as well as engaging in mutual aid) neighbourliness does not of itself determine the choice of friends and hence also of guests at events such as *Khatam Koran* rituals. The congregations at *Khatam Koran* gathering are not entirely drawn on a territorial basis, as *slametans* are in Java (where, according to Jay, dyadic friendship as we, or indeed at Pakistanis, conceive of it is not a recognized type of relationship – see Jay 1969: 201–6).

Only some neighbours from among those living nearby become friends, and of course, many friends are not neighbours at all. Some family friends are past neighbours who have moved away, others are former acquaintances from work or from Pakistan. The residential turnover in the central cluster is quite high (see Werbner 1979), and people do not simply discard friends because they have moved away, although they see them less frequently. Moreover, kinsmen seldom live on the same streets, although they often live nearby; nevertheless they are regularly invited to ritual and ceremonial events.

The range of friends a family has in the neighbourhood will be illustrated in the following case study. Although the family at the centre of the study is in many ways an exceptional one, since the number of friendships it has is far greater than that of most families in the central cluster, the pattern of neighbourliness-cum-friendship which this family has essentially conforms to that of other extended families with smaller social networks. The family is a focal one which links together many other Pakistani families living in the neighbourhood. I here examine what has given the family of Hafiza such a focal position in the central residential cluster, and consequently also in the community at large.

Focal families and women of influence: a case study

The family at the centre of this case study has a large *biraderi* (localized intermarrying caste group) in Manchester, many of whose members have remained living in the central cluster or on its periphery. Three women from this *biraderi* are Koran instructors: Hafiza, her sister-in-law, and a classificatory relative from the same town. The three women live about ten minutes walking distance from each other, in the central cluster (see Figure 9.1).

The most prominent member of the *biraderi* is Hanif, Hafiza's husband. He is a university graduate, a graduate of a religious seminary, a teacher, and a scholar. When the family first arrived in Manchester he was appointed as the main religious official at the mosque (*maulwi*). During that period he and his family lived in a flat attached to the mosque, and in the course of his official duties they got to know personally very many Pakistani residents in Manchester – rich and poor, newcomers and old-timers. Among the closest friends of the family were those members of the local Pakistani élite who run the mosque committee. After some years as *maulwi*, Hanif resigned to become a high-school teacher. However, he continues to officiate at weddings and to give advice on religious matters.

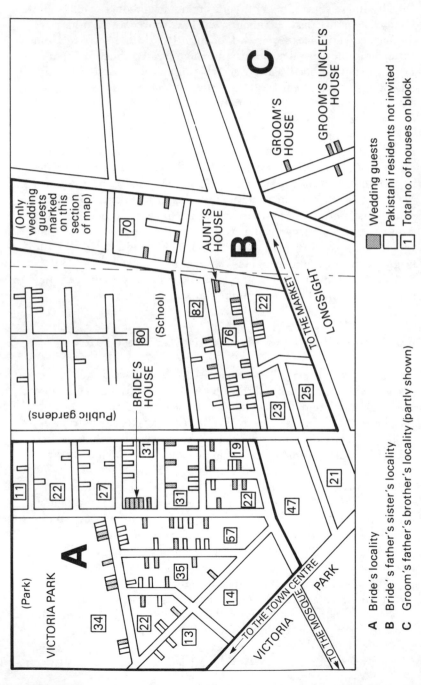

VICTORIA PARK

(Park)

(Public gardens)

A

11
22
34
22
27
31
31
13
35
57
22
14
19
47
21

BRIDE'S HOUSE

80
(School)

(Only wedding guests marked on this section of map)

70

B

82
76
22
23
25

AUNT'S HOUSE

VICTORIA PARK

TO THE TOWN CENTRE

TO THE MOSQUE

TO THE MARKET

LONGSIGHT

C

GROOM'S HOUSE

GROOM'S UNCLE'S HOUSE

▨ Wedding guests

☐ Pakistani residents not invited

1 Total no. of houses on block

A   Bride's locality

B   Bride's father's sister's locality

C   Groom's father's brother's locality (partly shown)

Figure 9.1 Neighbourhood wedding guests of bride's family in the central residential cluster (Hanif)

Furthermore, he is an active member, and for some years UK president, of a religious organization. This association involves him in a good deal of travelling, occupying much of his spare time. His wife's brother, who is also his first patrilateral cousin, officiates as *maulwi* on Fridays in the Cheetham Hill mosque, where he lives. Hence, the family's religious prominence in the community has always been very clear. Some of Hanif's close kinsmen are successful manufacturers, regarded as affluent by other migrants.

This part of the family is not very religious, and on the whole they keep apart from Hanif and his immediate kinsmen. They live on the periphery of the central cluster or in the inner suburbs where other businessmen live. They do, however, attend each others' life crisis rituals and other large events.

Hanif is a busy man and has little time for nurturing the many social relations that he and his wife had built up when he was *maulwi*. However, his wife has continued to cultivate these relations with women all over Manchester; and particularly with those resident in the central cluster within walking distance of her home. From my very first meeting with her she talked of the large number of 'friends' she had, and this was a continuous source of pride for her. The family is not well-off financially, and at that time they lived in a rather dilapidated large Victorian terrace house, which no amount of painting and wallpapering seemed able to rescue from its depressing shabbiness. There were numerous children in the family, and because much of its income was spent on religious activities the children were shabbily dressed in second-hand clothes. The house conveyed a general sense of poverty and decay. But for Hafiza her numerous friends are like a protective wall around her and her family. There are always people knocking at the door, and the telephone – an essential possession despite the shortage of money – is constantly ringing. Hafiza, and often her sister-in-law as well, are invited to virtually all the *Khatme Koran* taking place in the residential cluster. She is also regularly invited to attend the many *Khatam* events held by the wealthy 'old timers'. These are mostly successful businessmen in the clothing trade who live in the inner suburbs. Indeed, her daughter complained to me that 'sometimes she can be called to four *Khatams* in one day. During *Ramzan* she is never home to cook for the family, she goes to a *Khatam* every day'. Hafiza herself told me that at many *Khatam* gatherings she attended she didn't even know the people, she had been asked by friends to come to them. Her daughter also complained to me that she gets '. . . fed up with preparing food for all the visitors we have'.

At the time of the study Hafiza's activities were not confined merely to the religious sphere. She ran a fabric shop in the back room of her house (this later closed as she said it had proved unprofitable). Women coming to choose materials would sit around gossiping for many hours. She had also been the secretary (*kommittivali*) of several *kommittis*, which again meant that people were continually dropping by with their weekly payments, sometimes staying to chat. This combination of shopkeeping with *kommitti* management is not uncommon. Some of the largest and most costly *kommittis* in Manchester, to which many prominent businessmen belong, are managed by a woman who also runs a material shop in the back room of her terraced house. Another *kommitti* known to me was managed by a grocery shopkeeper in the central cluster.

During the period of my research, in the latter part of the 1970s, a large number of weddings took place in the central cluster, and also among old timers in the suburbs, many of whom had once lived in the central cluster. The weddings were usually of first sons or daughters and were consequently large, ostentatious affairs – the first major display events that families had held in Manchester. Attending weddings was a regular pastime among people I knew in the central cluster, who met each other again and again at one wedding after another.

The reason why the same 'set' of neighbours seem to have attended the different weddings is to a large extent bound up with their relations with one another via their children. Most girls and boys in the central cluster attend the same schools. At weddings girls invite their Pakistani classmates and their families. Girls and boys, it will be recalled, play an important role in the *mhendi* ceremony. Since boys also organize the serving of food and drinks at wedding receptions, they usually mobilize their friends to help serve at their sisters' weddings, and this entails inviting their friends' families to attend the weddings. Because in most Pakistani nuclear families there are many children, commonly four or more, parents of children within a certain age range inevitably get caught up in relations of mutual acquaintance and hospitality via their children, even if they had not known each other previously.

When Hafiza's first daughter married, she held a very large reception (*vyah*). The guest list included nearly 1,000 invitees and, as her husband explained, many people had to be excluded. The marriage was between two related families, both resident in the central cluster. There was a great deal of overlap in the circles of friends that each family had, but the size of Hafiza's family network was much larger. Apart from the *biraderi*, hailing both from Manchester and from various other English towns, Hanif invited his religious friends from various parts of Britain, while most other guests came from Manchester. These included some of the prominent community leaders and businessmen whose *Khatam Koran* gatherings Hafiza was constantly attending. Most other guests were neighbours. Since the wedding took place on a Sunday, many of the wholesalers did not, in the end, attend, but sent their apologies. In order to hold the wedding Hafiza had saved money in a *kommitti* for months, working as a machinist as well as earning some money from her shop. She had also borrowed substantial sums of money from a friend and from a relative.

As mentioned, most of the other guests at the wedding were neighbourhood friends in the central cluster. Figure 9.1 shows the residential distribution of guests invited to the wedding from the immediate locality of the bride's house. When I asked Hafiza and her husband to define what they thought of as their 'neighbourhood' they defined a locality bounded by main parks, somewhat larger than that marked in Figure 9.1[5]. But the clustering of invitations was within a more limited 'locality' marked (A) on the map. They also invited people living in an adjacent locality where Hafiza's sister-in-law (husband's brother's wife) lives (B). Other friends they invited included those mutually shared with the family of the groom's uncle who lived in a third locality (C), adjacent to that of her husband's brother's wife. To give a more vivid picture of the way the family defined its relationship with its neighbours I quote from an account of the wedding guests from the neighbourhood given to me by Hafiza and one of her daughters.

1 We've known them for ages. They're kind of close, Mrs H. and Mrs F.
2 We don't know them a lot but since they keep coming and going [to our house] we just invited them.
3 The mother here was my mother's best friend [Hafiza's]. She died 2–3 years ago. Her son is my brother's good friend.
4 and 5. They're just friends, mother's friends. We didn't know their husbands' names. We took the card and filled it in there.
6 She's just a friend. Her husband wasn't speaking to her once and she came to our house, and that's how we met her. You see, my father – when husbands' and wives' things are not well – I mean, don't get on well together, my father tries to make them friendly, good together.

(For lack of space I eliminate here some of those invited.)

37 The daughers come to read to our house and go to our school and are friends as well.
38 The daughter comes to read and they are my father's friends and now her mother is mother's friend.
39 She's been our friend, I don't know for how long. She comes to our house loads of times. You know, when there are religious festivals, *khatams* – people do *khatam* at our house, bring things with them. Someone dies. They want it done nearly every month and mother can't go there and they can't call everyone.
40 She used to live next door to us but now she's moved. Mother taught her to do machine work [sewing].
41 They go to our school and they come to read. Not very close really, but the girls are very close to us.
42 Just a friend through [40].
43 My aunt and her son's wife live here [note reference to women only].
44 She goes to my aunt's house to read. Came to buy cloth a few times from us. My aunt teaches only one or two girls who live near her and can't come to mother. Her [married] son is moving out soon.
45 N., our relations. Not very close, just *biraderi*.
46 and 47. The daughters used to read Koran with mother. Just friends.
48 Y. She was at school with B. [older sister, the bride]. Her cousin was at school with me, my friend [the cousin lives on the other side of the residential cluster].
49 They are *biraderi*, *Darzi*. A little close. Quite far really. From Wazirabad. H. and A. are also from Wazirabad but are very close relatives [referring to other relatives].
50 My younger sister's friend. We just met them once and A. [younger sister] wanted to invite them so we did.
51 We invited the food store owner as well from this road [in third locality, where groom's family live].

The main categories of persons invited from the neighbourhood were thus: school friends of the family daughters and sons: Koran students of Hafiza; friends of Hanif or of his brother and brother-in-law (through work or associational activity); employers or employees in the garment trade and other businesses; friends of Hafiza made over a long period; friends of relatives of friends; friends of relatives; relatives. Figure 9.1 indicates that even in the case of this family who 'knew everyone', only certain select neighbours were invited to the wedding. Pakistani newcomers to the neighbourhood were not well known and were not invited. A short time after the wedding took place Hafiza's mother died, and the same range of neighbours who had attended the wedding also participated in a funerary *Khatam Koran* (people outside the locality were not invited to this second *Khatam*, except for select close relatives and *biraderi* members).

Hence, within the general area of the central residential cluster, about one and a half miles long and less than half a mile wide, there are sub-neighbourhoods or 'localities' where people shop in the same neighbourhood stores, use the same routes to the market, travel from the same bus stops, etc. Somewhat larger neighbourhoods, including a number of adjacent localities, are school catchment areas. It is here that most friendships with neighbours are forged, and within this area mutual help is most frequently extended. I obtained several wedding guest lists of families living in the central cluster and all showed a similar pattern of informal 'locality' areas where most friends were concentrated. The actual boundaries of the locality vary from informant to informant, but usually within a space demarcated by major roads and parks, or council housing. However, families like Hafiza's who 'know everyone' – that is, who know many people living beyond the immediate confines of their locality – make for a greater degree of communication between Pakistani families living throughout the residential cluster. Thus, in another wedding staged by a family living on the other side of the central cluster, about a mile away from Hafiza's house, some of the guests invited were from the immediate locality but many of the guests were described as 'people we know through Hafiza'. In this way Hafiza and her husband fulfil an important 'connecting' role in the neighbourhood.

Hanif's intense public involvement and preoccupation with external affairs means he takes little part in domestic household chores. These are handled almost entirely by his wife and elder daughters. The demarcation of the house into sex-specific areas is also strictly maintained: the back area and room are the domain of women, entered only by male relatives. The front room is usually occupied by men. The constant stream of both men and women to the house, many of whom are strangers, as well as the religiosity of the family, dictate this continued separation between the sexes. Nevertheless, the type of purdah maintained by Hafiza and her family differs radically from the purdah which restricts movement and isolates women in the home, under the domination of a single male.

Male and female, public and domestic

A radical opposition between the cultural images of male and female, and the prescribed roles of men and women, may be true only of a specific phase in the domestic life cycle (La Fontaine 1981). Quite often, as La Fontaine argues, it is married women with young children who epitomize the female image. This image is contrasted with the male image achieved by mature men who gain prominence in the world of public affairs.

For Pakistanis, the complementary of the two worlds, the world of women and and the world of men, seen in terms of a strictly defined division of labour between the sexes, has been modified for many by the migration process. It is, nevertheless, still anchored in key phases of the domestic life cycle. It is also crucially related to certain phases of migration.

Thus, recently arrived pubescent brides or women with young children are most likely to be secluded, sometimes isolated, in their homes. This isolation is particularly extreme if they live outside the central enclave (Werbner 1979). Husbands are most likely to favour the seclusion of their wives if they are factory workers who work alongside other Pakistani men. This 'bundle' of features fits the Mirpuri women studied by Saifullah Khan.

Extreme female seclusion is, however, in most instances only a phase. Several women with extensive networks told me that when they first arrived in Manchester 'there were no women here'. As women settle down and their children reach school age this isolating tendency is, in most cases, gradually displaced by increasing sociability. Men's control over their wives' movements and circle of acquaintances decreases correspondingly, with significant social implications. As the residential enclave moves outwards, peripherally resident women are joined by Pakistani neighbours. Religiosity in this context takes a new form. Veiling and physical seclusion become matters of respect and sacred activity, reserved for honoured guests, strangers, prayer, and religious observance. The expression of religiosity through religious gatherings increases, however, as women become more 'rooted' locally.

Purdah has undergone an even more radical change for second-generation migrants. Although young Mancunian Pakistani girls are often chaperoned and watched, they enjoy a kind of freedom unusual in the Pakistan their mothers left. If their brothers are market traders, they often accompany them on trips to distant markets, and assist in selling on the stalls. Many have driving licences. Within the residential enclave they move around freely, visiting school friends. The abandonment of the *burqa* has transformed chaperoned trips with brothers into enjoyable outings. For young married Mancunian women the inevitable long hours of housework and babycare are relieved by visits and telephone calls to sisters or school friends. A girl's mother usually lives nearby and is a constant source of comfort and support.

As their children reach school age, the time women have for work and sociability increases quite suddenly and dramatically. They then move into a phase of network building and consolidation. Their impact and influence on the family's affairs and reputation increase accordingly. As mediators, they not only support or confirm their husbands' status. They also share with their husbands the task of negotiating affairs back home, in Pakistan. Whereas in Islamic societies women rarely have the exclusive mediatory role assigned to women in exogamous patrilineal groups (Strathern 1972), labour migration has here created a new mediatory role for women. On trips to Pakistan they arrange marriages, property investments, and other affairs on behalf of their family in Britain. They alternate with their husbands in mediating with kinsmen in Pakistan.

Migrants women's 'careers' in purdah may be summed up in Figure 9.2.

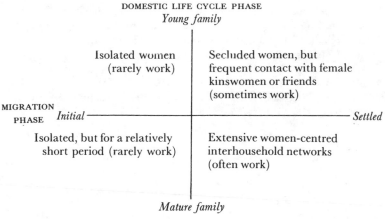

Figure 9.2 Variations in purdah

Conclusion

The image of a shy, modest, retiring young woman is still idealized amongst Pakistanis. It is part of a cultural lore of gender-related 'natural' stereotypes (La Fontaine 1981): the seductive or promiscuous woman, the domineering mother-in-law, the ever-giving mother, or the woman of fortitude. In contrast is a repertoire of male images: the man of honour, the protector of his family and its reputation, the man of violence, of enterprise, or of social responsibility.

As I have shown, the actual roles fulfilled by a woman, and her domestic influence, vary over her lifetime, and the domestic household division of labour is pragmatically negotiated (see Yanagisako 1979). Stereotypes, enduring values, and actual roles remain in some tension (Strathern 1972). But on formal and sacred occasions the strict separation between the worlds of men and women is upheld. Thus the image of a dual, segregated world persists, anchored in enduring cultural notions regarding the 'natural' attributes and proper roles of men and women.

Notes

1 I conducted fieldwork amongst Pakistanis in Manchester between 1975–78. I am grateful to the ESRC (then SSRC) UK for its generous support.
2 The *burqa* is not commonly worn in Britain, but local Pakistani women continue to cover their heads with chiffon scarves (*dupatta*) in the presence of – Pakistani – male strangers.
3 Purdah is most marked amongst the lower middle class in urban Pakistan. Work for women of this class background outside the home is predominantly menial and degrading (Papanek 1973a).
4 This contrasts with client-based female networks in urban Morocco (Maher 1976). In Manchester, most households are economically independent, if not wealthy.
5 For further discussion of the notions of 'sets' and 'localities' see Richard Werbner (1975)

References

Anwar, M. (1979) *The Myth of Return: Pakistanis in Britain*. London: Heinemann.
Bujra, J. (1974) 'Introductory: Female/Solidarity and the sexual division of labour' in P. Caplan and J.M. Bujra (eds) *Women United, Women Divided*, London: Tavistock Publications.
Eglar, Z. (1960) *A Punjabi Village in Pakistan*, New York: Columbia University Press.
Jay, R.R. (1969) *Javanese Villagers: Social Relations in Rural Modjukoto*, Cambridge: MIT Press.

Granovetter, M.S. (1973) 'The strength of weak ties', *American Journal of Sociology*, 78, 6: 1360–80.

Jeffrey, P. (1979) *Frogs in a Well: Indian Women in Purdah*, London: Zed Books.

La Fontaine, J.S. (1981) 'The domestication of the savage male', *Man* (NS) **16**: 333–49.

Maher, V. (1976) 'Kin, clients and accomplices: relationships among women in Morocco', in D.L. Barker and S. Allen (eds) *Sexual Divisions and Society: Process and Change*, London Tavistock Publications.

Papanek, H. (1973a) 'Purdah: separate worlds and symbolic shelter', *Comparative Studies in Society and History* **15**: 289–325.

—— (1973b) 'Men, women, and work: reflections on the two-person career', *American Journal of Sociology* **78** (4)(852–72.

Rosaldo, M. (1974) 'Women, culture and society: a theoretical overview', in M. Rosaldo and L. Lamphere (eds) *Women, Culture, and Society*, Stanford: Stanford University Press.

Saifullah Khan, V. (1975) 'Asian women in Britain: strategies of adjustment of Indian and Pakistani Migrants', in A. de Souza (ed) *Women in Contemporary India*, New Delhi: Manohar.

—— (1976) 'Purdah in the British situation', in D.L. Barker and S. Allen (eds) *Dependence and Exploitation in Work and Marriage*, London: Longman.

—— (1979) 'Mirpuris and social stress: Mirpuris in Bradford', in Saifullah Khan (ed.) *Minority Families in Britain: Support and Stress*, London: Macmillan.

Sharma, U. (1980) *Women, Work, and Property in North-West India*, London: Tavistock Publications.

Strathern, M. (1972) *Women in Between*, London: Seminar Press.

Vatuk, S. (1972) *Kinship and Urbanization: White Collar Migrants in North India*, Berkeley: University of California Press.

Werbner, P. (1979) 'Avoiding the ghetto: Pakistani migrants and settlement shifts in Manchester', *New Community*, 7: 376–89.

—— (1981) 'Manchester Pakistanis: Lifestyle, ritual, and the making of social distinctions', *New Community*, 9: 216–29. Reprinted in E. Butterworth and D. Weir (eds) (1984) *The New Sociology of Modern Britain*, London: Fontana.

—— (1984) 'Business on trust: Pakistani entrepreneurship in the Manchester garment trade', in R. Ward and R. Jenkins (eds) *Ethnic Communities in Business: Strategies for Economic Survival*, Cambridge: Cambridge University Press.

—— (1985) 'The Organisation of Giving and Ethnic Elites: Voluntary Associations Amongst Manchester Pakistanis', *Ethnic and Racial Studies*, 8, 3: 368–88.

—— (under consideration) 'The developmental cycle of social networks: Positive and negative transitivity in the friendship networks of Pakistani migrants', in B. Kapferer and K. Garbett (eds) *Essays in Honour of Clyde Mitchell*.

Werbner, R.P. (1975) 'Land, Movement and Status among Kalanga in

Botswana', in M. Fortes and S. Pattersons (eds) *Studies in African Social Anthropology*, London: Academic Press, 95–120.

Yanagisako, S. (1977) 'Women-centred kin networks in urban bilateral kinship', *American Ethnologist* **4**(2): 207–26.

—— (1979) 'Family and household: the analysis of domestic groups', *Annual Review of Anthropology* **8**: 161–205.

Name index

Subject index

Afro-Caribbean culture: and black
    British behaviour 158–60; narrow
    definition 173; self-employment 23, 31
Afro-Caribbean women: as immigrants
    4, 153; in labour market 7; teenage
    motherhood 153, 154, 156–8, 161–2,
    165
Aliens Act (1905) 61
Asians: unemployment 30
Asian women: arranged marriage 155;
    childcare problems 10; in clothing
    industry 29; in labour market 7,
    132–3; paid work 132, 149; roles 24,
    132, 149; self-employment 22; trade
    unionism 30; working culture 8

Bangladeshi men: in clothing industry
    28
Bangladeshi women: in labour market 7
bhaji 181
biraderi 185, 191
'black' as term 1, 104–5
blacks: as deviant 159, 162, 171; ethnic
    solidarity 171
black women: childcare problems 10;
    and daughters 169, 170, 172; feminism
    1; unemployment 167–8, 169; young
    153, 154–5; young motherhood 165
brides 106; *see also* marriage
Britain *see* Great Britain
British Restaurants 62
Brixton riots (1981) 22
burqa 180, 199

capitalism, and patriarchy 104
Caribbean people, *see* Afro-Caribbean
    culture
catering industry: Chinese 58, 59, 64–5,
    67–8, 71–2; Cypriot 44, 48–9; fast
    food 59, 62–4, 67; labour force 63, 67;
    wartime expansion 62–3
celebration, shopfloor 116–19
change, cultural 11, 97
childcare 9–10, 15, 16–17, 69, 70, 80, 81,
    87–8, 93, 136, 138, 141–7

childminding facilities 70, 143, 144,
    146–7
Chinatowns 61
Chinese laundries 61–2
Chinese men: role 68–9
Chinese people: catering industry 58, 59,
    64–5, 67–8, 71–2; industrialization
    60–1; isolation 58, 69; as migrants
    61–2, 63–4; second generation 70–1;
    self-employment 23, 61–2, 68
Chinese women: childcare problems 15,
    69, 70; exploitation 59, 72–3; and
    family businesses 5, 15, 66–71, 72;
    housing problems 66; as migrants 65;
    resistance 71–2; roles, changing 59–61,
    68, 71–2; second generation 71–2;
    social life 68–89; *see also* Asian women
class *see* social class
clothing industry 27–31; Cypriot 46–8;
    insecurity 43–4; labour costs 29;
    labour disputes 30; homeworkers 28;
    Pakistani 188; wages 29
colonial exploitation 3, 59, 73, 103
colour, and culture 159
Commonwealth Immigration Act (1962)
    41, 64, 65
conception, ideal time 164–5
Conservative economic policy 22
cultural change 11, 97
culture: Afro-Caribbean compared with
    black British 158–60; broad definition
    160–1, 173; diversity 104–5; as
    dynamic entity 11, 17, 97, 111, 153,
    160; narrow definition of 154, 158–60,
    161, 162, 164, 169, 171, 172, 173; of
    resistance 161; shopfloor *see* shopfloor
    culture; white as norm 159, 162
Cypriot men: honour 34, 36, 40–1, 47,
    48, 54; role 48–9; self-employment 23,
    44
Cypriots: Greek 42; immigration 41–2
Cypriot women: as captive labour 25–6;
    in catering 44, 48–9; in clothing
    industry 43, 44, 46–8; in Cypriot
    businesses 43, 44, 46, 50, 52, 54–5;